WILLIE FERNIE (Celtic and Scotland)
22

WILLIE FERNIE

Putting On The Style

by

David Potter
& John McCue

THE CELTIC STAR

Willie Fernie - Putting On The Style
by David Potter & John McCue

Published by The Celtic Star
in conjunction with Matt Corr Media.

First Published in the UK in 2022 by Celtic Star Books.

ISBN 978-1-8380207-4-3

Printed by Replika Press.

A catalogue for this book is available from the British Library and the Irish Library in Dublin.

Cover & page design and typesetting by Stephen Cameron.

Inside cover collages by Mark Lewis.

Edited by Niall Wilson.

Foreword by Tom Campbell.

Special thanks to the Fernie family for
editorial assistance and photography.

Publisher - David Faulds: email editor@thecelticstar.co.uk

Bookstore Website – https://celticstarbooks.com

Visit https://thecelticstar.com for the best Celtic news and views every day,

Contents

Acknowledgements

I am grateful to a lot of people for making this book happen, and in particular I would like to single out Alex Fernie, David Fernie, Mary Gillies, Diane Brownlee, Norman Douglas, Matt Corr, David Faulds and Niall Wilson.

All Celtic Star books can be purchased from the website celticstarbooks.com and from Celtic FC stores.

David Potter, 14 September, 2021

Introduction

Before reading this book, many of you will be aware of the influence Willie Fernie had on the Celtic teams of the 1950's in particular, the Coronation Cup and Hampden in the Sun. You may even be aware of the later training ground impact he had on the emerging Lisbon Lions and the Quality Street Gang, something no less than Kenny Dalglish commented on recently. But whatever you think you know about Willie Fernie, you will add many wonderful layers by the time you finish reading this exceptional account of one of Celtic's greatest entertainers.

From his unexpected early club allegiances, to the admiring interest in his talents from a surprising source, and the horrific injury that ultimately helped rather than hindered his signing for Celtic. The incredible tales of rudimentary coaching alongside the intrusive selection practices of the time, that thanks in no small part to the individual talents and of players like Willie, were negated to an extent, brought Celtic success, while also leaving unanswered questions hanging of unfulfilled team potential. The playing as an experienced foil for a precocious young striker, one who would become a managerial legend, before laying the groundwork for the one who became immortal. Then there is the gracing of the pinnacle of international football without a manager at all, whilst in graver danger of dehydration than national team glory. From Fife to Glasgow, to Middlesbrough, Paisley and Ayrshire, this journey has absorbing stories from them all. There is little doubt Willie Fernie was a natural footballer and your author mirrors that ability in the natural way he navigates his life for his readers.

David Potter, his books, and the Celtic legends of the club's illustrious history he describes in such wonderfully crafted detail, have accompanied myself and countless others from the armchair of the front room, through airport lounges, beaches and many a location besides for several years. This account of a Celtic Great is a wonderful and most welcome addition.

This summer after a lost summer for us all, I had the company of Willie Fernie on holiday in North Yorkshire, where I had the pleasure to not only read this fine story but also the great honour of scarcely required editorial input, in a part of the country, I learned whilst reading this book, Willie Fernie himself would have known well. It was entertaining company to keep and a privilege to have David Potter to guide me through Willie Fernie's journey with the detail and historical context for which the author is much renowned and deservedly so.

You too are about to start that journey through the life of one of Celtic's finest and most loved footballers and men. It is a story that deserves to be told and one that can now be handed down the generations as the history baton is passed on.

Willie Fernie could dribble and weave his way through any defence, and David Potter will manoeuvre you through his story with a similar grace. I hope you enjoy this book as much as I did. I am absolutely certain you will.

Niall Wilson, 7 September 2021

Foreword

It is an unfortunate fact of life that many so-called football heroes, admired and revered for their skill on the field, do not live up to that image off-stage. I can recall being in an Edinburgh pub and having to listen from an adjoining table to a former star (and not a Celtic player) mouth off obscenities about past incidents, complain about past injustices, and boast about his exploits on and off the football pitch.

And then there is Willie Fernie...

In 2000, Pat Woods and I arranged for an interview with Willie at his home in Glasgow's Newlands Drive. It was highly satisfying for Pat and I to meet and talk with somebody who lived fully up to his image. As a young man, Willie Fernie was a genuine player, and a perfect sportsman; older, he was a gentleman (in the best possible meaning of the word).

Audrey, his wife and who had been Jimmy McGrory's long-time secretary, had greeted us almost apologetically; Willie, apparently, was out, driving a visitor home and had not yet returned. Much worse was the news that he had very recently been diagnosed with 'early-onset Alzheimers' (and might at times be forgetful). Willie arrived, immediately recognisable and still trim and fit-looking in his 70s; Audrey told him we had been informed about his diagnosis. He shrugged fatalistically, and admitted to a slight difficulty in pronouncing the name of the condition:

"I'll just call it 'Oldtimers.' No great problem. Audrey'll look after me. She's been doing that for years, anyway."

During the interview, Audrey at times hovered nearby, but Willie needed little prompting from her (or us). What we saw that night was an elderly man, happily married, polite and gracious, appreciative that we had taken the trouble to come and interview him and the evening went beautifully. Willie's memory did not fail him, and he regaled us with stories of his days at Celtic Park (and also at Rugby Park). What impressed us most was his modesty about his own accomplishments in the game and his tolerance; it was clear that he, a non-smoker and non-drinker, had not cared too much for the habits of some of his playing contemporaries...but he was at pains not to criticize.

He had always been one of my favourite Celtic players and my admiration stemmed as much from his genuine sportsmanship as his undoubted skill and artistry. I saw him make his debut against St Mirren at Love Street on a miserable, rain-swept day, and was reasonably impressed with his promising display at inside-right in a 1-0 win (and I believe that Bertie Peacock made his second appearance at inside-left the same day). A month or so later, at Celtic Park on a sunny afternoon, both youngsters starred in a 4-1 win over East Fife and the denizens of the Jungle, notoriously hard to please, roared their encouragement and approval.

I am a few years older than Pat (Woods) and on the way home after the interview I reminded Pat of his great days: pride of place must go to his display (at right-half) in the famous 7-1 triumph in the 1957 League Cup final, but close behind came a scintillating performance (at outside-left) in the Coronation Cup final, when he roasted Hibs' renowned full-back Jock Govan...and, of course, there was a remarkable balancing-act along the bye line in the 1954 Scottish Cup final to set up the winning goal against Aberdeen (inside-right, that day). Sturdily-built with square shoulders, an erect posture, a graceful stride, perfect balance: a genuine player, no matter what position he played.

And a perfect sportsman from the start to the end of his football career.

I have another personal memory of Willie Fernie. I had been touring Scotland with a party of some 30 Canadian high-school students, and had arranged for a visit to Celtic Park. It was a Monday morning, and Jock Stein's Celtic had been surprisingly held to a draw by Hearts on the Saturday in the Scottish Cup and the replay was due at Tynecastle that night. Things were busy at Celtic Park that morning but the manager was agreeable to the visit going ahead: Jimmy McGrory gave the visiting Canadians a talk about Celtic's history…Jock Stein dropped in, and invited the youngsters to wander around Celtic Park, and take as many pictures as they wanted.

I found myself in a cubby-hole of a room where Willie was chatting with some of the visitors. He was comfortable with them, asking about Ottawa and where in Scotland they had visited. All the time he was folding the team's jerseys for that night's game. One young lady (Christine Trepannier) asked him in all innocence if that was 'the team's uniforms.' Willie, perhaps a little surprised, quietly pointed out, *"These are the Celtic jerseys. Lovely, aren't they?"* Christine was impressed and described Willie to me later as *"a really nice man"* and added, *"He was folding those jerseys gently, the same way my mother does after the ironing."*

"A really nice man" and a Celtic legend, indeed.

Tom Campbell, 7 September 2021

The Authors

David Potter was born in Forfar in 1948 and first saw Celtic at Dens Park, Dundee in March 1958, but had supported them before then, thanks to a severe indoctrination at the hands of a 'Celtic-daft' father who was just as rabid about them as David himself is now.

He lived through the awful days of the early 1960s but emerged into the glorious sunlight of the Stein era, after Billy McNeill and Bertie Auld propelled them to glory in the 1965 Scottish Cup final. In 1966, he went to St Andrews University and attended the 1969 Scottish Cup final along with a Boro supporter called John McCue. He became a teacher of Latin, Greek and Spanish at Glenrothes High School. Now well into his 70s, he acknowledges that the condition of being Celtic-daft is both endogenous and terminal, and there is no cure. One of his regrets is that he never saw enough of Willie Fernie in his prime, and another is that he was just too young to go to the 7-1 game in October 1957.

John McCue was born a stone's throw from Ayresome Park, Middlesbrough in 1949, and he was taken to matches by his dad around 1959, whatever the weather. He hung around the stadium during training days for autographs and remembers the legends that were Clough and Peacock. Sadly, the Wilf Mannion and George Hardwick days preceded him, but John watched Willie Fernie while he was with the Boro and even knocked on his family front door for his autograph when he wasn't collecting football cards and playing the Wembley board game.

John went off to St Andrews University where he met David Potter, returning to his native Teesside after graduation to teach Physics, Mathematics and Astronomy. These early days coincided with Jack Charlton's magnificent reign as Middlesbrough manager and many happy matches are remembered, many involving Bobby Murdoch.

CHAPTER ONE

FROM KINGLASSIE TO PARKHEAD (1928-1950)

Cosily reclining face to face
Sandwiched between Lochty burn and pithead.
The twin rows almost embraced
Through front gardens, only an access
Road inhibiting greater intimacy.
Consequently, the snug closeness
Of these Coal Company abodes
Built just beside the colliery itself,
Simply guaranteed that a community
Was delivered virtually ready-made.
Starved of mains electricity,
Domestic survival depended upon
Bowhill-piped gas and water
Filched directly from deep within
Those underground working next door.

Andrew Farmer; *The Pit Rows.*

Andrew Farmer is a talented local poet from Kinglassie. His poetry - as exemplified in two books *"Lamping the Flame"* and *"Mine Roots"* - is typical mining stuff about how hard a job mining is but yet how much of a community Kinglassie is, and how proud they are of men like Willie Fernie. In a poem called *"Come Awa' the Colliery"* proclaiming the virtues of Kinglassie colliery, Mr Farmer tells us;

'Twas the Celts wha snapped up Willie Fernie
An' the Pars wha signed Big Jimmy Michie
Twa local lads wha went awa'
Tae jine the ranks o' senior fitba'
As recruits frae a prood Kinglassie Colliery

The name Fernie is a very common one in Fife. There is of course Fernie Castle, just north of Freuchie on the road from Kirkcaldy to Dundee. It was first recorded in 1353, and it is now a hotel which can host very expensive weddings. Lower down the social scale, one will find many people called Fernie in Kirkcaldy, Glenrothes and Dunfermline, and in the case of Willie's family in the village of Kinglassie.

Kinglassie is a mining village. It is not far from John Thomson's Cardenden, and it is an undistinguished village to drive through. It can now no longer really be called a "mining" village, for mining has now long gone from Fife. Its population exploded in the 19th and early part of the 20th century, particularly when the Kinglassie Pit was opened by the Fife Coal Company in 1908. Willie Fernie was born on 22 November 1928 in Kinglassie, Fife, the son of William and Jean Fernie. William Fernie senior was a miner. Willie (who was usually called Bill in his family) was the third of five children. Andrew (Aund) was the oldest in 1924, Tom came next in 1926, then Bill in 1928 followed by David in 1930 before eventually in 1935 a girl called Mary came along.

The mining community into which Willie Fernie was born was, in 1928, beaten and broken. Miners had done well in the Great War. Coal had been much required and high wages had been paid to ensure that miners kept working and that the war effort never lacked coal. But of course, it all stopped in 1918 when not only was there immediately less demand for coal at home, but also the mine owners in the early 1920s tried to reduce wages and the number of workers that they needed. Not unnaturally, this was much resisted and there was a dreadful strike in 1921, and an even worse one in 1926 which lasted from May to November when the miners were starved back into submission. The 1926 Miners' Strike had of course caused the General Strike. The General Strike lasted less than a fortnight, but the miners were on strike for six months.

Magnanimity was not in great supply when the owners won the strike. Wages were reduced, well known troublemakers and agitators were not re-employed and victimisation was the order of the day. There was little that the workers could do. Even the most dignified of complaints could lead to another dismissal. They had lost. Poverty was the order of the day. *"Vae Victis"* (Woe to the conquered!)

The mining community in Kinglassie, like most other mining communities in Great Britain, stood together in adversity. This statement, although generally true, needs to be qualified. It is tempting to fall into the trap of assuming that miners were all decent, saintly people who respected education, religion and each other with a grim determination to help each other out of these unhappy times. Yes, there was indeed a great amount of that, but there was also theft, violence, drunkenness and incest. Such things were, sadly, found in mining communities as well.

The Fernies were typical miners in that they kept greyhounds, usually racing them at the Thornton track a few miles to the east, and one thing that one can rely upon in Fife mining villages is a plethora of footballers. Celtic in particular have done well out of Fife, and of course when Willie was less than three years old, there occurred the most tragic day of Celtic's history when goalkeeper John Thomson met his death on 5 September 1931 in a game at Ibrox against Rangers. The scenes at his funeral were hard to parallel even in the awful history of the Fife coalfield, but less than two months later, Bowhill Cemetery was again the scene of intense mourning when 10 miners met their death in a disaster at No 2 pit, Bowhill, one of the victims, by a coincidence, being a young 19-year-old man by the name of Charles Baxter Fernie.

Happier Celtic memories from Fife can centre on men like Chic Geatons, John "Jean" McFarlane, Peter Johnstone (tragically killed in the Great War in 1917) and in later years, George Connelly and Scott Brown, and that is not to mention hosts of Fifers who went on to play for other clubs, not least a man who grew up in the same street as Willie Fernie called Jimmy Bonthrone, who became an absolute legend both as a player and a manager with East Fife. He also, with less success, was manager of Aberdeen.

His sister Mary remembers "Bill" as being very fit and full of fun. She recalls the time when, impressed by a magician who was able to pull a cloth off a table without disturbing any of the plates and cups, he tried the same and it did not work, with disastrous consequences. He also once knocked out a lamp in the living-room while trying to walk on his hands, and there was another occasion when the four brothers took their little sister in her pram to a place called the Kirkcaldy Dykes, which was a steep brae. They then took their little sister out of the pram and left her at the top of the brae while they raced down the brae in the pram!

One thing that Fernie's parents were very keen on was that their children should all have the opportunity to learn how to play a musical instrument, even though the cost of lessons would have been expensive. Willie himself was proficient at playing the piano, while his sister Mary earned her certificate from the Licentiate of the Royal Academy of Music in 1957, and became a Church organist, playing at Tullibody Church for 47 years before retiring.

It would have been surprising if Willie had not grown up with some interest in football, but he was the only one in his family who played the game at a professional level. At one point, Andrew was picked to play for Scotland at youth level, but his mother wasn't very keen because he wore glasses! Neither his father nor any of the other three brothers were good enough players, however much they would have been obsessively interested in the game, but we are surprised to hear from Willie himself in an interview given to a journalist called Willie McTaggart in his Middlesbrough days that in his primary school days at least, football took second place to running, a sport in which he won a few prizes. And yet, as a Celtic player, although he was not slow, he was never a speed merchant in the sense that Bobby Lennox, for example, was.

However, his primary school headmaster noticed that he was a good football player, making the famous comment that he had *"more brains in his feet than he had in his head,"* and Willie played both for his primary school team in the days leading up to World War II and also for the Life Boys, the junior version of the Boys Brigade. He himself claims that he learned his *"versatility"* in this tough football environment, for although he was always good enough to get a game, and many a spectator commented on his ball control, he soon discovered that the big boys claimed for themselves the "best" positions, like centre-forward, in the team and the smaller guys had to be content with what was left.

On one occasion when he was about eight years old, he was playing at right-back, and had to take a goal kick. He summoned up all his strength, ran forward and miskicked, so that the ball barely trundled out of the penalty area amidst gales of laughter and a voice was heard saying, *"Puir wee laddie! They should gie him a tennis ball to play wi."*

It was of course a tennis ball that was used in the constant and interminable street games that went on in the streets of Kinglassie. There was not a great deal of vehicular traffic around in Kinglassie in the 1930s, so the games were relatively unmolested. No doubt the occasional window was broken, and the odd hammering was given out by irate mothers for wearing out and scuffing his good shoes, but that was the way that it was in Scottish working-class communities in those days, and Willie would always claim that his years of playing with a tennis ball would teach him a great deal in how to play with a real football when an organised game came along.

Willie's school Kinglassie Primary was used for Secondary Education as well and Willie would stay there until he left at the age of 14 in 1942. World War II had broken out with its inevitable consequences in 1939. Mining towns like Kinglassie were possible slightly less affected than other places because most men were still required to dig up the coal. Some did of course join up or were conscripted, but in Fernie's case when he left school around 1942, he went to work on a nearby farm, involved in the equally important task of providing food to nourish the nation. His parents were keen on this idea, and he was eventually followed by his younger brother David, and Willie tells us that he gave up football for a spell because there wasn't at that time a local team to play for. He did however spend his lunch hour dribbling a tennis ball round pigs and chickens and "selling a dummy" to the odd carthorse!

Once the war was over, he began playing football in a proper, organised way. He came under the influence of a man called Wull Kerr, a miner whose hobby it was to run football teams, and who had a wide network of contacts in the world of senior football to whom he could recommend young talent. Fernie started off playing with Bowhill West End, who included in the ranks of their old boys George "Dod" Aitken who played with distinction for East Fife in their half-back line of Philp, Finlay and Aitken before moving on to Sunderland. Fernie described them as a *"tough village club"* but he did not play with them for long. Fernie moved on to Leslie Hearts, playing for them on the right wing and did well enough to attract the attention of several major clubs.

As often happens with talented football players, he was not a very good football watcher. He tells the story of how he was 18 before he attended his first senior game, a Cup tie at the end of the bad winter of 1947 when East Fife lost 0-2 to Motherwell. *"I can't say I was terribly thrilled,"* he says. *"I just wanted to hurry back and get a game for my own team."* East Fife themselves had heard stories about Fernie and on several occasions tried to persuade him to sign, but for the moment at least he was glad to keep working on the farm and to play for Leslie Hearts.

At that point, Willie (in spite of never having seen them!) was a supporter of the other Hearts, from Edinburgh. He was a particular fan of Tommy Walker, who was reputed never to foul an opponent, and he was of course famous for taking the penalty kick for Scotland at Wembley in 1936 when the wind kept blowing the ball away from where it was meant to be on the penalty spot! In playing terms, Willie would have had more in common with another Walker of Hearts, an earlier one called Bobby who was known as "Houdini" because of his body swerve and general trickery.

Hearts had been a well-supported but under-achieving club in the 1930s with many fine players but never winning any trophies. Their last trophy was 1906, and during the First World War, their first team had enlisted en masse for the conflict. Hearts had never really recovered from the loss of these players. They had been anonymous during the Second World War, and had not shown any great sign of recovery in the few years after the war.

But it was the other Hearts in whom Fernie was for the moment interested, because in season 1947/48 we find him playing for Leslie Hearts, at that point the holders of the Scottish Juvenile Cup, which they had won on Saturday, 21 June 1947 at Easter Road when they defeated Campsie Black Watch in a replayed final. Their success had been hailed all over Fife, for it was a great achievement for the team from the *"paper making"* town of Fife, as it called itself.

Fernie soon settled into this team, and by dint of some strong performances, they reached the final of the Scottish Juvenile Cup again the following year, this time to play Dumbarton Vale Emmett on Saturday, 19 June 1948. Again, the final was at Easter Road, but this time the weather was absolutely atrocious, with heavy rain all morning and during the match itself. In spite of all this, some 5,500 were still attracted to Easter Road (a ground with no shelter other than the stand) in the middle of summer to see this game. Such was the love that Scotland had for football in 1948!

The Leslie Hearts team was Malcolm, Watson and Lister; Nairn, John Rutherford and Methven; Glancey, Fernie, Grubb, Hamilton and James Rutherford. Several of the Leslie players were being watched by senior clubs, with strong rumours that Falkirk were poised to make a bid for Fernie after the game. The game started with Hearts playing down the Easter Road slope, which possibly was not as pronounced then as it is now. And by half-time they were 3-0 up with two goals from James Rutherford and one from Grubb. Fernie had played superbly but had had to go off the field with a "facial injury" between the second and third goals. By half-time he had not returned.

What seems to have happened was that Fernie and an opponent jumped for the same ball. Fernie got there first, and headed the ball but on his descent, his jaw collided with the head of his opponent who was still rising. It was a grizzly injury, the very thought of which can make one wince.

At half-time, it was learned that the "facial injury" sustained when he *"bumped into an opponent"* as he himself would put it years later was in fact a broken jaw, but *The Fifeshire Advertiser* reports that Fernie refused to go to hospital and *"insisted on sitting on the trainer's bench to see his team win the day."* It was indeed a tight second half but the 10 men of Leslie held out against sustained pressure to see the game out. At full-time, the rain having now stopped, the cup was presented and Fernie was taken off to hospital.

One remembers in this context the Scottish Cup final of 2017 between Celtic and Aberdeen, when Kieran Tierney sustained a similar injury, went to hospital, but returned to Hampden in time to collect his medal and take part in the trophy celebrations at full-time. Such things require courage! History does not however tell us whether Willie was well enough to take part in the celebrations in Leslie that night when the cup was paraded through the streets along with the Leslie & District Silver Band, who had themselves won the Challenge Cup for the Fifeshire Amateur Band Association that day in Dunfermline. It was like VE Day once again!

This accident to Fernie had one major consequence. He was treated in hospital and allowed home. His broken jaw was painful, but it did eventually heal, as broken jaws do. His sister recalls that it must have taken about six months, as he had to have all his teeth wired together, and had to eat his food through a straw and there were only certain things that he was able to eat. It certainly stalled his footballing career. Falkirk now lost interest, as did Heart of Midlothian and anyone else who might have been keen. Rangers were reputed to be interested as well at this point, but no more was heard.

But one club did not give up on him. Willie himself says that there was a man *"there waiting for me"* when he came home from hospital, but it may have been a week or two later. This was a man by the name of Pat Duffy, a representative of Celtic FC. He immediately asked Fernie to sign for them. Fernie then says, *"My face was so painful and swollen that I could hardly speak. I just nodded my head in excitement, mumbled my thanks and put my name on the form as quickly as possible."*

A young Scottish boy would usually have no second thoughts about signing for Celtic. Some may have worried about the religious sectarian aspect of playing for one or other of the Old Firm – his mother initially expressed concern, apparently - but Fernie himself (and indeed most of Scotland, certainly the east of Scotland) rightly despised that. What might have been more of a problem was that Celtic in 1948 were far from the best team in Scotland. Their glory days of 40 years previously - when they had Jimmy Quinn, Patsy Gallacher and Jimmy McMenemy and their golden half-back line of Sunny Jim Young, Willie Loney and James Hay - had long gone, and even their great Empire Exhibition Cup-winning team of 1938 had broken up. The war years had not been kind to Celtic, and even though, Jimmy McGrory was now the manager, there were few signs of any comeback.

Indeed a few months previously, they had flirted with relegation, famously rescuing themselves on 17 April with a 3-2 win over Dundee at Dens Park. Things were possibly not quite as drastic as all that, for even if they had lost, other teams still had games to play, and one suspects that the Leagues might have been re-structured or some other device would have been found to get Celtic in with the big boys. They were indeed a very large goose that could lay quite a lot of golden eggs!

For a youngster, there was still the attraction of the name, a huge support and the green and white jerseys. Fernie had little hesitation in signing, even though he would be injured and unable to play for some time. A few days later, a man from Heart of Midlothian did appear to talk to Fernie, but by then it was too late, Willie having agreed to join Celtic. Clearly Celtic's scout Pat Duffy had been very persuasive, but Fernie tells us that Duffy gave him a piece of advice to the effect that he should never pass a ball unless he had it under control. By this he meant that the ball was not something to be got rid of like a "pass the parcel" children's game. Before one passed the ball, the ball had to be under control and the passer needed to have time to think about what he intended to do with it. It was a wise piece of advice and interesting in the context of Fernie's future career, where one of the frequent criticisms of him was that he tended to hang on to the ball too much!

Willie Fernie himself, writing in Charles Buchan's *Football Monthly* about 10 years later, says that the reason why he signed so readily for Celtic was because he was impressed by the fact that Pat Duffy came to see him even when he seemed to be out of the game for the foreseeable future. The other teams seemed to have allowed their interest to cool, but Celtic were still bothered about a player even though he was injured.

The Fifeshire Advertiser has a snippet of information that a *"benefit dance"* will be held in Leslie on August 20 for Bill (sic) Fernie who presumably had lost a little of his earnings on the farm with his injury. Things were now healing up however and on 12 October 1948 he appeared at Celtic Park, now officially a part-time player for the club.

As was the habit in those days, Willie, although technically a Celtic player, was "farmed out" (to use an appropriate metaphor for a man who was now a full-time farm worker!) to a local team, in this case to a newly formed team called Kinglassie Colliery. This was a sensible idea, for it gave the youngster competitive football rather than getting just the occasional game for the reserves. It also meant that he could live at home, and his weekly wage and the ability to put food on the table was not yet totally dependent on how he performed on a football field.

All the time, however, regular reports were sent back to Celtic Park, and now and again, a stranger might arrive at a game unobtrusively, pay his entrance money just like an ordinary supporter, talk to the locals as if he were one of them, bring the conversation round to how Fernie had been playing recently, and listen to what was said before watching some of the game and then depart as quietly and as insignificantly as he had arrived. He would then report back to Celtic Park.

Life in Kinglassie was gradually becoming a great deal better than it had been before the war. Coal was still needed after the war for the national recovery, and there were none of the labour disputes that we had after the Great War, for the simple reason that the pits were now out of the hands of the wicked coal-owners and were being run by the National Coal Board, which was more likely to be sympathetic to the miners. Overtime was frequent, and there was a buzz and even a certain air of prosperity around Kinglassie and Fife in general, and, even though rationing was still in force, things were getting better all the time.

That last statement however did not apply to Celtic. Fernie may well have wondered what had got into him for signing with such a poor team, who came close enough to relegation in 1948 and showed little signs of improvement in 1949 when Rangers were allowed to lift a Scottish treble with only feeble opposition from Celtic. Hibs, Dundee and even East Fife put up some resistance, but the form of Celtic was a constant source of despair to the huge army of fans who could do little other than live in the past, and pray for the return of better days. On the other hand, they had enlisted one new player in summer 1948 from Belfast in Northern Ireland who looked extremely able. This was Charles Patrick Tully.

Meanwhile, in the backwoods of Fife, Fernie was consolidating his form with Kinglassie Colliery. The first thing that one noticed about Fernie was indeed his versatility and his ability and willingness to play wherever he was asked to. For a man who was often wrongly accused of being "selfish" in his perceived reluctance to release the ball, it is ironic that in fact there was no more committed team man than Fernie. He had great dribbling ability, excellent ball control and the know-how to take a goal. His broken jaw had healed up, and he had a certain heading ability as well, but what counted for as much as anything else was his attitude.

He was always a teetotaller, never smoked and always appeared for training, ever willing to help out some other youngster and to learn from those who knew what they were talking about. Football, he appreciated, was a marvellous game, and what a privilege it would be if he were able to earn his living, even for only a few years, from playing the game that he loved. In summer 1949, after a year with Kinglassie, he was called up to Celtic Park.

He was invited to play in the Celtic trial match in early August 1949, and duly went through to Glasgow. He tells the story of how he knocked on the front door, but the commissionaire on the door did not recognise him and told him to go away. Fernie persisted and asked to speak to Jimmy McGrory. McGrory duly arrived but, similarly, did not immediately know who he was and Fernie had to show him his letter of invitation for the trial match. The time would come when everyone would know who Willie Fernie was!

CHAPTER TWO

EARLY DAYS AT PARKHEAD (1949-1954)

Following the 1949/50 winter of playing sometimes for Celtic Reserves and sometimes for Kinglassie under the vague supervision of a Parkhead representative or scout, Willie Fernie played his first game for the club on 18 March 1950 against St Mirren at Love Street. It was a season that had gone wrong (yet another such season!) for Celtic, particularly in the wake of their defeat to Aberdeen in the Scottish Cup at the end of February. Even as early as 1950, the Scottish Cup, won by Celtic 15 times (oftener than the 12 of Rangers and the 10 of Queen's Park) was still considered to be a "special" tournament for Celtic.

Celtic were fourth in the League but well behind Hibs and Rangers. Rangers would eventually do a League and Cup double (East Fife, of all teams, had won the League Cup!) but Celtic were nowhere. Yet their crowds remained high and surprisingly loyal. On Fernie's debut for example, the 20,000 Love Street crowd contained a large Celtic representation to see Bonnar, Boden and McAuley; Evans, McGrory and Baillie; Collins, Fernie, McPhail, Peacock and Haughney take on the Paisley Buddies.

Celtic won 1-0 thanks to a strange goal breasted in by Mike Haughney from a Bobby Collins cross, but what was as significant as anything else was the comment by The Sunday Post reporter that there were four young men on the field that we would hear more about – Lawson and Brown of St Mirren and for Celtic, Willie Fernie the debutant and the Irishman Bertie Peacock, playing only his third game for the club. Fernie was described as *"simplifying his colleague's passing by utilising the open space."*

Thus, we get an early indication of Fernie's ability to "read a game" and he and Peacock were considered good enough to be retained in the team for the rest of the season. Whether this was a pre-decided idea to keep him in the team for the remaining games, or whether he was in any case simply considered good enough, we cannot be certain, but he was indeed kept in the team and even by the end of the season, won a medal!

There were three remaining Scottish League games. Fernie played in his first game at Parkhead before a crowd of 25,000 when Celtic beat East Fife 4-1, all the goals coming from John McPhail. The hero of the hour was quite clearly McPhail, but on occasion the Parkhead crowd showed their appreciation for the effort of Fernie, who showed a welcome willingness to go and look for the ball. He had a less successful game at Partick Thistle on the Holiday Monday, when the team lost 0-1, but finished the League season in style by scoring his first goal for Celtic.

This was on the rather remarkable day of Saturday, 15 April 1950. Celtic's game against Clyde was played at Shawfield, but it was absolutely dwarfed by the Scotland v England game played about half a mile away at Hampden. The International was, of course, 134,000 all ticket with loads of fans stranded outside Hampden unable to get a ticket and reluctant or unable to pay the extortionate prices demanded by the touts and the profiteers. Quite a lot of fans then decided to cut their losses and head to Shawfield instead, and as a result, the turnstiles clicked merrily all through the first half and eventually the game attracted a crowd of 25,000 to see a fairly meaningless match.

It was meaningless but it was more entertaining than the Hampden one. England won 1-0 at Hampden and it was a game that would haunt Hearts' Willie Bauld for the rest of his life. On one occasion, he was through everything and hit the bar! It would have given Scotland a draw and a trip to Rio for the 1950 World Cup, because the SFA, in one of their craziest decisions of them all, stated that they would go to Brazil, but only if they were British champions! A feature of this game incidentally is that the Scotland forward line of Waddell, Moir, Bauld, Steel and Liddell were all Williams! Steel and Liddell were more commonly known as Billy, but the other three were Willies, as it were.

But just down the road at Shawfield, another Willie scored his first goal for Celtic. It was a double header and it came about following a cross from Tully which was headed on by Collins and came to Fernie who headed the ball into the right place. Unfortunately, Fernie then had the misfortune to get in the way of a Clyde forward's drive and conceded an own goal, but he was outstanding in the second half in a very entertaining 2-2 draw.

And thus ended Celtic's League season. It had been poor, but Fernie felt that he had made a good start to his Celtic career. For a young man from Fife, Glasgow and Glasgow football in particular takes a little to get used to, not least in its intensity and all-encompassing importance, but Fernie was intelligent enough to realise that it all takes time. He realised very quickly too that Celtic fans, although bitter and unforgiving in some ways, were very supportive of youngsters and that a man's background and religion meant absolutely nothing. What mattered was the green and white jersey, and whether a man was fit to wear it.

There was still a competition left to be played for in this season. This was the Glasgow Charity Cup, or more particularly, the Glasgow Merchants' Charity Cup. In some ways, it was a relic from the Victorian era in which the season finished rigidly at the end of April and players' contracts finished then as well. Thus, with the Charity

Cup being played in May, players were meant to play for free with all of their wages and the attendance money going to deserving causes.

It did not work out like that of course, and by 1950, football was a thoroughly professional business. Nevertheless, there was always the feeling that this trophy wasn't taken quite as seriously as it might have been. On the other hand, the weather was always that little bit better by the month of May, and for a club like Celtic, this Cup became important. They had won nothing since the Glasgow Cup in autumn 1948, and they had not won the Charity Cup itself since 1943. In addition, it gave the players a chance to win a medal, something that was very important for the new players who had joined the club recently, Sean Fallon, Bertie Peacock and Willie Fernie.

The six Glasgow teams – Celtic, Rangers, Third Lanark, Partick Thistle, Clyde and Queen's Park – all took part and Celtic's first game was against Clyde at Celtic Park. This game, on 29 April did not even play second fiddle to any other game. It was more like third, some distance behind the Rangers v Hibs game at Ibrox which was billed as a "League decider" and the English FA Cup final between Arsenal and Liverpool at Wembley. The Ibrox game ended up as a 0-0 draw and failed to settle the League Championship (although Rangers would eventually do it), and Arsenal beat Liverpool 2-0, but at Parkhead, Celtic beat Clyde 1-0 before a good crowd of over 20,000. Fernie played well, earned a few plaudits from the appreciative crowd and Mike Haughney scored the only goal of the game.

And so Celtic were into the semi-final. It was against Third Lanark and was played at Hampden on Wednesday, 3 May. Celtic scored in the first minute through John McPhail and stayed on top even though Third Lanark missed a barrowload of chances. Rangers beat Partick Thistle in the other semi-final very easily and, now Scottish League, Scottish Cup and Glasgow Cup winners, were confidently expected to get the better of Celtic in the final on the Saturday to win a quadruple of honours.

81,632 turned up at Hampden on Saturday, 6 May 1950 to see whether they would or not. It was, by some distance, the largest crowd that Fernie and quite a few of the Celtic players had ever played before or even seen, and there was another attraction as well in that the Glasgow Charity Cup committee had invited the American actor and comedian Danny Kaye (who happened to be in Great Britain) to entertain the crowd.

Danny Kaye was well received, but he had to take second place to Celtic whose first hour at least was one of the best performances that their fans had seen for some considerable time. Tully was outstanding, but he was well backed up by Collins, Peacock and Fernie in a sprightly Celtic forward line. McPhail scored twice and there was an own goal, and it looked to all the fans of both clubs that a new Celtic was at last emerging to challenge Rangers, and that Willie Fernie was an integral part of this new team who played with such enthusiasm and clear enjoyment. The Iron Curtain defence was in tatters, and what a sight it was to see Woodburn, Shaw and Cox chasing shadows!

But this Rangers team fought back. They were not, after all, champions for nothing and Gillick pulled one back. Panic now set in to this immature and young Celtic side, and Willie Thornton scored another. It looked as if Celtic were about to throw it all away, but they rallied, regained a little control and held out for an exciting 3-2 victory which was greeted by the green and white hordes as if it were a Scottish Cup rather than a less important Glasgow Charity Cup. It was one of the very few nights at this era of history where there was dancing in the streets of the Gorbals and Garngad. It was at least something, and Willie Fernie had at the end of his first season gained a medal to show off to them all in Kinglassie! Any apprehension that anyone in his family may have held about him playing for Celtic was now washed away in a tide of pride. *"Just Like the Celts We Used to Know,"* was the way that Jack Harkness (with Danny Kaye and American musicals in mind, presumably) put it in *The Sunday Post*.

The teams were:

Celtic: *Bonnar, Haughney and Milne; Evans, McGrory and Baillie; Collins, Fernie, McPhail, Peacock and Tully*

Rangers: *Brown, Lindsay and Shaw; Little, Woodburn and Cox; Gillick, Paton, Thornton, Duncanson and Hubbard*

Referee: *Mr W Davidson, Glasgow*

A great future seemed to be beckoning for Fernie and Celtic. There were at least two historical precedents (1903 and 1913) when a Glasgow Charity Cup triumph after a period of non-success had been the springboard for triumph in other competitions, and hopes were now high that a good team was beginning to emerge. That summer saw an unhappy trip to Italy for a dreadful 0-0 draw with Lazio in a "friendly" in which John McPhail had to be sent off to appease the Roman crowd when an Italian was sent off as well!

Season 1950/51 could hardly have started better for Celtic and Fernie. For the first time ever, they qualified for the quarter-finals of the League Cup, winning their section of Third Lanark, East Fife and Raith Rovers. That was actually, in 1950, a very strong section. East Fife were in fact the holders of the Scottish League Cup, Raith Rovers had reached the final in 1949 and Third Lanark, with men like Jimmy Mason, were a consistently strong team in that era. In fact, given Celtic's less than illustrious pedigree in the last few years of the Scottish League Cup (and other competitions) no-one would have predicted that Celtic would qualify with more than a game to spare.

There was of course a certain poignancy for Fernie in knowing that he was up against two Fife teams, and that may well have inspired him to play some of his best football, as he contributed to the team of Bonnar, Haughney and Milne; Evans, McGrory and Baillie;

Collins Fernie, McPhail, Peacock and Tully. That Celtic side won four of the six games in that section and drew the other two, both of them in Fife and both looked back upon with affection by those who saw them as being excellent games of football, with Celtic's right wing of Collins and Fernie being consistently lauded by both Press and public with phrases like *"delightful sweetness," "astonishing speed"* and a *"high degree of skill"* being employed. Fernie was not a tall man, but he was still a few inches taller than the "Wee Barra" as Bobby Collins became known.

East Fife were beaten first at Parkhead 2-0 on a day that the ball burst! Fernie and an East Fife player were both running for it when a sudden "pop" was heard and the ball collapsed pitifully on the grass. (It was no uncommon occurrence in those days in spite of the tough leather used). Then Fernie scored at a packed Cathkin on Wednesday night as he *"cracked home a magnificent counter"* early in the second half, and by the time that Celtic beat Raith Rovers 2-1 on Saturday, 19 August 1950 (although *The Fifeshire Advertiser* tries manfully to claim that Raith were worth a point,) Celtic supporters were openly talking about the team having *"arrived"* and that the Celtic renaissance was now underway.

In heavy rain at a dangerously overcrowded Bayview, Celtic drew 1-1 with East Fife, and their qualification was confirmed the following Wednesday night when they beat Third Lanark 3-1 at Parkhead. The section was rounded off by a visit to Stark's Park in which Celtic were 2-0 up with inside-forwards Fernie and Peacock totally dominating. When these two youngsters tired, Raith came into the game and earned a 2-2 draw. Not that it mattered, for Celtic had qualified with a degree of ease.

But it may be that at this point Fernie's bright start began to stall. They beat Lazio 4-0 in the return match of that awful game played in the summer, then went down 3-4 to Morton at Parkhead (a game in which Neil Mochan scored a hat-trick for Morton!) then beat Queen's

Park rather unconvincingly in a Glasgow Cup tie before the two-legged encounter in the League Cup quarter-final against Motherwell.

It was the first game at Celtic Park that was a total disaster and had a major effect on Fernie's subsequent development that season. He had sent over a splendid cross for McPhail to score in the first minute, but then after that, Celtic simply collapsed against a fine Motherwell side (who would go on to win the Scottish League Cup that season). 60,000 were there to watch this unexpected and unpredicted catastrophe as Motherwell won 4-1 with the last quarter of an hour being played in sullen silence, most of the crowd having disappeared. Fernie was poor, and latterly he and Collins had to switch positions to see if Collins could get going in the middle, for clearly Fernie was simply not doing anything in that position.

Someone has to take the blame after such a humiliation, and it was centre-half John McGrory and Willie Fernie who were dropped. Willie played only another half a dozen games in the rest of the season, normally as a cover for injuries. But no effort seems to have been made to offload him, as often happened in such cases, nor did Fernie himself make any "spoiled brat" effort to move elsewhere. It was clear that both Celtic and Fernie saw some value in the continuation of his employment, and Willie, for his part always a team player, realised that this need not go on for ever and that he had to stick in and work hard at his game, playing for the reserves, even although he may quietly have disagreed with the club's assessment that Donald Weir and Jock Weir were better players than he was.

It was a difficult season to quantify as far as the club themselves were concerned. On the one hand, they at last got back on the major trophy trail by winning the Scottish Cup. They beat Motherwell 1-0 in the final. On the other hand, the good start to the season was not maintained and League form was haphazard and unpredictable, with Celtic ending up nowhere near champions Hibs. The Glasgow Cup final replay against Partick Thistle was eventually played in

March and lost in a hideous manner when the team threw away a 2-1 lead late in the game to lose 3-2.

Fernie might have made a difference if he had been persevered with, but he realised within himself that all he had to do was bide his time. And he cannot fail to have been impressed by the events of Saturday, 21 April 1951, when Celtic won their first Scottish trophy since World War II. If he had not realised before what Celtic was all about, he would have known it then.

In later days, he would have been a substitute, but such things did not exist in 1951. So, from his seat in the stand, he would have observed the huge 134,000 crowd, the frenzied support and cheering of the team, the goal scored by John McPhail in the first half, the long second half as Motherwell piled on the pressure while Celtic defended for their lives, the countdown to the final whistle with the anxious prayers and pleas for the referee to blow for time up. And then, the joy at the end, the sight of Big Captain John lifting the trophy, and the sincere congratulations from all the reserves to the eleven who had done the job.

The congratulations were indeed sincere, but Willie would not have been human if he had not wished that he had been playing. His time would come, but it had not come yet.

Nor did it really come the following season, 1951/52 and Fernie's second full season with the club. But before that, there was a wonderful recompense in the shape of a tour to America and Canada. Fernie was considered good enough to be taken on that tour, which sailed out on the Queen Mary in early May and returned in late June, having taken the Scottish Cup with them (in a shopping bag, apparently) and having lost only once, and that was to Fulham. Tours are not always well chronicled but it appears that he played in only one game – a 2-0 win over Kearny All Stars on 17 June. Nevertheless, a trip to the USA was a great thing for a boy from

Kinglassie. Not many people from the Fife coalfield could boast that they had travelled on the Queen Mary!

There was also the St Mungo Cup, played before the start of the season. Celtic duly won it, but Fernie was not in the team. Indeed, he played only six games during the season, but it was significant that towards the end of the season he played at right-half, alongside the centre-half who had arrived from Wales in December, Jock Stein.

It was still a poor season, however. As far as Celtic were concerned, the main action seemed to centre on the fight between Celtic and the SFA about whether Celtic should be allowed to fly the Irish tricolour at home games. There were several dynamics at work here – not least a personality clash between Celtic's chairman Bob Kelly and the SFA secretary George Graham, but to most Celtic supporters, however praiseworthy the stand of the chairman was, it looked very much as if it was a cover to hide what was, in fact, a dire season and a very disappointing one following last season's Scottish Cup success. Perhaps symbolically, the affair arose out of trouble at the New Year Day game at Parkhead when a very poor Celtic team went down 1-4 to Rangers.

Nevertheless, it was all good fun to see Mr Kelly, with the unlikely support of *The Glasgow Herald*, various politicians and Rangers FC, take on the establishment in the shape of George Graham and Harry Swan of Hibs (Yes! Hibernian FC, whose very name means "Irish" trying to stop someone waving the Irish flag! You couldn't really make that up, could you?) and win. No-one really cared all that much what flag one displayed – Celtic also displayed the Scottish flag and the Union Jack – but it was hilarious to see pompous officialdom making a public fool of itself. It is ridiculous to insist on something that cannot be enforced, and Mr Graham soon backed himself into a corner of having to expel Celtic from Scottish football - a clearly impossible scenario - or be quiet. He quietly did nothing. As they said, the flag was like a man with constipation, no power on earth could pull it down!

But as we have said, however much it increased Kelly's popularity, the "flag flutter" did nothing to solve Celtic's major problems on the football field. Hibs won the League in 1952, Motherwell the Scottish Cup and Dundee the League Cup. The only comfort was that Rangers did not win anything either. Everyone in the Press hailed this as a triumph for Scottish football with words like *"democracy"* being bandied about because the Old Firm were not doing so well. This may have been true, but Celtic needed a boost.

It came at the end of the following season and it was spectacular. Fernie had claimed a place for himself at inside-right and had managed to hold it down for most of the season barring injuries. He had begun to impress the crowd with his dribbling skills, his passing ability, his ball-winning capabilities, and even his goalscoring. On 13 December 1952, for example, he scored a hat-trick in a 5-0 thumping of Dundee at Parkhead, but this was still not a good Celtic side. To an extent, an excuse can be made for them because of the tragic death at an early stage of the season through a burst appendix of Jackie Millsopp, something which naturally had an adverse effect on performances. But there were other, footballing, reasons as well, not least the inability of the management to decide on a settled team.

There was, however, one good point about this Celtic team, and that was their captain, Jock Stein. He was by no means the best centre-half or player that Celtic had ever seen, but he did have some leadership qualities, and Fernie and he had many talks about football in their spare time. Both similar characters, from mining backgrounds and strict teetotallers, they had a lot in common, and they struck up a good and beneficial relationship.

On 20 December, Celtic beat Falkirk 3-2 in a tight game at Brockville, a result that put them second in the League and with a real chance, apparently, of winning the League for the first time since 1938, but then they immediately blew up and lost four games on the trot, one of them being an unlucky 0-1 defeat by Rangers on

New Year's Day. There followed a revival of sorts, but then a defeat by Rangers in the Scottish Cup became contagious (as it were) and caused another series of four League defeats which caused them to finish a miserable eighth.

The Scottish Cup, so often Celtic's saviour in the past, saw a disappointing exit to Rangers at Ibrox at the quarter-final stage 0-2 before an astonishing crowd of 95,000. And yet it could have been so different. Rangers scored early, but then for the rest of the first half Celtic, inspired by Fernie, took over – but tragically couldn't score with several great chances being missed. The second half was even, and the consensus of neutral opinion was that Celtic deserved a replay, but it was Rangers who scored at the end.

Three weeks previously, Saturday, 21 February 1953 had seen the famous game at Brockville, Falkirk. The inadequate ground was dangerously overcrowded (in spite of a few threats of a boycott by Celtic fans in protest about prices) and at half-time Celtic were 2-0 down with ex-Celts Jimmy Delaney and Jock Weir outstanding for the Bairns and Celtic full-back Frank Meechan booed by his own fans for fouling Jimmy Delaney! Things looked very bad for Celtic until Charlie Tully scored direct from a corner kick twice (the first being disallowed by the referee Mr Gerrard of Aberdeen because of the ball being in the wrong place or perhaps because of a crowd encroachment which distracted the goalkeeper while the ball was in the air) and then Willie Fernie *"rose like a jack-in-the-box"* (according to *The Evening Times*) to head home the equaliser.

At this point, and indeed at several points in the second half, it looked as if the game might have to be abandoned because of repeated crowd invasions (thanks to crush rather than violent intent) but the game did continue with Celtic grabbing a winner when Fernie shot for goal, the ball rebounded off a Falkirk defender, and John McGrory headed home the rebound.

The significance of that Scottish Cup game in what was ultimately a losing cause in the next round was that it showed just what a massive backing Celtic, in spite of some rather disappointing and indeed dismal form, could command. The support was by no means uncritical of the team, and contained just rather too many hooligans, as the local newspapers on a Monday after an away game at Falkirk or Dundee or Raith Rovers would tend to indicate, but it was vocal, loyal and kept turning up in huge numbers to any part of Scotland where Celtic were playing.

It was soon after this that Willie Fernie earned his first representative honour, when he was selected to play for the Scottish League against the English League at Ibrox on Wednesday, 25 March 1953. Such games were restricted to Home Scots (i.e. those who played for Scottish clubs) but a good performance in a "League International" could lead to a call-up for the full International in a few weeks' time. These games were taken very seriously and clearly on this occasion 60,000 people thought so, for that was the crowd that Wednesday afternoon to see a strong Scottish side of ***Cowan (Morton), Young (Rangers) and Cox (Rangers); Evans (Celtic), Dougan (Hearts) and Cowie (Dundee); Collins (Celtic), Johnstone (Hibs), Reilly (Hibs), Fernie (Celtic) and Ring (Clyde) take on Merrick (Birmingham City), Green (Birmingham City) and Smith (Arsenal); Wright (Wolverhampton Wanderers), J Froggat (Portsmouth) and Dickinson (Portsmouth); Finney (Preston North End), Broadis (Manchester City), Lofthouse (Bolton Wanderers), R Froggat (Sheffield Wednesday) and Elliott (Burnley).***

It was a good game with the Scottish League just worthy of their 1-0 victory on a bright and windy Scottish spring day. Scotland's only goal came after an error from the English goalkeeper Gil Merrick, and Lawrie Reilly of Hibs pounced to score. Fernie, playing at inside-left (rather than his more normal inside-right) is described by *The Dundee Courier* in terms of *"he tried hard all the time and started some good moves"* – possibly damning with faint praise, one feels.

He did not win a place at Wembley for the full International, but that was hardly surprising as this was only his first full season in the first team at Celtic, he was in the wrong position in the Scottish League game and indeed was only called into the Scottish League side as a late replacement.

Indeed, he was the third choice after first Jimmy Bonthrone of East Fife (who incidentally had lived only a few doors up from Fernie in Kinglassie!) and then Eddie Turnbull of Hibs called off. Nevertheless, it was a good start to international football for Willie and indicated a part of him that was beginning to be apparent at Celtic Park – namely that he was versatile and could play on the other side of the field if he had to. This part of him would be put to good use soon, for he was given the huge honour of being asked to be "travelling reserve" for Scotland v England at Wembley on 18 April.

This was a "position" that only made sense in the pre-substitute days. He would go with the team to Wembley and be on hand just in case someone took ill or was injured in the warm-up for example and before the game actually started because once the referee blew the whistle the eleven players had to remain the same, even though, as happened on this occasion, left back Sammy Cox was injured and had to leave the field after 70 minutes. Willie would have enjoyed this somewhat frustrating experience better than he might have, for Scotland equalised late through "last minute" Lawrie Reilly to earn a 2-2 draw and preserve their unbeaten record at Wembley, where they had not lost since 1934. He clearly did this job well for he was given a similar role at Scotland v Sweden in 1953. His international career would come, however, but for the moment it was back to club duty and a remarkable time in the life of Celtic FC.

A massive indication of the power of Celtic's support had come in early March, when it was decided to celebrate the Coronation of Queen Elizabeth II with a trophy to be played in Glasgow between the best four teams of England and the best four teams of Scotland.

It would be a short competition more or less along the lines of the Empire Exhibition Trophy of 1938, the famous prize won by Celtic and which kept so many Celtic supporters going during the dark days of World War II and the awful Celtic teams of the late 1940s.

England sent *"four of the best"* (as the song would have put it) in 1953, League Champions Arsenal, the last two League Champions in Manchester United (1952), Tottenham Hotspur (1951) and Newcastle United, who had won the FA Cup in 1951 and 1952 and whose proximity to the Scottish border made them an obvious choice as well. As far as Scotland were concerned, Rangers and Celtic were entered automatically. They would be accompanied by the winners of the 1953 Scottish League and Scottish Cup. Rangers, as it happened, won both, so the respective runners-up Hibs and Aberdeen were given places.

But Celtic? Why were they there? Their League campaign in 1953 was nothing short of shocking, with their final position being literally mid-table (eighth out of sixteen), they had won only one trophy since the war, the Scottish Cup in 1951, and had yet to even reach the final of the Scottish League Cup. On the basis of recent form, East Fife, Motherwell and Dundee, to mention but three, had far stronger claims. But, not for the first or last time in Scottish football history, we must look at decisions made, shake our heads ruefully but then nod sagely at the undeniable truism that money talks really rather loudly, and a great deal more loudly than fairness. The tournament was to be played in Glasgow on May evenings. It needed to make money. With all due respect to the gallant and worthy East Fife, a crowd to see them take on Arsenal at Hampden would have been a paltry one. Celtic's fans earned Celtic the right to play in this tournament – possibly it was this phenomenon that led Celtic's then captain Jock Stein to remark for the first, but not the last, time that *"football, without fans, is nothing."*

For all that, Celtic's influential fans (or indeed their players, Fernie included) can hardly have been looking forward to the competition with anything approaching optimism or even sang-froid as the League season finished piteously. Fernie, give or take the odd game missed through injury had played throughout the season, and had enhanced his reputation. He was not yet, however, a superstar – nor could that have been said of anyone in the Celtic team, apart perhaps from the quixotic, mercurial and totally unpredictable Charlie Tully. But not for the first time in history we can see in 1953 the "springboard" effect of the Glasgow Charity Cup.

It all started on the wet Wednesday night of 28 April, when a small crowd of little more than 8,000 saw Celtic beat Clyde 4-0 in the first round of the Charity Cup. It is often felt that Celtic play well in the rain and they certainly did that night with the forward line of Walsh, Fernie, White, Peacock and Tully playing some superb football, and the crowd departing to ask the legitimate question of why they had not seen more of that earlier in the season.

Less satisfactory, although still a win, was the semi-final at Celtic Park on Saturday, 2 May 1953. The opponents were the stuffy Third Lanark team who resisted for a long time before a larger crowd in slightly better weather. Not only that, Thirds actually scored first in the 75th minute but were only in the lead for two minutes until Fernie headed home a Collins cross. The game was then decided on the somewhat primitive method of tossing a coin! This game was played on the same day as the famous Stanley Matthews FA Cup Final and a phenomenon of the new age was the appearance of supporters clustering round someone with a "portable" (sometimes called a "Portobello!") radio and cheers punctuating the air at odd times.

And so to the final against Queen's Park on Saturday, 9 May. Queen's Park had beaten Rangers in midweek in the same way as Celtic had beaten Third Lanark on the Saturday - by the toss of a coin – but this did not stop a large crowd of 40,000 turning up on a gloriously hot day to see the final.

The teams were;

Celtic: *Bonnar, Haughney and Rollo; Evans, Stein and McPhail; Collins, Fernie, Mochan, Peacock and Tully*

Queen's Park: *SH Weir, IG Barnett and T Stewart; R Cromar, A Bell and W Hastie; J Callan, S O' Connell; C Church, R Dalziel and W Omand*

Referee: *W Brittle, Glasgow*

The Queen's Park players are listed with their Christian name initial to indicate that they are Amateurs and in addition they played with their jerseys outside their pants. Even as early as 1953, all this was generally considered to be a quaint anachronism but generally looked upon also with benign tolerance, even by the Celtic support on the grounds that if Celtic are to be allowed to fly the Irish flag, Queen's Park must also be allowed to respect their traditions. It was a strong argument, but also sadly advanced by a few people who should have known better to justify the Rangers policy of refusing to sign Roman Catholics.

Great interest was shown in Celtic's recent capture. This was Neil Mochan, who had played for Morton and then Middlesbrough but who had wished to play for Celtic all his life and now got his wish. His entrance into the club's history could hardly have been more dramatic. Celtic won 3-1 with a degree of ease, and Mochan scored twice and made the other one for Willie Fernie to score from short range. It was a great Celtic performance, and was much celebrated by their support that weekend. Once again, it was the Glasgow Charity Cup for Celtic (the 26th time), a second medal for Willie Fernie and huge (possibly even disproportionate) celebrations in the Celtic heartlands of the Gorbals and the Garngad in Glasgow, Lochee in Dundee, the "Celtic" villages of Holytown, Cleland, Croy and by other Celtic supporters all over Scotland.

Fernie was listed as one of the stars, although *The Glasgow Herald* makes the point that "he was inclined to think that the ball belonged only to him." If this is a criticism, it is only a minor one, for it reveals a great deal of his ability to hold on to the ball and challenge the opposition to try to take it from him. On a hot day, this is a footballing skill much appreciated by one's team mates, and it was a ploy much used by Jock Stein some 15 years later when he told his players that if they were getting tired, they should give the ball to Jimmy Johnstone on the grounds that he could hold it for long enough to give everyone a much-needed breather!

And so Celtic won the Glasgow Charity Cup. The Coronation Cup would be an entirely different matter, for there was hardly enough time to draw breath, as it began on the Monday immediately after the Charity Cup final when Celtic returned to Hampden to take on Arsenal. Jokes were made about Hampden being Celtic's *"other home ground"* and indeed there was a curious point here involving Neil Mochan who actually won two medals for Celtic before playing a game for them at Celtic Park!

But Fernie was not playing in the first game against Arsenal on Monday, 11 May 1953. It is hardly to be believed that he was dropped, and so we must assume that he had picked up an injury against Queen's Park. Thus, it was that the forward line read Collins, Walsh, Mochan, Peacock and Tully for a game that in some ways was one of the best in the club's history, as a huge crowd of 59,500 saw Celtic beat the English League champions 1-0 thanks to a goal scored by Bobby Collins. It was a tough game, and Arsenal were visibly taken aback by the passion of the crowd and the sheer enthusiasm (which did not exclude some robust tackling) of the Celtic players.

Already there was an indication that things were not going to plan if the idea was to have the two champions of Scotland and England, Rangers and Arsenal, the two rich, royalist, establishment teams of Great Britain playing in the final of the Coronation Cup. And more discomfiture came to the establishment when Manchester United got the better of Rangers, thus setting up a semi-final with Celtic on Saturday, 16 May.

Once again, Fernie was not in the team and once again Celtic beat top-class English opposition in Manchester United. This time it was a sterner sort of game when Celtic had to work hard to get their 2-1 result on a windy day. They scored twice through Peacock and Mochan but then when Manchester United pulled one back, Celtic had to defend desperately... but held out to the delight of the 73,000 crowd.

And so, it was Hibs in the final, for they had defeated Tottenham Hotspur and Newcastle United. The irony was terrific. It was possibly just as well that the young and as yet uncrowned Queen was not invited to present the trophy. (Would she have been if the final had indeed been between Rangers and Arsenal?) Jokes went around that it might have been better to invite Eamon de Valera of the Irish Republic to do the honours! He would have been quite at home amongst 117,000 people wearing green and white and quite a few of them waving the flags that the SFA and the Chairman of Hibs, Harry Swan, had tried to proscribe less than 18 months ago!

The song of the time reports how the Royal Family themselves were, allegedly, disappointed at this turn of events;

"But, alas for the hopes of our two Royal blues
The Celtic beat Arsenal and Manchester too
Then Hibs in the final, all lo and behold!
All Hampden was covered with green, white and gold!"

Most newspapers tipped Hibs to win. Frankly, they were a splendid side with their Famous Five forward line of Smith, Johnstone, Reilly, Turnbull and Ormond and a good defence into the bargain. Several trains brought their fans in large numbers from Edinburgh confident that they could win the Coronation Cup to make up for their narrow miss in the Scottish League where Rangers pipped them at the post and prevented them from winning three Championships in a row. They did however seem to have a problem with Cup ties. They were aware that now 51 years had passed since they last won the Scottish Cup in 1902, and, like Celtic, they had never won the Scottish League Cup, although they had lost to Motherwell in the final of 1950.

Celtic had an injury problem in that Charlie Tully had pulled a muscle. He would be much missed and Tully himself was totally devastated, but this did at least solve a selection problem for Celtic. Willie Fernie might have played instead of Jimmy Walsh at inside-right – and that would have been hard on the sparkling Jimmy Walsh – but now, there was no choice. The versatile Fifer came in at outside-left while Bertie Peacock stayed at inside-left, where he had excelled so far in the competition.

It had rained quite a great deal during the day of Wednesday, 20 May, but it cleared up spectacularly at around teatime and it became a very fine night for a very fine game of football. Television had not quite arrived in sufficient strength and quality for the game to be televised live, so, for the fans, it was either go to the game or listen to it on the radio, as indeed the great Patsy Gallacher, reputed to be the best of them all but now with only weeks to live, did.

The teams were:

Celtic: *Bonnar, Haughney and Rollo; Evans, Stein and McPhail; Collins, Walsh, Mochan, Peacock and Fernie*

Hibs: *Younger, Govan and Paterson; Buchanan, Howie and Coombe; Smith, Johnstone, Reilly, Turnbull and Ormond*

Referee: *Mr H Phillips, Motherwell*

Those who congregated at the King's Park or "Celtic" end of the ground saw most of the action, for Celtic were marginally the better team in the first half and Hibs were overwhelmingly superior in the second. It was 1-0 at half-time, and Fernie played a part in the goal. A long clearance from Stein came to him, and seeing some Hibs defenders converging, Fernie deftly flicked the ball on to Mochan who ran on and scored a marvellous goal from about 30 yards, giving goalkeeper Younger no chance. It was a goal fit enough to win any Cup, let alone this one, but it was not the major talking point of this game.

It was only the second half which was broadcast on the radio – the Scottish Home Service – so, the game having kicked off at 7.00 pm, it was 7.45 when radios were switched on all over the country – and the next hour was excruciatingly anxious for all concerned as the talented Hibs side piled on the pressure in search of that elusive equaliser. Wave after wave of Hibs attacks hurled themselves on that Celtic goal and it seemed that the defence must yield to the concerted attacks of that superbly able forward line. But the Celts were organised with Haughney and Rollo dealing with the wingers as best they could, and crucially Stein getting the better of Lawrie Reilly more often than not while behind them all, Johnnie Bonnar played, quite literally, the game of his life. Fernie found himself playing further back than he would have liked – not quite an out-and-out defender, but needed to help out his defenders and to be ready to create something at the other end when required.

Hibs best and most unlucky player that night was Bobby Johnstone who rejoiced in the unlikely moniker of "Nicker" and on at least three occasions he was "through" and a goal seemed inevitable until Bonnar once again saved the day. Three minutes remained when once again, Fernie was responsible for a Celtic goal when he picked up a somewhat desperate clearance from Evans and charged up the left wing with no other intention than to use up time by "taking the dog for a walk" to the corner flag, when he suddenly noticed that Jimmy Walsh was available. He slipped the ball across to Walsh who scored at the second attempt.

There was now no way back for Hibs and minutes later the full-time whistle went, and soon after that Jock Stein was receiving the Coronation Cup from Lord McGowan. Words cannot really describe the scenes of ecstasy in the Celtic support, and for Willie Fernie, the recollection of that lovely early summer night, would stay with him the rest of his life. Once again, there was dancing in the streets of the Gorbals that night.

One night in March 1977, one of the authors was travelling back from a Newcastle v Middlesbrough match on the Edinburgh train, when he caught sight of Willie Ormond, then manager of Scotland. He went up to and talked to the amiable and unpretentious little man about all things football from his playing career with Hibs to being manager of St Johnstone and now Scotland. He did not hold back from a few volleys of criticism of the SFA and some of the current Scotland players either! But when he was asked about his biggest disappointment, he did not, surprisingly, mention anything about Scotland's departure from the 1974 World Cup, but harked back to the Coronation Cup final of 1953. *"We couldna get one by that bugger Bonnar"* was the way that he put it. *"There was one near the end when I connected wi a baw frae Gordon Smith, and said tae myself 'That's a winner, but no, he clawed it awa!'"*

Coronation Day itself on 2 June was miserable and cold, but Celtic supporters, most of them looking upon (not literally of course, for television had not yet really arrived) the pageantry in London with either polite disdain or benign tolerance rather than outright hostility, were still revelling in their great triumph and the glow of triumph lasted all summer. It was one of these summers when players and supporters could not wait for August and the resumption of the football season, for there was now the genuine belief that a great team was in place, and that this team was going places.

So it did – to an extent, but the late summer and autumn of 1953 were disappointing, and very soon disillusionment set in after a few poor results. Celtic seldom did well in the Scottish League Cup and this was no exception. A defeat at home to Aberdeen on the first day was never really recovered from and the worst blow of all was a 0-4 hammering in the Glasgow Cup semi-final replay from Rangers at the beginning of September. It was all the more disappointing for it came after an honourable 1-1 draw in the first game, and *The Glasgow Herald* unreservedly pointed the finger of blame at Jock Stein!

It looked like back to square one, but the team and Fernie in particular took it all on the chin and began to string together a few results beating Aberdeen, Raith Rovers and Hearts for example, but also losing to teams like East Fife, Queen of the South and Stirling Albion, with the supporters showing signs of bewilderment rather than anything else. But there were a couple of consolations for the puzzled Celtic fans – one was that no other team had asserted any dominance (at the turn of the year, Queen of the South, of all people, were top of the Scottish League!) and the other was that Willie Fernie was playing consistently well, and it was reckoned that his ball-playing skills were enough to attract an extra few thousand to the crowd.

For example, on Boxing Day 1953, the last game of that remarkable roller-coaster year, Celtic beat Clyde 7-1 at Shawfield. In spite of a Glasgow bus strike and pouring rain, a more than respectable crowd of 21,500 turned up, and *The Evening Times* talks about *"ball brilliance" "a remarkable player" "What a player!"* and a *"A splendid match with Fernie written all over it"* in the context of the Fife genius. He did not score, but had a hand in most of the seven goals, and Celtic fans who were compelled to walk in the rain to distant parts of Glasgow or to railway stations had quite a lot to cheer them up, not least in the play of Willie Fernie who had now seemed to add ball distribution to his other skills, and was now beginning to lose his reputation of holding on to the ball too much.

New Year's Day 1954 saw Celtic beat Rangers 1-0 in a game that was far more one-sided than it seemed and effectively ended Rangers season with more and more questions being asked about the aged Struth at the helm at Ibrox. Fernie once again starred, but the gilt was taken off the gingerbread by the events the following day at Pittodrie when Celtic went down 0-2 to a good Aberdeen side. They then lost to Raith Rovers and Hearts and things were beginning to look bleak until, as it were, someone pressed a switch, but the switch was called Willie Fernie.

On Saturday, 6 February 1953, Celtic went down 2-3 to Hearts at Tynecastle. They ought to have done better, but it meant that Hearts were now eight points clear of Celtic. But crucially, Celtic had games in hand, as indeed had Rangers. Basically, all it needed was for one team to go on a run, and the League would be theirs. Celtic had nine games left. They won them all, and predictably, as often happens when you go on an unbeaten run, your challengers are affected by this and begin to drop points, even when you are not actually playing them! Hearts in particular wilted in the face of this onslaught.

Dundee, East Fife, Airdrieonians, Partick Thistle, Stirling Albion, St Mirren, Falkirk, Hibs and Hamilton were the teams who were swept aside, all by more than one goal, as the Celtic juggernaut roared into action. Goals were lost at the back, but the forward line of Higgins, Fernie, Fallon (replacing the injured McPhail), Tully and Mochan took off. Sean Fallon, normally a full-back and the last man one would have thought of as a striker, silenced his doubters by scoring goals. Neil Mochan was similarly effective, Higgins was a superb revelation on the wing, Tully was simply Tully, but the man who was making it all happen for Celtic was Willie Fernie, who now added goalscoring to his already extensive repertoire.

He was such a dominant player. He wanted the ball (always a good sign in a footballer) and the rest of the team were particularly keen to give the ball to him, and he was well supported by the excellent wing-halves Bobby Evans and Bertie Peacock. If there was any criticism of the team it was in the defence, but the support who had been so depressed after the Tynecastle result in early February slowly became more and more animated and even confident that the Scottish League might be coming to Celtic Park for the first time since 1938. Captain Stein assessed the situation and radiated confidence, his close relationship to McGrory and Kelly guaranteeing that he had at least some input into team selection. Reverses to opponents helped, and two Wednesday evening results at difficult grounds of St Mirren and Falkirk in early April meant that the League could be won at Easter Road on 17 April.

A crowd of over 50,000 seemed to be crammed into Easter Road that spring day, knowing that a win would guarantee Celtic the Scottish League. Celtic clearly meant business, for Mochan scored in the first minute and after that, Celtic never looked back. Mochan scored again, and then Higgins made it 3-0 and the joy of the Celtic fans was complete, but no-one was happier than the artist of it all, Willie Fernie, the man who had made all things possible. Willie himself, always a team man, would never have claimed any more credit than anyone else but in the opinion of the Press and the supporters, Willie was "the bhoy." Seldom had Edinburgh seen such rejoicing as the Celtic fans sang and danced all their way to Princes Street and Waverley Station. *"There's not a team like the Glasgow Celtic! No, not one – and there never has been one!"*

But that was only half of it. If anything, the Scottish Cup this season was even more thrilling, and now Celtic supporters after so many years of hunger, suddenly found themselves at a feast. The road to Hampden consisted of three difficult away fixtures at Falkirk, Stirling Albion and Hamilton Academical. They did not sound all that difficult but all of these teams had caused trouble in League games to Celtic and other "bigger" teams, and in each one of them, Celtic eased home by the odd goal 2-1 at Brockville, 4-3 at Annfield and 2-1 at Douglas Park.

The game at Falkirk ought to have been played on Saturday, 13 February but was postponed because of a waterlogged pitch and played on the Wednesday afternoon. (Floodlights had not as yet arrived at Brockville in 1954.) This did not in the slightest lessen the tension or the large crowd and they were rewarded by a great game of football in the tradition of games between these two clubs. Fernie opened the scoring for Celtic when the goalkeeper could only parry a free-kick and played well throughout.

Stirling Albion were next on 27 February. The clubs had not met very often (Stirling Albion had only been founded in 1945) but amazingly it was a ground on which Celtic had never won before! The sequence of goalscoring was odd. 2-0 for Stirling Albion became 4-2 for Celtic but then the Albion pulled one back and Celtic had to defend desperately.

It was a similar story at Douglas Park on 13 March. This time, there was evidence of serious overcrowding - such was the enthusiasm of the Celtic support - and at one point a crush barrier collapsed. Fernie was brought down in the penalty box and Mike Haughney converted, then Fernie himself scored late in the game to seal the tie, apparently. But Hamilton pulled one back and once again Celtic were glad to hear the final whistle.

The other quarter-final winners were Rangers, Aberdeen and, eventually after a replay, Second Division Motherwell, who struggled to beat Partick Thistle. It was Celtic's good fortune to draw Motherwell, but it did not really look that way in the semi-final on 27 March when Charlie Aitken of Motherwell headed an equaliser just at the very death after Celtic, with Fernie totally dominant, had failed to put the game to bed.

102,424 watched that game and the replay which was played on Monday, 5 April (the Glasgow Holiday Monday) attracted 92,662. It was a tight game, 1-1 at half-time, but then Fernie scored with a goal that Motherwell thought was offside. Celtic then took control to reach the Scottish Cup final for the second time since the war and the 25th time overall. They had won the Scottish Cup 16 times, twice oftener than Rangers.

The other semi-final was between Aberdeen and Rangers. Celtic had no game that Saturday of April 10 (other than a friendly with Kilmarnock), so Celtic chairman Bob Kelly and captain Jock Stein turned up to see the semi-final. It was generally agreed that this was not one of Rangers better seasons, but no-one could possibly have predicted this score line of Rangers 0 Aberdeen 6 – and it should have been more! Aberdeen's hero who scored a hat-trick was a Celtic supporting youngster from Bridgeton called Joseph O'Neill. Amazingly, it was the first time that Aberdeen had beaten Rangers in a Scottish Cup tie and they certainly made a good job of it this time!

This was an earth-shattering experience for everyone, and although Celtic fans rejoiced in the humiliating discomfiture of their rivals, their joy was tempered by the thought that they were now up against a good Aberdeen team who knew how to win in Glasgow. Fernie and others might have even preferred to have been playing Rangers in the final, for Rangers were not having a good season, whereas the fast-developing Aberdeen were very efficient, and indeed had given Celtic a great deal of trouble in League and League Cup games.

But the week before the Scottish Cup final, Celtic had won the Scottish League and the momentum was with them. It was an astonishing statistic that the last time that Celtic had won the Scottish Cup and League double was 1914, some 40 years and a couple of dreadful World Wars ago when Alec McNair, Sunny Jim and Patsy Gallacher were all around. Celtic were looked upon as marginal favourites because they were League champions and had in Fernie and Tully two of the genuinely artistic ballplayers of the season, but Aberdeen also had some great players in Bobby Leggat, George Hamilton and Paddy Buckley. They did however suffer one blow when it was announced that their hero of the semi-final

Joe O'Neill was injured and out of the final. This did at least solve a problem for Joe and his family. Joe, naturally, had to keep his mouth shut, but his family now had no doubts or inhibitions. They were supporting Celtic!

In circumstances of the greatest excitement and anticipation, the city of Aberdeen virtually emptied itself that weekend with buses leaving as early as Thursday night in some cases. The Dons had won the Scottish Cup once in 1947, and there were still many people around with vivid memories of the previous time that Celtic had played Aberdeen in a Scottish Cup final in 1937 when Celtic had won 2-1. Aberdeen had since then changed colours. They had then played in black and gold, but now they played in red, and what a nice scene they made as they poured out of Buchanan Street Station, and in the concourse of Hampden where they mingled happily and harmoniously with those wearing the green and white of Celtic.

Celtic and Aberdeen supporters had traditionally got on well together. Aberdeen is far enough away from the awful sectarianism and religious divide of Glasgow to be almost living in a different world, and traditional Glasgow hospitality and friendship meant that the red men and women (a huge number of women as always in the red army of the north) were made welcome, and of course this year there was another point of contact as both sets of supporters loved Joe O'Neill and his hat-trick in the 6-0 demolition of Rangers a fortnight ago!

Joe of course was not playing and was replaced by Jim Clunie, a centre-half rather than an inside-forward, but that was curiously balanced by Sean Fallon, a tough, rugged full-back playing in the centre-forward position for Celtic. The weather was pleasant without being too sunny, and the pitch was in fine condition as the crowd of just over 130,000 made their way to Hampden Park to see a game which was generally regarded as one of the best Scottish Cup finals of them all.

The teams were:

Celtic: *Bonnar, Haughney and Meechan; Evans, Stein and Peacock; Higgins, Fernie, Fallon, Tully and Mochan*

Aberdeen: *Martin, Mitchell and Caldwell; Allister, Young and Glen; Leggat, Hamilton, Buckley, Clunie and Hather*

Referee: *Mr C Faultless, Glasgow*

The first half saw Celtic playing to the King's Park end of the ground. One is tempted to say towards "*where their own supporters were standing*" but that would not be true because the crowd was agreeably mixed with red rosettes and favours mingling with green ones. Scarves were not yet a major feature of supporters' gear as they would become a few years later (it was in any case a day which hardly lent itself to such winter clothing) but rosettes were common and a particular manifestation of one's affections in 1954 came in headgear with bowler type hats, lum hats, tammies and bonnets all made out in either green or red depending on one's preference, and frequently knitted by one's grandmother. The crowd was about equally divided, but there was also, as often in the 1950s, a considerable contingent of neutrals, people who would normally support Clyde or St Mirren, perhaps, but who made it their business to attend the Scottish Cup final, no matter who was playing.

For Fernie, this must have been the greatest moment of his footballing life. The meeting at a hotel, the light and early lunch, the usual banter on the bus going to Hampden tempered by nerves, last minute fitness checks, arrival at the ground through masses and masses of fans, having a walk on the pitch and talking nervously to the Aberdeen players who were going through the same emotions, looking to the stand to see if the family had arrived yet, then back to the dressing-room to get ready.

The absurd superstitious rituals of putting your left boot on before your right, the thrill even more pronounced on a day like this of pulling the green and white jersey over your head and realising just exactly what this meant to so many people, then the best wishes from chairman Bob Kelly and manager Jimmy McGrory before the final pep talk from the man who was clearly the leader of the party, captain Jock Stein. Willie had grown to like big Jock. An occasionally abrasive exterior and certainly not a man to get on the wrong side of, Jock with his encyclopaedic knowledge of the game, his instant recall of players, his awareness of tactics and above all his love of football and desire to win games and trophies made everyone listen to him, even potential mavericks like Charlie Tully who had needed some time before warming to his captain.

As far as Fernie was concerned, the tactics were simple. Play your own game, let them see your dribbling skills but recognise that dribbling would not in itself score goals. Dribbling bought time for teammates to get into position for the eventual pass, and that had to be a good one. Fernie nodded sagely to what McGrory and Stein said, everyone wished each other *"good luck,"* everyone shook hands, the religious made their devotions and a knock came to the door with the referee saying *"Right, lads."*

The wall of noise as they entered the arena, more handshakes, the best wishes (the teams ran out separately in 1954) to teammates – all this passed in a flash, and the game started. The first half similarly passed in a flash, and it was difficult for Fernie to recall much about those 45 minutes. The radio commentator said that "there was not a piece of paper between the two sides." Both teams had had chances, but no clear-cut ones, the standard of entertainment and sportsmanship had been high but everyone knew that the second half would decide it all.

It was Celtic who went ahead soon after half-time, and the goal had a large slice of fortune about it. Neil Mochan shot from the right, the ball deflected off the luckless Alec Young and went into the net.

It was lucky, although possibly not undeserved on the balance of play, but then within a minute the scales were balanced again when a long ball found Paddy Buckley who for once got to the ball before his "shadow" Jock Stein, and Aberdeen were level.

It was now clear that something special was going to be needed to settle this tie, and it came from Willie Fernie. He had not done anything wrong so far in the game, had always been well marked and hadn't really asserted himself either, but now he picked up a loose ball, made space down his inside-right channel, dribbled past a defender, looked up, saw Sean Fallon in a little space and immediately sent him an inch-perfect pass from which the "Iron Man" in the greatest moment of his career shot home past Fred Martin in the Aberdeen goal.

It was a good goal and it was tempting for supporters to look back on that goal as if it decided the Scottish Cup. So it did, but there were still another 15 minutes to go and Aberdeen inspired by their talented inside-right George Hamilton threw everything at the Celtic goal. But the same men who had done so well against Hibs in the Coronation Cup final of less than a year ago – Bonnar, Evans and Stein in particular- held out. Fernie's role in all this was to help the defence and if the ball came to him, to hold on to it for as long as he could. Nothing fancy or dangerous - just simple ball retention.

Life was tense both inside the ground and in Scottish living-rooms, as the radio was listened to with avidity. One of your writers, not yet 6 years old, heard the commentator say something about *"Johnnie Bonnar in the Celtic goal slides across his line to save"* and promptly showed his father how it was done – only to be rebuked for so doing, for the moment was far from conducive to levity at this point.

The 15 minutes passed, referee Charles Faultless (well named today for he was spot on) allowed a minute or two of injury time, and then blew for time up to indicate that Celtic had won a League and Cup double, had won the Scottish Cup for the 17th time and that Willie Fernie had now won a Scottish Cup medal. Life could not get much better for the man from Kinglassie! Life could not get much better either for the 5-year-old who was presented with the silver teapot (which did indeed have a passable resemblance to the Scottish Cup) by his mother at just about the same time that Jock Stein was lifting the real thing, while his relieved father, with tears in his eyes, clapped, cheered and talked about Willie Fernie and Patsy Gallacher.

There were, however, two slight downers to end the season. One was a narrow 0-1 defeat to Rangers in the Glasgow Charity Cup on 1 May and the other was a rather heavy defeat for the Scottish League at Stamford Bridge on the Wednesday before that. Three Celtic players were involved – Fernie, Evans and Stein – and it must have been a particular disappointment after the successes of the past two Saturdays. Fernie and Evans would play again for Scotland and the Scottish League, but it turned out to be Jock Stein's only representative honour. It would have to be said that the experience possibly exposed Jock's limitations at the top level. He did have other good qualities though! He had a sense of humour as well. He said he was a *"passable"* centre-half!

The teams at Stamford Bridge were ***Merrick (Birmingham City), Ball (Bolton Wanderers) and Willemse (Chelsea): Wright (Wolverhampton Wanderers), Owen (Luton Town) and Bell (Bolton Wanderers); Harris (Portsmouth), Sewell (Sheffield Wednesday), Jezzard (Fulham), Haynes (Fulham) and Mullen (Wolverhampton Wanderers)*** for the English League and ***Martin (Aberdeen), Lapsley (St Mirren) and Binning (Queen of the South); Evans (Celtic), Stein (Celtic) and Coombe (Hibs); Leggat (Aberdeen), McMillan (Airdrie), Bauld (Hearts), Fernie (Celtic) and Ormond (Hibs).*** Mr AH Blythe of London was the referee.

Fernie would soon find himself winning a full Scotland cap, but it was a mixed blessing, as we shall discover.

CHAPTER THREE

THE MID 1950s (1954-1957)

Summer 1954 had seen Willie Fernie in an odd roller-coaster of emotions, one would have imagined. On the one hand he had played a major (some might even have said the main) part in Celtic's first League and Cup double for 40 years. Celtic supporters had enjoyed the summer, relishing the thought of what had just happened with their team that contained just so many fine players – Bobby Evans, Willie Fernie, Neil Mochan, Bertie Peacock, Bobby Collins and Charlie Tully – who were fit to grace any footballing company, and they were looking forward to the glorious future that seemed to beckon.

On the other hand, Willie had also seen at first-hand how NOT to run a football club, and in this case an International team that was supposed to represent a football-daft nation. In particular, the 0-7 hammering from Uruguay was hard to take. As in a similar situation in 1978, a foreign catastrophe and a World Cup debacle meant that the game struggled to regain domestic credibility for a while, and although men like Willie Fernie and Neil Mochan were hardly to blame for what went wrong, they were nevertheless associated with what had happened and were inevitably the subject of remarks about 7-0 *"and it should have been 27-0,"* sometimes delivered in a kindly, good natured, sympathetic way, but sometimes not.

Funnily enough, the club that emerged smelling of roses out of all this were Rangers. They had arrogantly considered themselves above all this and had taken their players off on tour to America, so they could not be blamed for the Swiss fiasco. Indeed, some of their supporters, for all their banner waving and talk about "Scotland's No 1 team" gave the impression of having enjoyed it all! They had also changed management. Willie or Bill Struth who had been in charge since 1920 had now at last retired and had been replaced by ex-player Scot Symon who had enjoyed considerable success with East Fife and had recently taken Preston North End to the final of the English FA Cup where they lost narrowly to West Bromwich Albion.

But there were other good teams around – Aberdeen, Clyde, Dundee, Hibs, Hearts and East Fife were all respectable outfits – and in some ways the mid 1950s were Scottish football's best years, in spite of the disgraceful performances at International level which would continue for some time yet. Crowds had boomed in the years immediately after the War and showed no signs of diminishing. They would begin to fall away in a few years' time when the arrival of television would provide an alternative for a Saturday afternoon and people would begin to ask questions about why they had to put up with grounds with shocking facilities for shelter and toilets, let alone the lack of any adequate refreshment opportunities. But season 1954/55 was buoyant and interesting, and undeniably, with full employment, prosperity was in the air. People still moaned about poverty, but then again, people always do. One thing didn't change, though. As a topic of conversation, in male society at least, football absolutely dwarfed anything else.

It was often said that the reason why Celtic did not do well in the Scottish League Cup was because they were always slow starters to a season. The League Cup had been in existence since 1946/47 and Celtic had never won it, or even appeared in a final, while East Fife had won it three times! This season Celtic were drawn in a challenging section alongside Hearts, Dundee and Falkirk, and the season opened when Falkirk came to Parkhead on 14 August.

46,000 were there to see the League flag unfurled and Scottish Cup displayed. The weather was pleasant, and it was a happy Celtic crowd who saw their team win 3-0 over a decent Falkirk side. Fernie was once again at inside-right – indeed the whole team was as it had been at Hampden in April – and there was every expectation that life would continue as previously. Fernie once again earned a few rounds of applause with his dribbling skills and one or two lovely passes to other forwards.

But then for reasons that were fairly inexplicable at the time, let alone nearly 70 years down the line, Celtic just collapsed and won only one other point in the rest of the League Cup campaign. It all started at Dundee on Wednesday night when 29,000 (a huge crowd for a midweek game) saw Celtic go down 1-3 and The Courier's report fails to mention Fernie once, a significant and eloquent omission. Worse followed on the Saturday when Hearts came to town and won 2-1 with *The Evening Times* making the comment that *"Celtic were merely rugged while Hearts revelled in positional manoeuvres which were often delicately executed."* The 60,000 departed wondering what had happened to Celtic over the summer and particularly Willie Fernie who had seemed jaded and unhappy. Perhaps his experience in Switzerland had done him no favours.

What little chance Celtic had of qualification disappeared at Brockville with a 2-2 draw, not in itself a bad result but a win was required, and some of the supporters misbehaved as they would tend to do quite often there in the 1950s, leading to grim jokes that it should be called "Brickville" because of all the stones that the Celtic fans threw and that Celtic supporters' colours should be "bottle green."

The impressive Hearts side then beat Celtic again and, as it turned out, they went on to win the League Cup that year, and Celtic also failed to distinguish themselves in the Glasgow Cup where they went out to Partick Thistle at the third attempt, losing by the astonishing score of 4-5 after two feckless draws. The season had not started well, but there were signs that Fernie was coming back to his old self, although he had to prove his versatility by moving to inside-left to cover for an injury to Charlie Tully while Alec Boden, a good centre-half but a questionable forward, came in at inside-right.

A great deal was forgiven by the support (as is often the case) when Celtic won their first game of the season against Rangers. Rangers themselves had not started at all well under Scot Symon and a few days before the game at Parkhead, they found out that centre-half Willie Woodburn had been banned "sine die" by the SFA for a thuggish head butt on a Stirling Albion player.

The Old Firm game was on 18 September at Parkhead and Celtic won 2-0. The goals were scored by Jimmy Walsh and Johnny Higgins, but *The Evening Times* was in no doubt about who the star of the show was. The headline was *"Celtic's Fernie Tickles"* and the summing up says quite unequivocally *"Fernie stood out like a beacon. He was the most accomplished player afield."* Celtic supporters often look upon games against Rangers with a disproportionate sense of their importance, and anyone who is responsible for a victory against Rangers is looked upon as a hero for weeks and months afterwards – and will naturally be forgiven for the occasional poor game.

Three good wins followed at Raith Rovers, Aberdeen, then Kilmarnock at home, with Fernie well mentioned in newspaper reports, and it was little surprise that he was chosen to play for Scotland in the International at Cardiff on 16 October. Scotland won, but it was maybe not without significance that the form of Celtic, without Fernie, dipped a little that day with a 1-1 draw against Queen of the South.

Willie also played against Northern Ireland on Wednesday, 3 November 1954, and he continued to star for Celtic, mainly at inside-left in a forward line which normally read Higgins, Tully, Walsh, Fernie and Collins, although most supporters were of the persuasion that Collins and Tully should change places. Results continued to be good, although there was a defeat at Firhill in mid-November and a couple of insipid draws against Motherwell and East Fife.

But the team rallied in the dark days of December when, in the absence of floodlights, games had to kick off at 2.00pm with a particularly good 5-0 win over Hibs at Easter Road. Then there was a 4-1 defeat of Dundee at Celtic Park. The Easter Road display in particular excited admiration from the Press with Fernie scoring twice and, along with Charlie Tully, showing how football should be played – and this was against a good Hibs team! The following week when Dundee were put to the sword to the tune of 4-1, *The Dundee Courier* after searching manfully for excuses and quoting the ever chivalrous and gentlemanly Jimmy McMenemy that *"Dundee might have gone home with a point"* has to admit that Celtic were *"that wee bit better" and that the difference was Willie Fernie who "had ball control and needle-like penetration," "his goal, taken on the turn, was unsavable (sic) and worth the two points."*

Football was played on Christmas Day in 1954, and Celtic entertained near neighbours Clyde. It was this time a disappointing 2-2 draw and that was really Celtic's problem as 1954 gave way to 1955 – too many draws. They were still well placed however with 15 games played and 22 points, equal with Rangers, but behind the surprise leaders, Aberdeen who had 26 points from 16 games. *The Evening Times* of Christmas Day 1954 has a feature on Fernie, with the respected journalist Gair Henderson using political imagery of Fernie, since his wonderful performance against Hibs on 11 December resolving to give up his *"private enterprise"* in order to improve the *"welfare state"* at Parkhead.

It was something that Fernie, a solid Labour man (Tories don't really exist in Kinglassie or anywhere else in the Fife coalfield!)

would have approved of. Jimmy McGrory is also quoted as saying that Fernie had given up some of his *"all my own work"* touches, and has learned now, McGrory hopes, to co-operate and collaborate with men like Tully and Walsh for the benefit of the team. This apparent change in approach may well have had something to do with him not being picked for the Scotland game against Hungary in early December – ironically against a team (currently regarded as the best in the world in spite of their defeat by West Germany in the 1954 World Cup final) who were full of ballplayers and great individualists like Fernie.

But in spite of being sidelined for the Scotland team, 1954 finished on a high note for Fernie, and 1955 promised even more of the good things. Yet it did not start well with a 1-4 defeat by Rangers at Ibrox. *The Glasgow Herald* is of the opinion that the faults for this defeat lay mainly in the defence rather than the attack with Jock Stein, never a favourite of *The Glasgow Herald*, in particular singled out for having a poor game, but it was also true that the attack did not get going either and it was a particular disappointment after so many good performances in the latter part of 1954.

But the mark of a good team and a good player is often that they have the ability to bounce back. The rest of January saw four competent wins with Fernie in top gear, scoring twice, for example, in the 2-0 win over Queen of the South in Dumfries (always a difficult fixture) and playing a significant role in a 2-0 win over Hearts at Parkhead. That was on 29 January, and effectively removed Hearts from the League race. On the same day, Rangers lost 1-2 to Dundee, but there was still Aberdeen, winning consistently and now five points ahead of Celtic, although Celtic did have a game in hand.

February saw another point dropped at the bogey ground of Brockville. The conditions were difficult with frequent snowstorms and Fernie scored first for Celtic, but then after he had another shot cleared off the line by Alex Parker, Falkirk equalised. It was generally believed to be hard luck on Celtic, but Aberdeen continued their relentless winning run with a 4-0 defeat of Partick Thistle at Pittodrie in conditions that were equally wintry.

It was that same unpredictable Partick Thistle who had folded at Pittodrie that next took a point off Celtic a month later. Feckless finishing was the reason, and it was all the more frustrating for Celtic because Aberdeen lost that day 0-2 to Hearts, so Celtic had only made up one point rather than two. (Until the 1994-5 season it was only two points for a victory in the Scottish League.) Six games were left, one of them Aberdeen at Parkhead, and the feeling was that Celtic might yet pressurise the Dons to lose. Aberdeen had never before won the Scottish League, and their result against Hearts showed clearly that nerves were beginning to play a part.

In the meantime, Fernie was beginning to struggle with an ankle injury, something which compelled him to withdraw from the position of travelling reserve for the Scottish League game against the English League on 16 March, thereby guaranteeing that he would not be chosen for the big International at Wembley, and he also missed two Celtic games in which the team edged home narrowly without him, the quality of their play clearly indicating how much they were missing their talisman.

It all unravelled for Celtic as March turned to April. Fernie returned on 26 March when Celtic drew 2-2 with Airdrie in an undistinguished Scottish Cup semi-final at Hampden. He scored with a header and set up Walsh for the other goal, but then picked up another injury, this time to his back, in the course of the game and missed the next two games. Celtic beat East Fife narrowly at Methil on Wednesday, 30 March, but then the League challenge collapsed as, still without Fernie, Celtic lost 1-2 to Hibs at home, on the same day that Aberdeen beat a poor Rangers team 4-0 and an outclassed Scotland went down 2-7 to England at Wembley. It would be safe to say that 2 April 1955 was not the highlight of the life of anyone at Celtic Park!

The irony was that when Aberdeen came to Celtic Park on 16 April, they had the League title already wrapped up, but Celtic beat them 2-1. Fernie was once again out injured (he had been comparatively injury-free most of the season, but he was struggling with this one to his back and was clearly being kept for the Scottish Cup final next week) for this game which was remarkable for the long and sustained welcome given to Aberdeen by a chivalrous and sporting Celtic crowd who had lost their title to Aberdeen, but at least recognised their worth, and they also reckoned that if the Dons won the League, at least it wasn't Rangers! The good relationship between Celtic and Aberdeen – players and supporters – was one of the features of the 1950s.

But there was still the Scottish Cup. The passage to the final had been far from easy and far from impressive. Alloa at Recreation Park were no huge problem, but then two games were needed to get the better of Kilmarnock when they might well have lost on the hard, frozen pitch at Rugby Park before they won through 1-0 at Parkhead. 50,000 were at Parkhead to see the quarter final against Hamilton, again won by a veritable whisker when Fernie scored the winner.

The two semi-finals - Celtic v Airdrie and Aberdeen v Clyde - ended up 2-2 draws, and the replays for both games were set for the Monday Holiday on 4 April at 4.15pm. Fernie and Walsh both passed fitness tests, and it was just as well, for Airdrie fought hard. It was, however, the old warhorse John McPhail who scored twice to put Celtic into the final for the second year in a row. In the other semi-final, played at Easter Road, Clyde surprisingly beat champions-elect Aberdeen 1-0, and thus the scene was set for an 'all east end of Glasgow' Scottish Cup final between Celtic and Clyde on 23 April. This had not happened since 1912.

For the first time in Scottish football, the new medium of television played a part in the build-up to the Scottish Cup final. The BBC were very keen to show the game and sent Kenneth Wolstenholme to do the commentating (this was part of their policy at the time not to encourage Scottish or English regional voices!), but the SFA, conservative and awkward as always with the disliked George Graham in charge, would only allow the game to be televised if a given percentage of tickets were sold in advance. As it happened, 106,831 turned up, it still not being clear on the very morning of the game whether the game would be on TV or not. There were in any case still very few (although their numbers were growing) people who possessed a TV set in Scotland in 1955.

Those who attended Hampden and the TV audience watching on their tiny, flickering "sets" (as they were called) were very disappointed. Fernie's injuries had all disappeared and thus Celtic put out their best available forward line in Collins, Fernie, McPhail, Walsh and Tully, although there were those who argued that a place should have been found for Neil Mochan. Celtic, second in the Scottish League, were clear favourites and for a long time it looked as if they were going to win.

The day was sunny but with rather too much of the wind for which Hampden was notorious in those days. It was Fernie who set up Jimmy Walsh to score a fine goal in the first half, but that was about the only good piece of football in the whole game. The ball kept going out of play and there were loads of "throw ins" as even the better players like Fernie and Tully struggled to retain control of the ball, a feature of the game being the amount of litter that was seen blowing across the field.

Nevertheless, Fernie was singled out as man-of-the-match by several observers, but there was little going on. Clyde scored but were clearly offside, and Bobby Collins at least provided a laugh by indulging in a "bumping" contest with Clyde goalkeeper Hewkins (the diminutive Collins reminding some spectators of Charlie Chaplin taking on a burly bully in the silent celluloid films of 20 years ago), but as time wore on, Celtic although now playing against the wind and the sun, looked as if they had things under control. Crucially, however, they were unable to add to their goal tally, which would have settled the matter. It was a classic case of an accident looking for a place to happen.

It was three minutes from time when disaster struck. Clyde won a corner on the right. It was taken by Archie Robertson and drifted gently and safely, as it appeared, into the Celtic goalmouth but well away from any Clyde forward and goalkeeper Bonnar rose to collect, as it seemed. Sadly, the ball held up in the capricious wind, the sun may have got in Bonnar's eyes, and the man who had been the hero of the Coronation Cup two years previously, suffered the horrors of hell as the ball squirmed out of his reach into the net. It was a grim Celtic moment, and a replay was necessary the following Wednesday night. Fernie was thus denied his second Scottish Cup medal. He would be fated to lose three Scottish Cup finals for Celtic, and this one was possibly the hardest to take.

Celtic, however, were still the favourites for the Wednesday night replay. But this was one of chairman Bob Kelly's worst nights when he decided to drop Bobby Collins, apparently because of his somewhat comic shoulder-charging episode on Saturday. It reflected badly, reckoned Mr Kelly, on the image of the club. The forward line was rearranged and Sean Fallon who, admittedly had scored the winning goal the previous year in the Scottish Cup final, was brought back in as centre-forward when he was clearly a better full-back. It was an appalling decision described unreservedly as a *"boardroom tactical blunder"* by *The Dundee Courier* and *"scarcely believable"* by other sections of the Press.

The Celtic fans could indeed scarcely believe all this, as the following teams took the field on the dark, wet, unpleasant night of Wednesday, 27 April 1955 for the 6.30pm kick-off. 68,824 were there, considerably down on Saturday and this time there was no interest shown by BBC TV. It was on the radio however - in a sort of a way. The broadcast started at 8.15 pm, just more or less at the time that the game was finishing! The broadcast was thus a summary rather than a commentary.

The teams were;

Celtic: *Bonnar, Haughney and Meechan; Evans, Stein and Peacock; Walsh, Fernie, Fallon, McPhail and Tully.*

Clyde: *Hewkins, Murphy and Haddock; Granville, Anderson and Laing; Divers, Robertson, Hill, Brown and Ring.*

Referee: *Mr C Faultless, Glasgow*

There are many candidates for the most painful Celtic night of them all - Inverness 2000, Milan 1970, Dunfermline 1961 and Rangers 1963 all spring to mind but this dark, almost Gothic night is definitely a strong candidate as well. The forward line had three men out of their normal position, and frankly, they never functioned well. They must have been affected by the strange team selection and although professional players must always do their best for their club and their supporters, there are times when the "head is not in the right place" (to use a modern phrase) and it is difficult to raise one's game especially when the opposition have had such an unexpected boost at the bizarre non-appearance of a potential matchwinner. Clyde players, many of them Celtic sympathisers, after the game confirmed that their dressing-room before the game got a huge boost when they heard that Collins had been dropped.

Fernie, who often fed off Collins and vice versa, did not have one of his better games. He was in one of his "fiddling" moods according to *The Dundee Courier*, meaning, presumably, that he was back to his old tricks of overdoing it and not releasing the ball when he ought to have done. Half-time came with no goals scored, however, and the Cup still up for grabs. Clyde had won the trophy only once, in 1939, whereas Celtic had won it 17 times and could call on the experience of last year, and it was believed by the green and white clad that Celtic might yet, in spite of everything, win the day.

But it was Clyde who scored what turned out to be the only goal of the game about five minutes into the second half. A free-kick from Harry Haddock found the Celtic-daft Tommy Ring on his own. For some strange reason, the Celtic defence had stood off him and he ran on, shot against Johnnie Bonnar, the ball rebounded to him and he netted the rebound.

The fat was now in the fire as far as Celtic were concerned and they piled pressure on the Clyde defence and the Mount Florida goal for the rest of the game. But while there was no problem about determination and effort, guile and craft were lacking. Fernie did his best but was sometimes a step or two ahead of the rest of the forward line, Fallon had hard luck near the end, and too soon Charles Faultless blew his whistle to signal woe for Celtic and the second Scottish Cup win for Clyde. For Celtic, it meant being runners-up in both major Scottish competitions – a disappointing outcome to a team like Celtic.

There was a sequel to this game for Tommy Ring who, as we have said, was a strong Celtic supporter and came from a staunch Celtic family. The following night he was invited to his mother's house for tea so that she could be proud of her son and dote on the newly acquired Scottish Cup medal. His younger brothers all shunned him and refused to talk to him! Tommy himself was quoted as saying that he wished it could have been Rangers that Clyde had beaten in the final!

It was a dreadful end to what had been a good season for Celtic. But, yet second in the two major Scottish competitions was not bad, especially when Rangers didn't win anything either! For Fernie, it had been a good season, although there were still too many reports of him overplaying the ball and not involving his team mates as well as he could have. Yet he was such a good player to watch as well with all the ball-playing skills of trapping a ball, controlling it, dribbling, shooting and even heading a goal now and again, a reasonable achievement for a small man.

But he would have been disappointed as well because Scotland played four games in that early summer of 1955. Fernie did not play in any of them, and that was a shame. It was also unfortunate for Scotland, for they did not do well. Indeed, there were some shameful performances in which it was hard to believe that a sparkle or two from Fernie might not have made a difference.

Season 1955/56 was almost a repeat of the previous one in terms of no domestic honours won (apart from the Glasgow Cup) and a major disappointment in the Scottish Cup. Fernie played well throughout but was now clearly out of favour with the Scotland selectors, something that provoked a few arguments among supporters, because he was now quite clearly one of the best players of a football in the land. Possibly playing in a team that was less than totally consistently successful was not a great point in his favour.

The season began with the usual disappointment of the League Cup. Celtic failed yet again to qualify, but this was quite a remarkable sectional performance and the eventual dismissal showed just exactly how much Celtic owed to Willie Fernie. Celtic's section contained Rangers, Queen of the South and Falkirk, but this year the arrangement of the fixtures was strange with Celtic playing Queen of the South home and away, then Falkirk at home, then Rangers twice before finishing up at Falkirk.

Without any great deal of bother Celtic won their first three games and then went to Ibrox on Saturday, 27 August and with Fernie on song, beat Rangers 4-1 even without the injured Charlie Tully. They played some great football to entertain the crowd and delight their supporters who now realised that a draw against Rangers at Parkhead on the Wednesday night would probably be enough to guarantee qualification.

But the game at Parkhead turned out to be a disaster, and not for the first nor last time Celtic were aware of just how much exactly they missed Willie Fernie. Willie had injured his thigh in the win at Ibrox, so joined Tully on the injured list while Matt McVittie took Fernie's place. But even so, Celtic looked capable of earning a draw and would have done so but for a bad ankle injury to Jock Stein, who was taken off in the first half and then spent the rest of the game hobbling ineffectively on the left wing.

Stein, so often the target of abuse from the fans when things were not going well, was missed in two respects. One was as a centre-half, where he had dominated proceedings and had totally mastered the Rangers forward line at Ibrox on Saturday and the other was as captain. He found it difficult to captain from the left wing and felt severely hampered by not being able to be in the centre of things. Celtic moved Evans to centre-half but he was totally out of joint tonight and Celtic lost 0-4. The injury to Jock Stein was a serious one, and although he made a comeback of sorts in the middle of the season, his career was now effectively over, and he soon moved on to coaching and management where he became a reasonable success!

The defeat to Rangers (for which excuses were possible in that there was no Tully, Fernie or Stein) meant that the section now boiled down to goal average, and Celtic simply had to go to Falkirk and win by as many goals as possible, and hope that they could outscore Rangers who were playing Queen of the South. Fernie and Tully both returned to the team, but they could not prevent what turned out to be a Celtic horror show. While Rangers were beating Queen of the South 6-0 (which rendered the Brockville game irrelevant anyway) Celtic could only draw 1-1 with Falkirk.

But that was not all. *The Evening Times* had a headline, *"The Battle of Brockville"* and although that is a clear journalistic exaggeration, the behaviour of the fans was truly shocking. Of course, it takes two to have a fight and some of the locals were equally culpable, but at several points, there were free fights on the terracings and at one point a Falkirk player was hit by a bottle. The behaviour on the field was by no means exemplary either (at one point a Falkirk player was ordered off and could consider himself "picked on" because several others on both sides might reasonably have been invited to join him in the queue for the early bath) and we had the sad spectacle of Willie Fernie and other Celtic players appealing to their fans to desist from bottle-throwing.

And thus ended yet again Celtic's sad quest for the Scottish League Cup. More progress was made in the Glasgow Cup with good wins over Clyde and Partick Thistle and then a 1-1 draw against Rangers in the final in which Fernie, playing at right-half, excelled. This game followed a 0-0 draw in the League, a couple of days earlier, and showed that there really was nothing between the two teams at the moment. But then someone had a rare brainwave and came up with the idea that playing the replay on Boxing Day Monday, 26 December, when most people were still on holiday,might not be the worst idea in the world. Boxing Day was one of the big football occasions in England, but not so much in Scotland, unless it fell on a Saturday.

Such rare positive thinking was rewarded with a crowd of nearly 40,000 on a cold day with wind and rain, and a rare phenomenon between Celtic and Rangers – a genuinely good and entertaining game of football in which everyone played their part by behaving! Stein was (temporarily) back in the side and Fernie was now back in his favoured inside-right position. He had a good game and Celtic won 5-3, Fernie capping a great performance by heading home the fifth goal late in the game to make victory certain, although the hero for Celtic was probably Jim Sharkey a grossly underused forward who scored two that day. It was Fernie's first-ever Glasgow

Cup medal (he already had two Glasgow Charity Cup medals) and the teams were;

Celtic: ***Beattie, Haughney and Fallon; Evans, Stein and Peacock; Smith, Fernie, Sharkey, Collins and Mochan.***

Rangers: ***Niven, Caldow and Little; McColl, Young and Rae; Scott, Simpson, Kichenbrand, Baird and Hubbard.***

Referee: ***J Mowat, Burnside***

It was sad to record a day or two after that the death of the Celtic great, Tommy McInally, the star of the 1920s and a man to whom Fernie was frequently compared. There were similarities in playing ability, style of play, dribbling, turn of pace, entertaining the crowd. Where they differed however was in attitude. Mercifully, Willie never shared the self-destruction streak, which was the bane of Tommy, but he was proud to be linked in the same breath as Tommy McInally.

Celtic then won at Queen of the South to finish the calendar year of 1955 on top of the League and things were looking good. Unfortunately, they then lost 0-1 to Rangers on 2 January. It was a narrow defeat, caused by a goalkeeping error, and might easily have gone the other way. It need not have been too serious a reverse but unfortunately the oldest Glasgow dynamic of them all kicked in at this point and the defeat became "infectious" leading to more defeats largely because players' and management's minds were still on the game that they had lost to Rangers.

A 0-1 defeat to Aberdeen at Pittodrie followed (again by no means a disaster to last year's League champions and still arguably the best ball-playing team in the League at the time) but then there were two miserable draws against Raith Rovers and Hearts at a time when Rangers were winning, and by the end of January, Celtic's League chances were looking forlorn – and yet it was a mystery to their supporters why it was that a team with so many able and intelligent players, not least Willie Fernie, were unable to play consistently well enough to win the League.

Man for man, Celtic were probably better than Rangers, or indeed any other team, but too often they let themselves down by failing to win when they really should have or really needed to. There were, of course, defects in the system at Celtic Park. Manager Jimmy McGrory had been a great player, and in truth he was not a bad manager on occasion, but he was too often overruled even in the matter of team selection by chairman Bob Kelly, a man whose commitment to the club could never be doubted but whose despotic attitude did not always work in Celtic's best interests. In particular, he was no judge of a football player, and often allowed considerations like "honour" and "the good name of the club" to over-ride the main business of a football club, which was winning matches and trophies.

Training was generally held to be not very good. It often appeared that other teams finished the game in much better shape than Celtic did, and stories circulated (and were widely believed) about players nipping into the "Jungle" (the hideously shaped cow barn of an enclosure on the Janefield Street side of the ground) for a smoke when they were meant to be lapping the track! Astonishingly, there was very little work with a football. It was all running, building up stamina, and being tough. It was felt that if you did not have ball skills, you shouldn't be at Parkhead anyway. And the lack of ball practice would make a player keener to get the ball on a Saturday! Maybe so, but even the best ball players in the world like Willie Fernie need to practise! Apart from anything else, players enjoyed playing with a ball, and training really has to be an enjoyable experience.

Not for the first nor last time, it was believed that the Scottish Cup represented Celtic's best hope of a trophy. It was their favourite trophy and they had won it 17 times, three times more than

Rangers and some considerable distance ahead of anyone else. Last year's unfortunate events against Clyde were still remembered with anger and angst. As it turned out, 1956 would be even more of a heartbreak to Celtic and their lovers than 1955.

First up was a trip to Greenock to play Second Division Morton on 4 February. Second Division or not, Cappielow is never the easiest of places to go to, nor would it be Greenock if there were not loads of rain. Indeed, eyebrows were raised by a few journalists at the game going ahead (several other games in Scotland were not so lucky) but referee Mr Gerrard from Aberdeen decided that play was possible. It was pantomime stuff and ball players like Fernie were never really able to get going on the difficult surface, which rendered a shock result all the more likely. However, Tully and Collins scored before half-time, and in spite of some determined efforts from Morton, who claimed to have had the ball over the line at one point, 2-0 was how it finished.

Fernie was injured when Celtic played their next tie, a 3-0 win at Somerset Park, Ayr, but he was back for the quarter-final on 4 March, when Airdrie came to Parkhead. It was a tight 2-1 victory with Fernie playing well throughout and scoring what looked like a good goal only for it to be chalked off for offside, but Tully and Collins scored legitimate goals which allowed Celtic to edge past the determined Diamonds. This particular result however, although very welcome for Celtic supporters, was dwarfed in importance by the news of another game played in Edinburgh, which finished Hearts 4 Rangers 0!

There was however a warning here in how good Hearts were, and Celtic were happy to avoid the Edinburgh men in the semi-final. Hearts were drawn to play Raith Rovers in a game which went to a replay before Hearts pulled through, while Celtic found themselves against last year's victors Clyde. It was a less than sentimental return for Celtic fans to Hampden to see them take on Clyde on a really dreadful day with a cold north-easterly wind blowing, but such was the physical layout of Hampden that the wind was a not unusual but totally capricious swirl.

65,200 were there and this time Celtic won in a most unsatisfactory game. Fernie was clearly seen as the key man for Celtic and was targeted brutally by Clyde. He was fouled a total of seven times before half-time, one of these challenges leading to a penalty kick in a challenge that was not far short of a body check. Mike Haughney finished the job, and that put Celtic two ahead, the first having come from Sharkey after goalkeeper Watson had collided with Collins and the ball squirmed out to Sharkey on the edge of the box.

That made it 2-0 but then Clyde pulled one back almost immediately with a similar sort of goal when Beattie collided with Billy McPhail, the younger brother of John, and Billy put Clyde back into the game. 2-1 at half time and it would be a fair assessment that the excitement increased as the standard of any kind of quality football disappeared. The wind seemed to get worse and worse and Fernie more or less disappeared from the game as the conditions did not in any way encourage his style of play. Clyde became definitely the better team and twice the ball was cleared off the line by Sean Fallon, once with his head and once with his foot to the relief of the frozen and soaked green and white hordes behind that goal.

Last year's Scottish Cup final was still haunting everyone, and in spite of the wind, one could almost hear the sharp intake of breath every time that Clyde won a corner kick! Those who loved football as distinct from those of us who had an irrational and all-encompassing love of Celtic might have been happy to see a Clyde equaliser on the grounds that it might have given us a chance of a better game of football in better conditions in the replay, but Celtic's defence, with goalkeeper Dick Beattie outstanding and also enjoying his fair share of luck, held out, and the final whistle saw Celtic into their third Scottish Cup final in a row. Clyde, as it turned out, were heading for relegation this year, but no-one would have predicted that on this showing.

The final, once Hearts disposed of Raith Rovers, attracted the attention of the whole country. It was made all-ticket and the method of ticket distribution brought an awful lot of criticism, but the irony was that 2,000 tickets seemed to be unsold for the crowd was "only" 132,000 when the capacity was 134,000. There does not seem to have been any attempt to televise this game. The Scotland v England game (a 1-1 draw) seems to have been the "ration" for this season!

For Hearts, this final meant an awful lot, for they had not been in a Scottish Cup final since 1907 and therefore it was probably true to say that every single one of their supporters who travelled from Edinburgh in huge numbers was attending a Scottish Cup final for the first time. They had won the League Cup final in October 1954, but this was the big one as far as they were concerned.

Celtic, on the other hand had tradition and history on their side, but they also had long-term injuries to two key players, Jock Stein and Bobby Collins. Both these players had been missed and although hopes had been entertained that Collins, at least, might just make it, neither he nor big Jock donned the hoops. Collins' trickery and Stein's leadership might just have made the difference.

It was how Celtic dealt with these two omissions however that caused the trouble. It will be recalled that, to the dismay of Fernie and others, last year chairman Bob Kelly had dropped Bobby Collins for the cup final. He went one better this time with at least two crazy team selections. On the right wing he brought in youngster Billy Craig for his fifth game for the club. Young Craig had shown promise, but this pitching him in against the competent and experienced Hearts side effectively ruined his career as well as costing Celtic the Scottish Cup. That was bad enough, but to partner him at inside-right, Kelly brought full-back Mike Haughney and played LEFT-back

Frank Meechan at right back alongside Sean Fallon. Haughney had at least played occasionally in the forward line before, but not often, and it seemed odd to play him there in a Scottish Cup final.

The fans were astounded by all this, and it was not as if Celtic had been forced into doing this. There were at least three experienced and capable forwards available in John McAlindon, Jimmy Walsh and particularly Jim Sharkey. They watched the game from the stand when they could have been on the field. It is different nowadays when there are substitutes, but in 1956 you were either chosen or you weren't.

Years later, Jim Sharkey a man who had played brilliantly in the Glasgow Cup final to beat Rangers, claimed that the reason he was not invited to don the green and white that day was because he had been seen drinking sherry with Charlie Tully a day or two before the game. Interestingly, Charlie Tully himself was not dropped. If this story is true, it says very little for the way the club was run. Far better, surely to summon the two of them into the office, fire a rocket or two at them and tell them that they now had a couple of days to prove their fitness.

As it was, the team selection bewildered the Celtic fans, puzzled the journalists when they were given the team sheets and even when the radio broadcast started at half time on the BBC Home Service, the team selection was described as "odd". Apart from anything else, the decision seems to have been made at the last minute, and this may well explain the disorientation of the three Celtic players who under-performed on the day to the detriment of the team – Dick Beattie, Bobby Evans and Willie Fernie.

The weather was bright and breezy as the following teams took the field;

Celtic: ***Beattie, Meechan and Fallon; Smith, Evans and Peacock; Craig, Haughney, Mochan, Fernie and Tully.***

Hearts: *Duff, Kirk and McKenzie; Mackay, Glidden and Cumming; Young, Conn, Bauld, Wardhaugh and Crawford.*

Referee: *Mr R H Davidson, Airdrie*

Fernie never really got going in this game. A few mazy runs which ended up with him losing the ball, a few passes to Mochan or Tully, an occasional good run, but there was nothing magical about him, and the general consensus was that he had a poor game. There was a certain fight from Celtic particularly after they went behind and then pulled one back, but Hearts were undeniably the better team throughout with even the goal that Celtic got looking as if it might have been a foul on goalkeeper Duff.

Hearts were 1-0 up at half time with a fine strike from Crawford. Early in the second half they got another after Bauld had beaten Evans to the ball and ran up the left wing with Evans running parallel to him. Evans then put in a weak tackle; the ball was crossed and it was headed on to Crawford again who hammered home with Beattie very slow to dive. Then came Celtic's goal, ironically from the grossly out of position Mike Haughney. It was a goal that would certainly not be allowed today and was lucky to be allowed in 1956 as it looked like a charge on the goalkeeper, but at least this goal gave the Celtic hordes something to be happy about and to hope for better things.

Celtic were now only 1-2 down and with a long stretch of the second half to go, there was a chance of an equaliser and a replay. But once again Fernie and Tully, Celtic's best players, failed to get going. Conn scored for Hearts with ten minutes to go and the game finished with the disappointed Celtic legions already on their way home.

It was a mystifyingly poor Celtic performance, partially at least to be explained by that bizarre and inexplicable team selection, but the dominance of Hearts in midfield was also disturbing. This performance presumably affected the players as well, for the last few games of the 1955/56 season were played out before miserable crowds who saw lacklustre, apathetic and dismal football from Celtic.

The trouble with Celtic supporters was that they expected better. But the Celtic support at the Cup final were subdued and dangerously quiet, and the tense atmosphere outside the ground indicated just what this meant to THEM. Two rows of Celtic supporters stood on each side of the street to the Mount Florida railway station as the Hearts fans, often in families with wives and young children, had to run the gauntlet in that eerie silence with the Celtic fans almost daring the Hearts fans to say something and provoke a fight. Fortunately, no-one said anything, and serious trouble was averted, but the whole scenario was one that would stay in the minds of so many people for a very long time.

For Fernie, it was a salutary experience. Success does not come automatically, but failure can very quickly become a success if it can be learned from. Fernie was determined to do just that, but it would be a long time before the penny dropped with the Celtic establishment.

Season 1956/57 was possibly Fernie's best season so far. He won his Scottish place back (deservedly) and was generally regarded as being Celtic's best player. He was virtually an ever-present, but it was not a totally successful season for Celtic ending in disappointment and indeed puzzlement. But it did start off well with Celtic doing something that they had been trying for ten years to do and had never managed. They won, at last, at the eleventh attempt, the Scottish League Cup.

It was not that they were drawn in an easy section. They faced Aberdeen, Rangers and East Fife – last year's winners, last year's League champions and the current record winners of the trophy (incredible, but true that East Fife had won the League Cup three times!) and won through with the loss of only one point. On

Some wonderful images of Willie's early days with his family.
Top left: Back seat driver with mum Jean and brother David. **Top right**: Willie up front and centre.
Above: The Fernie family with Willie to the right of his mum but on the left wing of the team!

Fernies on the beach. Note the striking resemblance Willie (front) would bear to his father.

Teenage Willie second from left in front row in the colours of Leslie Hearts in 1947/48. They would retain the Scottish Juvenile Cup that season at Easter Road, Willie suffering a broken jaw in the final.

Commemorative plaque.

Kinglassie Colliery, where many members of the Fernie family and local community worked. Willie was never employed here but he did play for their football team in season 1948/49.

The Celtic team which beat Rangers 3-2 in the 1949-50 Glasgow Charity Cup Final. Back row: Haughney, Milne, Bonnar, Evans, McGrory, Baillie. Front row: Collins, Fernie, McPhail, Peacock and Tully.

Willie wins his first trophy as a Celt on 10 May 1950 as the Hoops beat Rangers 3-2 at Hampden in the 'Danny Kaye final' of the Glasgow Charity Cup.

Danny meets another famous entertainer, Charles Patrick Tully, as Bobby Evans looks on.

Willie Fernie in Celtic training gear

Willie kicking high at training with Bobby Collins.

Willie with his back to the camera, leading his teammates
in a training session at Celtic Park

Willie is seated front left in this special Celtic photograph taken in September 1951. The two trophies on the left were secured on that summer's tour of the USA.
Back row: Desmond White (Director), John McGrory, John McAlindon, John Jack, Alec Boden, John Bonnar, John Duffy, Bob Kelly (Chairman), Jimmy Walsh, Alex Devanny, Mike Haughney, Gil Heron, Donald Weir, Roy Milne, Tom Devlin (Director) and Jimmy McGrory (Manager). **Front row**: Alec Dowdalls (Trainer), Willie Fernie, John Higgins, Bobby Collins, Jock Weir, Bobby Evans, Joe Baillie, John McPhail, Bertie Peacock, Sean Fallon, Charlie Tully, Alec Rollo, Jimmy Mallan and Jimmy Gribben (Assistant Trainer).
Seated at front: Jimmy Duncan and Jackie Millsopp.

Willie in action against East Fife's veteran defender Sammy Stewart at a packed Bayview.

Celtic's goalscorers Neil Mochan and Jimmy Walsh in action in the Coronation Cup final.

"Old Hampden was covered in banners of green!" Hibernian's Lawrie Reilly and Celtic's Bobby Evans tussle in the Coronation Cup final on 20 May 1953.

Goalscorers Neil Mochan and Jimmy Walsh admire the Coronation Cup.

The Celtic players celebrate after winning the Coronation Cup in May 1953. Willie is behind the trophy, between Bobby Evans and Jock Stein.

Three Coronation Cup heroes with the trophy. Goalkeeper John Bonnar, captain Jock Stein and goalscorer Jimmy Walsh.

Celtic at the start of the 1953/54 season with the Coronation Cup. **Back row:** Trainer Alex Dowdalls, Mike Haughney, Frank Meechan, John Bonnar, John McPhail, Bobby Evans, Charlie Tully and Manager Jimmy McGrory. **Front row:** Bobby Collins, Jimmy Walsh, Jock Stein, Neil Mochan, Bertie Peacock and Willie Fernie.

Willie with Charlie Tully and the Coronation Cup in 1953.

Willie proudly displays his first major honour as a Celt.

Willie sets Sean Fallon up for the winning goal in the 1954 Scottish Cup final.

Neil Mochan scores at Easter Road as Celtic clinch their first League Championship in 16 years on 17 April 1954, Willie's only title success.

Some images of Willie celebrating with the Celtic team and the Scottish Cup following the victory over Aberdeen at Hampden on 24 April 1954.

The team bus leaves Hampden Park after Celtic had defeated Aberdeen 2-1 in the 1954 Scottish Cup Final. Jock Stein shows the Cup to the waiting fans.

24 Celtic with the Coronation, League and Scottish Cups, 1954

Back row: A. Dowdells (trainer), Paterson, Haughney, Meechan, Evans, Bonnar, J. McPhail, Walsh, Peacock, Dr. Fitzsimons, J. McGrory (manager). *Front row:* Collins, Higgins, Fernie, Fallon, Stein, Tully, Mochan

A smiling Willie with the first Celtic team to win a Scottish League and Cup double in 40 years.

Willie and Celtic teammate Neil Mochan line up ahead of Scotland's match against Uruguay in Basel on 19 June 1954. It wouldn't end well!

Willie keeps his eye on the ball against Kilmarnock at Celtic Park on 2 October 1954.

Willie looking very dapper in his Scotland World Cup blazer in 1954.

Willie airborne in the Celtic reserve strip against Kilmarnock at Rugby Park in February 1955.

Celtic line-up before the League clash with Falkirk at Brockville on 12 February 1955.
Back row: Jimmy Walsh, Bobby Evans, John Bonnar, Mike Haughney and Frank Meechan.
Front row: Bobby Collins, Sean Fallon, Jock Stein, Bertie Peacock, Willie Fernie and Neil Mochan.

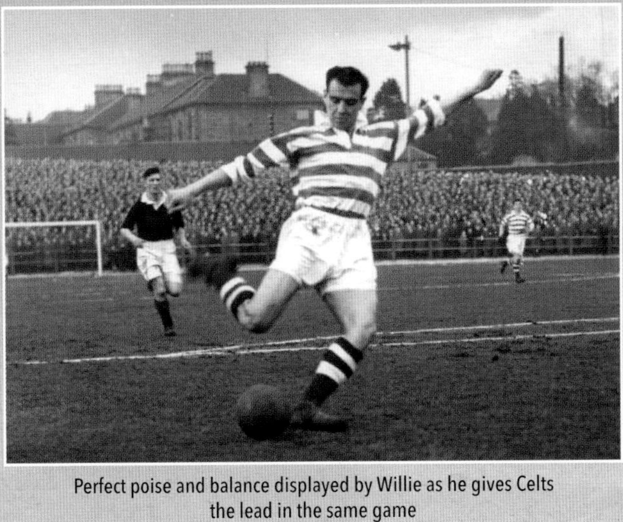

Perfect poise and balance displayed by Willie as he gives Celts the lead in the same game

Celtic's line-up for the home League Cup match against Falkirk on 20 August 1955. **Back row:** Mike Haughney, Sean Fallon, John Bonnar, Bobby Evans, Jock Stein and Bertie Peacock. **Front row:** Bobby Collins, Willie Fernie, Jimmy Walsh, Charlie Tully and Neil Mochan.

Willie and Bertie Peacock are airborne in the Glasgow Cup final replay against Rangers at Hampden on Boxing Day 1955. Willie headed home Celtic's fifth goal late on in a 5-3 win.

Willie jousts with Bobby Kirk of Hearts during the 1956 Scottish Cup final.

Scotland team line up ahead of the match with Wales at Ninian Park, Cardiff on 20 October 1956. **Back row:** Alex Parker, Ian McColl, Tommy Younger, John Hewie and Doug Cowie. **Front row:** Graham Leggat, Jackie Mudie, Lawrie Reilly, George Young, Bobby Collins and Willie Fernie.

Willie proudly poses in his Scotland kit at Ninian Park, Cardiff on 20 October 1956.

Willie equalises against Wales at Ninian Park in the above match, his only goal for Scotland

Willie lets fly at the Queen's Park goal at Celtic Park.

Willie heads for the Hampden turf following a clash with Scotland international colleague Jimmy Davidson of Partick Thistle in Celtic's first League Cup final, played on 27 October 1956. Celts would win the midweek replay 3-0 after a goalless draw, although Willie had a much bigger match in the interim!

opening day, Fernie scored Celtic's first goal of the season at a rainy Pittodrie – the new *"unselfish Fernie"* as *The Evening Times* puts it – and then he scored again against East Fife and Aberdeen when they came to Parkhead.

The first game against Rangers was on Wednesday 15 August, when Fernie inspired Celtic to a narrow 2-1 win, and the key game for qualification was the return at Ibrox. It was a goalless draw before 84,000 (a huge crowd for a Wednesday night) and that kept Celtic at the top, although they had to avoid defeat at Methil on the Saturday to guarantee it. Before an anxious and packed crowd at Bayview, Fernie might have put Celtic ahead in the early stages with a brilliant back-heeler from a distance which hit the base of the post. It would have been one of the most remarkable goals of all time if it had gone in, but in any event, it was new boy Billy McPhail (who had joined the club from Clyde more or less at the same time as elder brother John was going out the door) who scored the goal which saw Celtic into the quarter-finals of the League Cup.

It was another Fife team that they faced in Dunfermline Athletic, at that time an underperforming side playing on a poor pitch with primitive conditions. The quarter-finals were two-legged affairs in 1956 and the first leg was played at Celtic Park on Wednesday, 12 September. *The Glasgow Herald* talks about the *"cantrips"* of Fernie and Collins entertaining the 23,000 crowd as Celtic won 6-0, but then Celtic proceeded to horrify their travelling support and the thousands of Fife-based supporters who idolised them by going down 0-3 to East End Park on the Saturday. It was a game that didn't really matter too much, but it was a truly awful performance. It was not enough to say simply that they *"took the foot off the pedal."* This was an example of the quixotic Jekyll and Hyde performances that would characterise this season.

But, in spite of this, Celtic were now into the League Cup semi-finals which had three Glasgow teams and Dundee. The League Cup form was good, but against that Celtic had twice lost to Rangers – once in the Glasgow Cup in a high scoring and entertaining 3-4 defeat which hinted at awful defending and they also lost to Rangers at Parkhead in the League, followed a week later by a defeat at Motherwell. The League challenge was thus seriously impaired at an early stage of the season by this unpredictable behaviour.

But as far as the League Cup was concerned, success continued. It was old adversaries and neighbours Clyde in the semi-final at Hampden on 6 October. But this was a Clyde side whose teeth had been drawn and they were now in the Second Division, and, of course, their centre-forward of last year Billy McPhail was now with Celtic. 36,697 saw a poorish game but one in which Celtic did enough to justify a place in their first-ever League Cup final. Billy McPhail scored both goals, and their opponents were to be Partick Thistle, who beat Dundee after a struggle in a replay. It was a tie in which even the normally supportive and encouraging football Press found it hard not to use words like *"dull"* and *"boredom."*

And so, it was Glasgow's two unpredictables of Celtic and Partick Thistle for the League Cup final on 27 October 1956. The week before (when Fernie was away playing for Scotland) Celtic had played out a feckless 1-1 draw with Raith Rovers which showed their vulnerability, and Partick Thistle had always been the zany, crazy and gloriously unreliable team of Glasgow whose supporters simply did not know what to expect. *"Firhill for thrills"* was the slogan, but there were as many dull, sleepy days in the north of Glasgow as there were exciting ones. However, they were now managed by ex-Rangers legend Davie Meiklejohn and no-one could ever write them off. Like Celtic, they had never won the League Cup, but they had appeared in the final, losing to East Fife in season 1953/54. It promised at least to be an interesting final. Or so everyone thought.

58,794 turned up on a dull, windless day at Hampden to see a game that frankly did not have much going for it. It was played with a certain amount of international tension in the background as, in an unsavoury display of what can only be called international bullying, the Soviet Union prepared to muscle in on the rebellious Hungarians, and the British, French and Israelis prepared to do likewise on Egypt. If some of the crowd allowed their minds to stray to the possibility of World War III, they could hardly be blamed, for the football was terrible.

This was an awful Celtic performance with the team giving an *"object lesson in how not to score."* Fernie, playing unaccountably on the left wing, made a few opportunities but they were spurned to the anguish of the Celtic crowd, and even when the game went to extra-time, and Thistle were down to nine fit men, Celtic could still not break the deadlock. Indeed, Dick Beattie, who had spent 90 boring minutes in regulation time, was called upon to make a couple of saves, and Jack Mowat's full-time whistle came with the score 0-0. *The Glasgow Herald* tries to rationalise all this by making bizarre statements about the ball being white and lighter, and therefore it dipped and soared a lot more than the heavy brown one, but that was hardly any kind of excuse for what was, quite simply, a dreadful Celtic team in which only Beattie and Fernie emerged with pass marks.

The Aberdeen Evening Express is more direct about Fernie, whom it describes as a *"flop"* but Fernie could be forgiven in this case for not having his mind 100% on the task in hand. On Monday, 29 October 1956, two days after this League Cup final and two days before the replay and a few hours after Israel had invaded Egypt, Willie married Audrey Douglas, the secretary of manager Jimmy McGrory, at Christ the King church in King's Park, Glasgow. Mike Haughney was the best man. They had been courting for some time, but the timing of the wedding was distinctly unfortunate. The honeymoon was severely curtailed because of a League Cup final replay! Indeed, at one point the Saturday – the actual day of the League Cup final – had been pencilled in for the wedding. And the possibility of a third World War starting in the immediate future cannot have been a pleasant one! But the couple were happy and a large crowd of well-wishers including a few with green and white rosettes and favours were there to see them wed. It would be a very happy and successful marriage with four boys – William born 1957, Alex born 1959, Andrew born 1963 and David born 1970.

As far as the football was concerned, clearly a few stern words were spoken over the weekend, and Walsh was dropped, Fernie was restored to the inside-left position and the out-of-favour Neil Mochan was brought back on the left wing, with the result that the following teams took the field at Hampden on Wednesday, 31 October.

Celtic: *Beattie, Haughney and Fallon; Evans, Jack and Peacock; Tully, Collins, McPhail, Fernie and Mochan.*

Partick Thistle: *Legerwood, Kerr and Gibb; Collins, Crawford and Mathers; McKenzie, Wright, Hogan, McParland and Ewing.*

Referee: *Mr J Mowat, Burnside*

The final was a funny one for all sorts of reasons. It kicked off at 2.15pm because Hampden had no floodlights and they had to allow for the possibility of extra-time. It was a normal working day with even schools on. It was hardly surprising that only 31,156 were there at the start although it was noticeable that many schoolchildren arrived soon after half-time, thanks, perhaps, to a few co-operative headmasters! It was thus a somewhat unreal atmosphere for a cup final, certainly one of the lowest crowds that Celtic had ever played in front of, one imagines, when silverware was on offer.

But there was more than that. *The Evening Times*, which was able to give its readers an account of the early stages of the game, has as its headlines that British and French troops had invaded Suez. This sounded as if it were not a million miles away from war, and the small crowd would have been justified in feeling apprehensive about the future, particularly as so many young men were currently doing National Service, a form of conscription, and might soon be involved in this absurd military operation.

The first half of the replay was little different from Saturday, although there was a distinct improvement in the play of wing-halves Evans and Peacock and a firm determination from the team as a whole. It was early in the second half,with Celtic now attacking the Mount Florida goal, that it all happened. First Billy McPhail took advantage of a defensive error to lob the ball over Legerwood's head; then he scored again after a fine move involving Fernie, Tully and Mochan. By the 60th minute, a good through ball from Evans found Collins who rifled home a third.

Celtic were now well on top and coasting. Well before the full-time whistle, Davie Meiklejohn had congratulated his old adversary Jimmy McGrory and Celtic won comfortably 3-0. In the gathering gloom, captain Bobby Evans lifted the trophy, the first Celtic captain to ever do so. It was Fernie's first League Cup medal as well. That, and getting married meant that he had had a good week so far!

It was a satisfying occasion for Celtic, but the following days saw a few sadly predictable occurrences. The Suez intervention flopped piteously, and the British troops had to be withdrawn, and Celtic, with the players and the supporters high on a cloud, came down to earth with a loud thud as they travelled to Dundee and lost 1-2 to the heartbreak of so many of the 22,000 crowd. More seriously, the Russians crushed the Hungarians with brutal ferocity, and the great Hungarian football player, Ferenc Puskas, escaped by the skin of his teeth.

The League challenge then failed to ignite and eventually fizzled out, Celtic finishing a dismal fifth behind even Raith Rovers and Kilmarnock, and never really getting over a 2-0 defeat at Ibrox on

New Year's Day. Any further excitement this season came in the Scottish Cup, and there were quite a few good games there for Fernie.

The first game was at the unfamiliar venue of Mosset Park, Forres, where the local Forres Mechanics had the greatest day of their lives when about 1,000 Celtic fans arrived all decked in green to see their favourites win 5-0. It was an educational experience for quite a few of the Celtic supporters to travel to a part of Scotland that was not well known, and no doubt some of the players were similarly apprised as to how the rest of the world live.

But then two weeks later, it was like chalk and cheese in every sense when Rangers came to Celtic Park. The behaviour of the spectators inside Celtic Park was faultless (less so outside) as Celtic and Rangers drew 4-4. Fernie was always on song today and scored a brilliant fourth goal some 10 minutes from time to make the score 4-2 (the proverbial "turning on a sixpence" goal) and it looked as if Celtic were home and dry, but then centre-half John Jack had a shocker, conceding a needless penalty and then being in the wrong place as Rangers equalised to make the final score a barely credible 4-4.

Celtic felt ill-treated by fortune as a result of those two late blows but kept the same side and the same grim determination that they had shown on Saturday. 80,000 turned up at Ibrox this cold miserable Wednesday afternoon with icy winds to see a game played on a pitch that had distinct similarities to the Sahara Desert, for it was covered in sand. Celtic once again took a two-goal lead, before half-time this time, through Higgins and Mochan, and then spent the second half well on top, not making the mistake of lying back and defending.

Gair Henderson of *The Evening Times* is in no doubt about who the star of the show was – *"once again football's Mr Genius, Willie Fernie"* and Rangers obviously agreed for Sammy Baird and Bobby Shearer both targeted Fernie for their violent attacks, and were spoken to by the referee, but it was just so frustrating for them to have to chase the shadow that was Willie Fernie. The game finished with Celtic well on top and Rangers utterly demoralised, with the detestable Shearer and Baird unable even to get close enough to Fernie to foul him!

It was indeed one of the strengths of Willie Fernie and his style of play. He was never roused to retaliation, and never in trouble with referees. Often after a brutal tackle with the marks of injury still visible on his leg, he would say calmly to his attacker a remark along the lines of *"I hope you are proud of yourself"* or *"Happy now?"*

St Mirren now came to Celtic Park for the quarter-final on 2 March. The game was a thriller. Celtic started well on top and were 2-0 up before half-time, and when St Mirren pulled one back, excitement was guaranteed but Celtic held out and it would have been a shame if they had not gone through to the semi-final.

And thus we come to the semi-final against Kilmarnock at Hampden in late March, something that must have been one of the major heartbreaks of Fernie's career, and a game that prevented Celtic reaching four Scottish Cup finals in a row. 109,145 saw the first game on 23 March with Celtic wearing their white with green sleeves strip against a solid Kilmarnock team now managed by ex-Celt Malky MacDonald. It was a good tight game, but it might have been better for the green and white hordes if John Higgins had missed his header from that Mochan cross which gave Celtic their late and not really entirely deserved equaliser. Fernie was, frankly, off form that day. However, 76,963 came back again for the replay at the teatime kick-off time at Hampden on Wednesday, 27 March. It was an odd, disappointing and mysterious Celtic experience.

The wind was described as "capricious", but newspapers, not least the respected *The Glasgow Herald* unite in talking about the sheer amount of mistakes made by the Celtic defence, centre-half John Jack and goalkeeper Dick Beattie in particular, the latter described as a *"nervous wreck"* by the end. The highlights can be viewed on You Tube and one leaves the reader to make up his own mind, but it was all a huge disappointment. Years later in 1965, when Beattie was "done" for match fixing when with Portsmouth, Celtic supporters thought back to this match and said *"Ah!"* Some of them even wondered about the 1956 final against Hearts – but it must be stressed that no evidence of anything untoward has ever emerged, at least as far as Celtic are concerned. It is also true that it is a gut reaction for supporters to blame a bad defeat on corruption – the same was said about the 1926 Scottish Cup Final and the Glasgow Cup Final of 1908/09, again with no evidence. And it is also possible that Kilmarnock, a fast-emerging team with some fine players, quite simply were the better team! In any case, they won 3-1.

Fernie had a better game but was sadly unable to coax the rest of the Celtic forwards into taking advantage of his play. Celtic finished the game dispirited and distressed with most of their fans in the 76,793 crowd already departing in sullen silence to catch their buses and trains home. It meant that the season had now ended with Rangers winning the Scottish League by some distance and Falkirk beating Kilmarnock to win the Scottish Cup. A season which had started so well with the capture of the League Cup now fizzled out.

But not necessarily for Fernie. He was now well in contention in the Scotland squad and indeed had already starred for the Scottish League on 13 March at Ibrox. The result was a 3-2 victory for the Scottish League, but the Scottish Press is absolutely convinced that the score line was a travesty and that 6-1 would have been a fairer reflection with some sparking Scottish forward play from Bobby Collins in particular but also Willie Fernie and Tommy Ring as well. Fernie played in a team of ***Brown (Dundee), Parker (Falkirk) and Caldow (Rangers); McColl (Rangers), McNaught (Raith Rovers) and Mackay (Hearts); Collins (Celtic), Fernie (Celtic), Bauld (Hearts), Holmes (St Mirren) and Ring (Clyde) against Hodgkinson (Sheffield United), Howe (West***

Bromwich Albion) and Sillet (Chelsea); Clayton (Blackburn Rovers), Wright (Wolverhampton Wanderers) and Edwards (Manchester United); Hooper (Wolverhampton Wanderers), Thompson (Preston North End), Finney (Preston North End), Stokes (Tottenham Hotspur) and Pilkington (Burnley) with Hugh Phillips of Wishaw the referee.

The summer of 1957 saw Celtic tour America and Canada yet again (Fernie had already been there in 1951). He might have hoped to be in the squad for the Scotland tour of Europe in May, but he missed out, although Collins and Evans made the grade. He would have been very disappointed about that but there was ample compensation in the Celtic tour. They might by 1957 have opted to fly out but they sailed in the RMS Mauretania on 8 May and returned on the Queen Elizabeth on 13 June. Evans and Collins joined them after their Scotland commitments were over. As well as playing, Willie Fernie wrote regular "ghosted" reports for *The Evening Citizen*.

The tour was remarkable for the strange appointment of Bertie Peacock as captain in the middle of the Atlantic! He had already been appointed as captain for the tour because Evans was with the Scottish squad, but Peacock was suddenly called into a cabin and given the proper job as captain for the new season! It was a good choice for he was a good player and very popular with his teammates, although those who concerned themselves about such things were not slow to point out that Bertie Peacock was a Northern Ireland Protestant. (Oh dear! What were things coming to?) The tour itself consisted of eight games, four against local opposition whom Celtic defeated fairly easily and four against Tottenham Hotspur at various venues. The score of victories and defeats was, as it were, 3-1 for Spurs, but Celtic finished the tour on a high note by beating Spurs 2-0 in Montreal before sailing home.

CHAPTER FOUR

7-1 AND DEPARTURE (1957-1958)

By season 1957/58 Willie Fernie had earned the nickname "Tennessee Ernie". It was all due to Glasgow rhyming slang of course, in the same way that Bertie Auld in future years would become "Ten Thirty" to rhyme with "Wee Bertie". The real "Tennessee Ernie" was an American singer and television host called Ernest Ford. He is now a somewhat obscure character, but sufficiently well known in the 1950s in Glasgow to have his name used for this purpose.

This season was actually a lean time for Celtic as far as the Scottish League and the Scottish Cup were concerned. They disappeared out of the Scottish Cup at the quarter final stage to old adversaries Clyde, and ended up 3rd in the Scottish League, some 16 points behind winners Hearts, disappeared early to Rangers out of the Glasgow Cup and the Glasgow Charity Cup, (admittedly on the toss of a coin in the case of the latter), but it was all made up for by the Scottish League Cup which was retained from last year, and its final is probably the second most famous game ever played by Celtic, second only to the immortal events of Lisbon. It was of course the 7-1 win over Rangers on 19 October 1957, still commemorated in song and in folk lore.

The League Cup section this year contained Hibs, Airdrie and East Fife. East Fife, as is the way with provincial clubs, were now a shadow of the team that they had been a few years previously and provided little opposition, Airdrie were a little more obdurate and Hibs actually beat Celtic in the first game at Easter Road. But they too had passed their peak, and Celtic won the crucial last game of the section 2-0 at Celtic Park with goals from Sammy Wilson and Billy McPhail to send their 50,000 crowd home happy and looking forward to their two-legged quarter final against Third Lanark.

The team had changed a little. Fernie was now playing at right half, a position in which he excelled, for, playing further back, he was far more able to control the game, and he clearly did that here at this stage of his career. Celtic have been graced throughout their history with great right halves – one thinks of Sunny Jim and Peter Wilson before Fernie, and Pat Crerand and Bobby Murdoch after, but Fernie was as good as any with his ball winning skills, mazy dribbles, hard but fair tackling, visionary passing and, as important as anything, he was now very much a team man. The argument about whether he was a better midfielder or defender would rage endlessly in the Press, but there can be little doubt that, although he himself preferred the inside right position, he produced the goods at right half in 1957. He was in any case always Mr Versatile!

Bobby Evans, for his part, was now the centre half, a position to which he adapted very well and very quickly, while up front a new forward had joined the club in Sammy Wilson, an Uddingston man who, legend has it, recommended in later years that the club have a look at another Uddingston man called Jimmy Johnstone. Wilson had fitted in well and was now playing in the excellent Celtic forward line, and things were beginning to look good for Celtic.

The good news continued. Third Lanark were swept aside in both quarter finals, and then in a League match at Ibrox, Celtic beat Rangers 3-2 but the score should have been a great deal more than that. Ibrox was not a place Celtic normally did well at. It was their first League win there since Frank Murphy and Johnny Crum had done the business in 1935 and the one before that had involved Joe Cassidy in 1921!

Things were clearly looking up, and Fernie was superb.

Then at the end of September, when a flu epidemic began to sweep Scotland and affect team selections, Celtic reached the Scottish League Cup final by beating an understrength Clyde side 4-2, while in the other semi-final, Rangers, themselves suffering from the flu bug, were nevertheless good enough to beat Brechin City to make it to the first Old Firm League Cup final, a tournament in which neither of them had really distinguished themselves. East Fife were still the record holders of this young trophy with three wins!

Fernie was playing so well that he might even have expected a recall to the Scotland team for the game against Northern Ireland on 5 October 1957. That didn't happen, but the game would have repercussions for Celtic. Collins and Evans were chosen for Scotland and Peacock for Northern Ireland. It was a 1-1 draw, and generally agreed to have been far from the best International between these two. Indeed the word "rank" is used in some newspaper accounts.

Fernie maybe did well to miss this game, but Charlie Tully, with his International days behind him, was working for a newspaper covering the game and mentioned that very few of the Scotland players were worth their place in the World Cup squad. He gave a few exceptions, but Bobby Evans was not one of them, the implication being that Evans was not worth his place in the Scotland team. Whether or not this was a "ghosted" report (ie written by a journalist while Tully merely put his name to it) is irrelevant. It was Tully's name. It was incidentally not an opinion that was generally agreed with, for *The Glasgow Herald* although lambasting the Scottish performance in general terms, does give Evans some faint praise "Evans…may be regarded as a success" for keeping tabs on Irish centre forward McAdams.

But there may have been a little more to it than that. Evans, possibly already feeling prickly about the way that he was deposed from the captaincy in the summer, did not like Tully. Tully, like many players who were intensely popular with the fans, was not necessarily well loved by team mates who could resent the way that he overdid things with the ball and constantly sought the limelight. Evans, a dour Scotsman, was not always charmed by his Irish patter which could indeed sometimes be laced with selfishness and awkwardness.

How it actually came about, no-one knows but one day in the run up to the League Cup final, the two of them came to blows at training, and it fell upon captain Bertie Peacock (who, ironically played for the Northern Ireland opposition in that game!) and the more sensible of the squad like Fernie to sort things out. How Fernie reacted to this we do not know. He knew and understood both players, and was bright enough to appreciate the nuances of the situation, not least because he himself would have loved to play in the International match in question. He himself was tough. He came from a Fife mining background which was nothing if not hard, and no-one would have taken liberties with him, but he realised above all else that football is a team game, and that discord in the squad was a pernicious dynamic.

One way or other the matter was patched up, it never reached the newspapers until much later, and anyone watching the Celtic team that day would never have dreamt that there had been any discord. It was generally agreed that Celtic were the favourites, but it was a Celtic-Rangers game and anything could happen. No-one could have predicted just exactly what was going to take place that mellow autumn day of 19 October 1957.

Several songs and a book have been written about this game, so it is clearly well documented. What kept it so alive in people's memories was that it was, in fact, isolated. It was a beacon, standing almost alone in a decade of dire under-achievements. It was like a cry of laughter at a funeral service. Almost immediately after this game, the Dark Ages descended with a vengeance, and vengeance was indeed an appropriate term, for Rangers were able to get back at Celtic on many occasions, and the only ammunition we had to throw back at the insecure chortlers was "7-1". Sadly it only happened the once.

It really ought to have happened a lot oftener than once, for Celtic at that time had loads of great players, and man for man they were a lot better than anyone else. Bobby Evans, Bertie Peacock, Willie Fernie, Bobby Collins, Neil Mochan and Charlie Tully were as naturally gifted as one would find, but the team was badly managed. Jock Stein's playing career had now ended. If he had been Manager of the team at that time, Celtic would have won many Leagues and Cups.

As it was, it was not entirely a barren time. Celtic were the current holders of the Scottish League Cup, and the Double of 1954 was not yet a distant memory. It was just that it could have been a lot more. This was the day, however, in which the whole team came good, and the world saw Celtic at their best. It was almost an apology from the players to the fans for their previous under-performances.

It was a sunny day, but the crowd was a low one of 82,293 which was poor for the 1950s and certainly well below what one would have expected for an Old Firm Cup final. A six figure crowd would not have been out of the question, one feels. The attendance was blamed on the rather unseasonal flu epidemic which had hit Central Scotland over the past few weeks. It never seemed to affect Celtic at all, and such clubs as had been affected (like Rangers) had managed to get over it (as one would imagine would happen with fit young men) but it still was present in the population at large, particularly the large, unhealthy, dirty city that Glasgow undeniably was in 1957. It was blamed, according to one letter writer to a newspaper on the Russians who had sent their Sputnik into space!

Celtic had a more settled side than their rivals. Rangers seemed to have problems replacing centre half George Young who had retired in the summer. For this game they had chosen John Valentine whom they had signed from Queen's Park. Up front they had the ageing Sammy Baird, the under-performing Maxie Murray and their best forward appeared to be the Ulsterman Billy Simpson. Their recent form had not been great, and not all Rangers supporters were as optimistic as their raucous and offensive battle hymns would have suggested.

The teams were:

Celtic: *Beattie, Donnelly and Fallon; Fernie, Evans and Peacock; Tully, Collins, McPhail, Wilson and Mochan*

Rangers: *Niven, Shearer and Caldow; McColl, Valentine and Davis; Scott, Simpson, Murray, Baird and Hubbard*

Referee: *Mr J Mowat, Rutherglen*

This was without much doubt Fernie's best ever day. Everything seemed to start from him. The centre circle was virtually his own, as he sprayed passes to either wing, bewildering his Rangers opponents. His direct opponent was Sammy Baird. The abrasive Baird hardly got a kick of the ball that day. Fernie did less dribbling than he had done in the past, and the accuracy of his passing frequently drew gasps of admiration from the King's Park End and sighs of despair from the other end, while the gnarled old journalists in the Press Box nodded sagely and told each other that the world was now seeing Fernie at his best.

Celtic started off playing towards their own supporters, and almost immediately were on the attack. They had hit the woodwork on at least two occasions and it was a major surprise that they were not ahead. Indeed the pessimistic of the green and white hordes were beginning to fear that their moment had passed, but not a bit of it. Billy McPhail headed down for Sammy Wilson to bang the ball home. Wilson had joined the club in the summer on a free transfer from St Mirren. His career had not exactly been coming along with leaps and bounds until he joined Celtic but today was his day. Then as half time approached, and everyone was remarking how lucky Rangers were to be going in only 0-1 down, Celtic struck again. This time it was Neil Mochan who made ground on the left, racing past Bobby Shearer as if he weren't there, and when everyone expected a cross, he ran on himself and scored from an incredibly tight angle.

Half-time was spent in glorious euphoria with the only negative thought being that Rangers couldn't possibly be as bad as that in the second half. But they were, and Celtic, apart from one moment, simply tore them apart. Billy McPhail got into the act heading home a Collins cross, and then for one brief moment, Rangers came back with a good headed goal by Billy Simpson. This goal was not entirely unconnected with an injury to Bobby Evans caused by a couple of bad tackles on him from Maxie Murray and Sammy Baird.

It did not really matter. Rangers might have taken heart from that, but it was Celtic who re-asserted themselves. McPhail volleyed a Mochan corner, but his shot was parried by Niven straight back to him and he was able to get there ahead of anyone else and to make it 4-1. The next was Mochan again, driving home first time a cross from Wilson, and soon after that came the goal of the game when McPhail earned his hat trick by picking up a clearance from goalkeeper Dick Beattie, flicking the ball past the luckless John Valentine, and running half the length of the field to slip the ball past Niven.

6-1 really should have been enough, and Rangers fans were either throwing bottles, fighting with each other or going home when the seventh was scored. Billy McPhail was brought down in the box, referee Jack Mowat, ruthlessly impartial, did NOT listen to Rangers pleas for mercy and awarded a penalty. Some felt that hat-trick hero Billy McPhail should have been given the chance to make it four goals, but Willie Fernie was given the job. It was appropriate that Fernie finished things off, for no-one had contributed more than he did to the victory.

The song "Oh Hampden In The Sun" written a la Harry Belafonte in honour of this victory contains this stanza for Willie Fernie's late penalty

"Here comes Fernie cool and slick
He ambles up to take the kick
He hits it low and hard past Niven
The Tims are in their seventh heaven"

The greatest compliment for Willie Fernie that day came from Andy Cunningham writing in Monday's Scottish Daily Mail. Andy was an unashamed Bluenose having played for them in the 1920s before becoming Manager of Newcastle United. Well respected and even liked by the more sensible Celtic supporters, Cunningham knew what a good player looked like, and today he compared Willie Fernie to the immortal Patsy Gallacher, saying that Willie was as good a dribbler as Patsy had ever been, and if anything, "stronger on the ball". Frankly, it is not possible to get higher praise than that! Cyril Horne in *The Glasgow Herald* is of the persuasion that the Scotland selectors should build their team round Willie Fernie.

Sean Fallon, the left back that day was also wholesome in his praise of Willie Fernie... "Willie Fernie had a great game that day. He had brilliant skill on the ball, and you couldn't get it off him…" but there wasn't a single Celtic failure on the field, and the teamwork, discipline and cohesion were a thing to behold. It was Celtic at their best. In the stand that day were two grand old Celts, Jimmy McMenemy and Davie McLean, the last two survivors of Maley's great side of 1908. How they enjoyed themselves! Maley himself, now 90 was too old and frail to attend, but listened to the game on the radio, as indeed did Jock Stein who was now retired from the playing side of the game and recovering from an ankle operation.

Celtic however sent a car to bring Stein to the victory celebration.

Celtic supporters walked on air for days afterwards, and it is a pity that so soon after this game, injuries, old age and sheer greed for transfer fees saw this great team broken up and replaced by a "youth policy". Nothing wrong with a "youth policy" in itself, but it needed to be monitored and controlled a little better than this one was. As it happened, Celtic's next happy day would be 24 April 1965, and a Biblical "seven years of famine" ensued in the interval. But there was a short term gain for Fernie at least in that he won back his Scottish place, and of course he now had two Scottish League Cup medals.

Rangers were of course distraught, and took a while to recover but they got back into the habit of winning things more quickly than Celtic did. Not immediately however. The Scottish League was won by Hearts that year, and although Hearts had a good team, wise analysts of the game pointed to this League Cup final as the reason for Rangers' inability to sustain the pace. The psychological effects of it were considerable.

But, for Celtic fans, this game will always be remembered. It is a British record for a score in a national Cup final, and naturally, Celtic's biggest ever score against Rangers. It is curious too the significance the number 7 has on Celtic's history. The first League and Cup Double was achieved in 1907, the Scottish Cup was won in 1907, 1927 and 1937, 1967, 1977, 2007 and 2017. And, of course 1967 has its own significance as well! It was of course the squad number of Jimmy Johnstone and Henrik Larsson – and that says a lot, but for those supporters old enough to remember this game, No 7 will always be associated with this game on that sunny day of 19 October 1957.

Piling On The Agony
Puttin On The Style
That's what Glasgow Celtic
Have been doing all this while.

One, two, three, four, five, six, seven
Ways to make you smile
Watching Willie Fernie
Putting On The Style!

The 7-1 score line has its own significance. Fifteen years later in the latter stages of the 1972 Scottish Cup final Celtic were beating Hibs 6-1 and looking likely to score again. An old Irish supporter with no teeth and a whisky bottle which he shared liberally with fellow supporters, pleaded with Celtic NOT to score another because he did not want the immortal 7-1 score line to be shared! On the other hand, one day in the late 1980s when Celtic were beating St Mirren 7-1 in a League game at Parkhead, supporters were urging the referee to bring things to a close in order to preserve this mystic and magical score line!

The collapse of that wonderful team was abrupt. For a while all was well with some fine wins in November as Celtic basked in the afterglow of their triumph. But then came the fateful day of 14 December when Celtic went to Shawfield to play Clyde. The ground was grossly overcrowded, and a wall collapsed under the pressure of the crowd, killing one nine-year-old boy and injuring about 50 others, some of them seriously. The fact that the game was played out and Celtic won 6-3 seemed irrelevant, although it did seem the right decision at the time, as the abandoning of the game might have led to further problems.

But then, Celtic imploded. Whether it was because of the tragedy at Shawfield which affected them all, or for some other reason, no-one can say but the team now lost four games in a row. Astonishingly they were all at home. In the first of these games against Partick Thistle, Fernie was carried off with a bad knee injury and made the fatal mistake of trying to come back, and thus aggravating the injury. It meant that he was out until 25 January, by which time the League challenge had vanished with Hearts who had beaten

Celtic (without Fernie) 2-0 on 28 December, virtually out of sight. They would win the League very comfortably for the first time since 1897, and no-one could argue that it was not well deserved.

But the return of Fernie in late January made a difference to Celtic, and there was still the Scottish Cup. The game at Airdrie on 1 February was a thriller in which Celtic dominated the game for more than half the 90 minutes, scoring four times (including one from Fernie) but then losing their grip and struggling to hold on to their lead as Airdrie scored three times. Two weeks later they beat Stirling Albion 7-2 with Fernie outstanding, and for the next round, Celtic were drawn yet again to play the team that they always seemed to meet in Cup ties at this time, Clyde.

But February 1958 had seen one of football's saddest days when Manchester United's plane crashed in the snow at Munich killing such great players as Roger Byrne and Duncan Edwards, and putting the life of Manager Matt Busby, an unashamed Celtic supporter, in great danger. The whole sad business seemed to put the future of air travel to European matches in a great deal of doubt, and affected all of world football for a very long time.

The atmosphere was therefore generally very sombre, and the events of December rendered the Scottish Cup game v Clyde on 1 March an even more poignant and emotive tie. The decision was taken to move the game to Celtic Park, although Clyde were still technically the home team. It was a sensible decision and rewarded by a large 50,000 crowd. For this game, Celtic, plagued by injuries, made the decision to put Fernie back into the forward line at inside right, and to bring Eric Smith in at right half. This was not a good idea and Celtic were 2-0 down at half time. They rejigged the forward line for the second half, but that made no impact, and Celtic never really got back into the game.

It would not be fair to blame it all on the difficult background to the match. Credit must be given to Clyde who would go on to win the

Scottish Cup that year beating Hibs in the final, and thus bringing to an end four remarkable years of winning the Scottish Cup in 1955, being relegated in 1956, gaining promotion in 1957 and winning the Scottish Cup in 1958. There was never a dull moment in the East end of Glasgow in those days.

But the season ended dismally for Celtic. The remaining games were played out with no real urgency for there was little at stake. There were some good games, and Fernie himself turned in some good performances, but it was a curious anti-climax to a season which had seen Celtic's best ever single result. There was also a growing feeling that it was perhaps time for some changes and that the gradual introduction of youngsters might produce better results.

And thus began the ill-thought-out youth policy of the Kelly Kids, based on the Busby Babes of Manchester United. The policy would eventually bring great dividends, after many heart breaks and one particular volte-face when the Chairman had to admit that he was wrong in letting Jock Stein go to Dunfermline. Had Stein been given total control of the youth policy with Fernie as his "voice on the field" as it were, the late 1950s and early 1960s might have been a totally different story. But for the next few years Celtic floundered as overawed youngsters were brought in, suddenly dropped, then played again in another position – and Mr Kelly wondered why the team did not do well!

There was another dynamic as well as the 1958/59 season, an unsatisfactory and unhappy one for all concerned, began. The ground at Celtic Park was anything but the "paradise" that it was called by supporters. Money needed to be spent on it – the "Jungle" on the north side of the ground was a filthy, unhygienic experience and it had holes in the roof. Frankly it was a disgrace. Recently, at the Railway End, a shelter had been built, but, for bogus penny-pinching reasons, it only extended half way down the terracing, and the windows at the back were always broken and not repaired! And worst of all, the ground had no floodlights, something that meant that Celtic were lagging far behind many other clubs. They would find playing in Europe difficult, and could not now be considered for Scotland or Scottish League Internationals. And yet this ground had been built in the 1890s for no other reason than to be the best in the country and to host the Scotland v England games!

One way of paying for floodlights was the selling of players, and Collins, Fernie and later Evans were the men to go. Collins was still playing for Scotland as late as 1965, (seven years after Celtic considered him expendable!) and Fernie, although now 30, would return less than two years later and still play significantly in Scottish football for some time after that! The decisions were crazy. In addition, Tully was now more or less finished, and all in all, the 7-1 team had more or less disappeared little more than a year after the game.

But to begin at the beginning of the miserable 1958/59 season, one must recognise that football in Scotland was still by some distance the obsession of the country, but it was on a downer after the miserable performances in the World Cup in Sweden in 1958. As in 1954 and 1978, when things had been a lot worse on the World Cup front, these things did affect the domestic season. Celtic were drawn in the same League Cup section as Clyde, Airdrie and St Mirren. Fernie was still playing at half back. But the names were changing – Mackay, McNeill, Auld, Byrne, Jackson, McVittie, Colrain and Conway all made their appearance (some made it and some didn't!) – and, as is often the case with youngsters, results were unpredictable. Fernie, as we said, started the season at right half, but moved forward to inside right (certainly his own preferred position, although many people thought he was a far better right half) to accommodate Eric Smith for a spell and then a talented youngster called Pat Crerand.

The potentially difficult League Cup section involving St Mirren, Airdrie and Clyde was negotiated well with four wins, a draw and an odd 3-6 defeat at St Mirren on the last day when the section was already decided. So far, so good, and the play of youngsters Jim

Conway and Bertie Auld in particular was a cause for enthusiasm. There were a few stumbling blocks with an exit from the Glasgow Cup and a defeat in the first League match to Clyde, but a 2-2 draw with Rangers at Parkhead was satisfactory.

That game however on 6 September 1958 saw Glasgow at its worst. There has always been heavy rainfall in Glasgow, but today was something special with a huge thunderstorm and floods. Amazingly, the pitch was cleared and the game went ahead when wiser counsel might have suggested a postponement or at least a delay for an hour. The weather however was no-one's fault. What definitely was someone's fault was the hooliganism which dogged this game from start to finish, involving the burning of each other's flags, free-fights, bottle throwing and general disorder. Psychiatrists tell us that rain and water usually dampen down aggression and violence. Sadly not in this case.

There was of course nothing new in all this. Most Celtic v Rangers games at this time seemed to contain a certain amount of crowd disorder to a greater or lesser extent, but no-one seemed to have any idea of how to stop it. There were of course solutions – draconian and drastic ones – but they all seemed to involve the clubs losing money, and this they were not prepared to do. Those who would advocate corporal punishment had their supporters, but there was no point in anyone advocating National Service in 1958. It was still in force, and indeed National Service was the place where not very bright young men learned "proper" violence!

This particular game may well have made Fernie think. Later in the autumn he made a decision to leave the club (or he had the decision made for him by the Chairman) and one of the factors may have been the question of whether he really wanted to continue playing his football in an atmosphere like this. Players were usually well protected from the excesses of supporters, and were usually themselves well behaved (unlike the 2020s perhaps?) but there was always the chance of something really silly happening, and in any case, was this atmosphere in any way conducive to good football? The thought of playing somewhere else must have been attractive to the quiet man from Fife who was now approaching his 30th birthday and who had already done enough to earn a place in the Celtic pantheon.

Progress in the League Cup continued with beatings of Cowdenbeath in the quarter finals, but hopes of winning a hat-trick of League Cups crashed on Wednesday October 1 at Ibrox when Celtic went down to Partick Thistle in the semi-final. It was a frustrating experience for the Celtic fans in the 45,000 crowd, but one with which Celtic fans would have to get familiar with in years to come. Chances went a begging (even against a replacement goalkeeper!), then two goals were lost against the run of play, and by the time that Jim Conway did score in the 88th minute, it was too late. Fernie tried, but there was something wrong with the team, and a great deal of unhappiness among the support who did not really understand why Bobby Collins had been transferred. This game turned out to be very significant in the future of Celtic.

A week after this Fernie played what turned out to be his last representative game on Wednesday 8 October 1958 in a 1-1 draw against the English League before 31,000 at Ibrox. The teams were Scottish League; ***Brown (Dundee), Grant (Hibs) and Caldow (Rangers); Turnbull (Hibs), Toner (Kilmarnock) and Mackay (Hearts); Hamilton (Hearts) Fernie (Celtic), Bauld (Hearts), Baird (Rangers) and Auld (Celtic) and the English League team was Hopkinson (Bolton Wanderers), Bond (West Ham) and G Shaw (Sheffield United); Malcolm (West Ham), J Shaw (Sheffield United) and Iley (Tottenham Hotspur); Wilkinson (Sheffield Wednesday), Quixall (Manchester United), Clough (Middlesbrough), Greaves (Chelsea) and Pilkington (Burnley)***

The referee was RH Davidson, Airdrie, and it was generally looked upon as a poor game. Fernie had his moments. *The Glasgow Herald* says "Fernie flashed into prominence midway through the first half when a well-placed header going away from the goalkeeper was scrambled clear on the goal-line and again after the interval when he shot narrowly over the crossbar, but he had played better games in a dark blue jersey". It would be interesting to know what Fernie made of the English centre forward from Middlesbrough, a brash character with a lot to say for himself called Brian Clough. They would soon be colleagues, possibly even friends.

As far as Celtic and Fernie were concerned, events accelerated rapidly downhill in November. Two defeats at Dunfermline and then Partick Thistle brought matters to a head. Clearly something was wrong when Cyril Horne in *The Glasgow Herald* says "Fernie played with the lethargy one would associate with a frolic on the beach on a warm summer's day", and the Celtic fans in the 16,000 crowd were mystified by this, especially when it was Fernie's misplaced pass that led to the only goal of the game.

And then two weeks later another awful performance from Celtic and Fernie saw a 2-0 defeat from Partick Thistle at Firhill, and it was now clear that things were simply not functioning. One does not need to be an expert in football psychology to work out a connection between poor performances on the field and general unhappiness behind the scenes. Nevertheless, it was a bombshell to read in *The Evening Times* of Monday November 24 that Willie Fernie had asked for a transfer with the quotation given "because he wants to better himself" with Newcastle United already quoted as being interested.

"Because he wants to better himself" does not ring true. Nor was anyone 100% convinced that he really did want to leave the club. Perhaps pressure was put on him to ask for a transfer as part of the deliberate Kelly policy of clearing out the old players, and at 30, it was now beginning to look as if Fernie's better days were behind him. It had certainly been obvious for some time possibly since the Scottish League Cup semi-final defeat that he was not happy, and his unhappiness had been exacerbated by the departure of his friend and colleague Bobby Collins, now in the colours of Everton.

There were other factors too. His wife Audrey had of course been

McGrory's secretary, and there was possibly a feeling from Fernie that the atmosphere was just a little too close. Maybe he did feel that it was time to move on, particularly as he was no longer in the first flush of youth and he wished to sample English football as long as he had the opportunity.

One wonders too what the thoughts of Jock Stein were. Jock was now helping with the youth set up and had no direct involvement in the transfer of Fernie, but it is inconceivable that Fernie did not talk to Jock at some stage. They had a high respect for each other, and it would have been interesting to know what Stein's thoughts were about all this. Stein himself was always extremely reluctant to try his luck in England – he once lasted about 40 days as Manager of Leeds United – and simply loved Scotland, particularly after an unhappy spell in Wales in the early 1950s.

One factor, although widely touted at the time, can be disregarded as pure rubbish, and that was the religious factor. Some people (not the newspapers who tended, surprisingly, to ignore that rather obvious facet of Glasgow's football) pointed out that both Collins and Fernie were non-Catholic, and wondered whether there was some "ethnic cleansing" going on. Such feelings grew when in subsequent years Evans, Stein and Auld all took their departure, but they were clearly all the wrong decisions, as was proved when Fernie, Stein and Auld all returned!

And yet, there may be an element, although only an element, of truth in this. Many players, particularly Protestants who play for Celtic, have confessed to finding it difficult to play in Glasgow's sectarian cauldron. Some – Sunny Jim, Alec McNair, Bertie Auld and Jock Stein himself – almost gave the impression of enjoying it; others perhaps less so, and it may be that Fernie, from tough Fife mining stock where religious sectarianism is quite alien and indeed incomprehensible, felt that this nonsense was something that he and his career could perhaps now do without. He had proved himself (and more!) for both Celtic and Scotland and it was time for a change.

There was also the hooliganism of some Celtic fans. Those of us who have been brought up with the idea that "Celtic fans are the best in the world" have to temper this belief by the recollections of how they behave when things are not going so well. In recent years we have seen some awful behaviour directed at men like Neil Lennon and Peter Lawwell, and there were clear signs in late 1958 that some Celtic fans were beginning to turn nasty, and far too often their disapproval of team performances was backed by the throwing of bottles and stones. Did one really need that?

Most Celtic fans, however, were distraught at the thought of Fernie's departure. He still seemed to have something left in him (a good four years as it turned out) and the balance of opinion was that he was being pushed out the door for a large transfer fee to help fund the floodlights. This was in fact the bottom line as far as the club and Mr Kelly were concerned. Not for the first time, and certainly not for the last, it seemed that success on the field was being sacrificed for other purposes, and that once again, Mr Kelly had misjudged the mood of the fans. The fans, after all, come to football grounds to see good football players. They do not come to admire floodlights or enclosure roofs.

The affair was carried out with breath taking speed. By 1 December exactly a week after Fernie had asked for a transfer, he was on his way, not to high-flying First Division Newcastle United (a team with many similarities to Celtic) but to Second Division Middlesbrough. It was difficult to resist the conclusion that it had not been planned by Mr Kelly some time in advance. The transfer fee was said to be £16,000, although some reports went as high as £20,000.

As for Fernie's real feelings, no-one can know for certain. Certainly there were many photographs of him taken sitting on a train with Audrey, and others of him waving goodbye to his team mates at Celtic Park. He probably was sad to leave (and indeed most fans were sad to see him go) but maybe felt that there was less and less room for him at Celtic Park with the youth policy in place, and that Middlesbrough was a new challenge. It was not a place that he knew a lot about necessarily, but that was possibly a good thing. His arrival was certainly welcomed by the Teesside fans, who had not had an awful lot to be happy about in recent years. One often hears the cliché "pressure cooker" used about the atmosphere around football in Glasgow. In Middlesbrough, it would be no less intense.

At Parkhead, things went from bad to worse. Usually in football, awful seasons are self-inflicted. This one certainly was. There was one bright moment when they defeated Rangers 2-1 in the Scottish Cup, but then the raw youngsters reached the semi-final and went down 0-4 to St Mirren in one of the most piteous collapses of their whole history.

And then there were the virtually inconceivable events of the last day of the League season when Celtic excelled themselves by beating League challengers Hearts 2-1. Normally it would have been a cause for celebration, but this result meant that the 1959 Scottish League Championship would this year be won by Rangers! Rangers themselves lost to Aberdeen, and were duly booed off the park until they heard the news that they were Champions thanks to Celtic beating Hearts! No-one knew whether to laugh or cry! It was the day that Celtic won the League for Rangers, and it was rumoured that some Rangers supporters even said "Thank You" to Celtic fans (and bought them drinks) when they met in George Square, Glasgow that night!

One of the authors recalls coming home that afternoon from the matinee performance at the cinema to meet his father, who had been listening to the radio, saying that Celtic had won 2-1, but not looking very happy about it. "They've played a lot o' pish a' season! Could they no hae just lost the day?"

CHAPTER FIVE

MIDDLESBROUGH (1958-1960)

Middlesbrough's home match with Ipswich on 6 December 1958, the day after Britain's first motorway opened, was imminent and things were becoming desperate. Manager Bob Dennison and director George Winney were hoping for a turn of the tide in a mediocre season: despite a bright start, which included the 9-0 dismantling of Brighton in the opening game, there was a run soon of nine games with no wins. The relegation zone beckoned. Something had to be done. The Teesside club tried to sign Don Revie, a native of Middlesbrough and a future England manager, then playing for Leeds in the autumn of his on-pitch career. Leeds were disinclined, understandably, having just signed Revie the month before!

Undeterred, and no doubt impressed as well by Willie Fernie's international appearances against Switzerland, Wales and Paraguay during the previous season, the pair drove to Glasgow to sign the experienced Celtic man at the very beginning of December, 1958. £18,000 was the agreed amount, and it equalled Boro's record payment, for Bill Harris, four years earlier. Despite these ambitious efforts, against Ipswich they were to be disappointed. As an aside, history can play curious tricks. If Leeds had agreed to sell Revie, then he would have been playing alongside Brian Clough, Boro's centre-forward and goal machine. The later managerial rivalry between the two men might not then have been so poisonous.

After a noteworthy 315 games for Celtic, Willie Fernie had submitted an official transfer request. Feeling that the club's new youth policy would limit his future as a Celt, he was himself setting out plans for the next stage of his career, with a new club. The Scotsman newspaper goes further however, saying openly in Fernie's obituary in 2001 that the imperious chairman Bob Kelly sold him to pay for Parkhead's floodlights! Second-division Middlesbrough FC, nicknamed the Boro', were also known as The Ironsides, marking the origin of the town in the iron and steel industry. Iron ore mined in the Cleveland Hills during the nineteenth century was transported by rail to ironworks established in County Durham. Ironstone mines sprang up to exploit the rich brown seams in these evocative coastal areas, creating an inpouring of fortune-seeking entrepreneurs and job-hunting workers on a scale not seen since the famous American gold rush. One of the many settlements that bloomed to house the miners was even called California! In their prime, the Hills produced a third of the country's entire iron ore output.

To that time, the Boro's trophies cabinet was quite small, the only honours being amateur cup victories in 1895 and 1898, and Second Division wins in 1926-7 and 1928-9. Transparently, they were not prolific but made sure their fans noticed their deeds by winning the competitions twice!

The £18,000 fee to Celtic was no mean amount with the highest transfer fee then being £45,000. That sum was paid by Manchester United in 1958 for Sheffield Wednesday's Albert Quixall, football's youthful golden boy. He played with imagination and was United manager Matt Busby's choice as part of his team rebuilding after the Munich aircraft tragedy earlier in the year. The world was shocked by the crash of the plane on its third attempt at take-off in the middle of winter snow.

Into this environment, as we see, came Willie, his wife Audrey, and young son Billy. His first game, sandwiched between his signing and the worrying Ipswich league match was a friendly contest with the French side Nimes Olympique, presumably arranged to improve, hopefully, the confidence and cohesion of the misfiring Boro' side. The club at Nimes, almost on the French Mediterranean coast, had only been in existence in that present guise for twenty years. Perhaps Nimes will best be remembered for the brief time Eric Cantona played for them in December 1991. During a match for Nimes, upset by a decision, he threw the ball at the referee. A disciplinary hearing declared him banned for one month. Cantona promptly responded by calling each member of the committee, to his face, in turn, an idiot, earning himself a doubling of his suspension to two months. He quickly signed for Leeds, then equally promptly moved on to Manchester United where he settled, and forged his reputation as a football genius.

Maybe if the likes of Cantona were playing that day for Nimes against Middlesbrough and the newly signed Fernie, the result might have been different, but the Teesside team won 3-0 comfortably. A bigger than average crowd turned out to welcome Willie and, by all accounts, took him to their hearts, applauding his smooth-moving defence-splitting passes and majestic ball control. Boro' scored all their goals before half-time but failed to add to their total after the break. Maybe that was down to Willie tiring – he said afterwards that "after all the rush of the last few days, I had just about had it by half-time". He even managed to keep a cool head to calm a possible fistfight. Willie had passed to Brian Clough who had worked to a goal-scoring position, but Clough merely collided with the French goalkeeper, visiting upon him the need for medical treatment on the touchline. The French players, naturally unhappy, surrounded Clough and Fernie, but Willie, keeping his self-control, achieved a truce. Manager Bob Dennison said after the game, "He was every bit as good as we had hoped. He obviously has the experience to blend our young forward line, and I'm sure he will team up into the best right wing in the business with Billy Day, who is in the army, and couldn't play tonight".

Dennison was halfway through a nine-year residency as the Boro' manager, having built an attractive attacking team with the irrepressible Brian Clough as its star-performing centre forward and fellow England international Alan Peacock, an immaculate 6 feet tall player, at inside-left. It was said that the two did not get on well, a recurring theme in Clough's playing and subsequent managerial career! Attendance at the Boro's matches had been falling during a curate's egg of a season with the team struggling only two points above the bottom teams.

An extra 10,000 supporters though crowded into the home ground of Ayresome Park to support Fernie against Ipswich, his first league match in a Boro' red shirt. He played in every match thereafter, bar three, until his return to Celtic early in the 1960-61 season. Boro's form had picked up in the previous two home games with victories against Scunthorpe United (6-1, with Clough and Peacock harvesting a hat-trick each) and Derby County (5-0, with five different players scoring, including an own goal) so expectations were high, despite a 3-1 reverse at Bristol Rovers the previous Saturday. The swollen crowd encouraged Fernie and roared on the Boro'….and they lost 2-3. Brian Clough, scoring in the first minute, and right winger Ron Burbeck (though he could play on both wings), got the goals but the Boro' defence was pulled around too easily by the Ipswich attackers. To add to the home team's discomfort, right-back Ray Bilcliff scored an own goal. In Boro's history he has the unenviable record of playing in more matches than any other player without scoring a goal, that is to say, in the opponents' net! Willie could not be blamed for the defeat since, although he had a quiet debut, he created enough chances for his team-mates to win the match, if they had taken them. So Boro's sad position of only two points above the relegation zone was not eased.

Cliff Mitchell, the regular local press reporter opined two days later that "supporters were still in the process of recovery from the disappointment, even shock, of Saturday's game against Bristol

Rovers". Willie himself, even though he had a quiet game, created enough chances for the striking twins of Clough and Peacock to win the game had the two been sharper.

All players have their off days, but Brian Clough didn't have many. If Middlesbrough FC had a Hall of Fame, he would certainly be vying to be "in the top one". As with many who become driven on their chosen path he was controversial, not only during his playing years but also in the managerial career that followed. Looking back on his time in football during an interview, he was asked if he thought he was the best football manager ever. "I wouldn't say I was the best manager in the business, but I was in the top one", he cheekily replied. Clough's goal-scoring achievements were certainly breath-taking. Playing for the Boro' alone, he scored 204 goals in only 222 games. Only five months before Willie joined Middlesbrough, Clough had scored five goals in that 9-0 league match drubbing of Brighton, and almost achieved the same feat on another five occasions, only managing four nettings in those games.

When he arrived to play alongside Clough, Willie Fernie displayed his usual mesmerising skills on the ball, but that wasn't good enough for the often-selfish number nine, who demanded the ball incessantly. Clough was even known to barge his own players off the ball for a goal-scoring opportunity. Unsurprisingly, Willie was not the only Boro' player to be frustrated with Clough. During November, 1959, nine of the first team players signed a round-robin demanding his removal as captain quoting "harsh words on the pitch", and sulking after defeats. One wouldn't have blamed Willie if he had been one of the signatories! News spread about the incident (in fact, the writer remembers being told of it by his father!) and Clough was barracked by the crowd at the next home match, against Bristol Rovers, but he answered his critics by scoring a hat-trick in a 5-1 demolition. To rub it in, all three goals were scored from well outside the penalty area!

Fairness demands the mention of two other legends of the Ironsides whose shining repute reaches well beyond the club, even, or perhaps especially, in the modern age. 'Gentleman' George Hardwick preceded Brian Clough by a decade, and was his antithesis. Brought up in the iron-ore mining village of Lingdale, he was a hard-tackling left back, though calm and steady in his far-sighted approach to the game. Scoring an own goal though in the first minute of your debut match in front of a capacity crowd is not the ideal start to your career, and moreover, war broke out within a few games. Serving then as a sergeant in RAF Bomber Command, he was wounded in both legs in an air raid on his RAF base on the Isle of Sheppey, but despite these setbacks, George became one of the country's best known post-war players. He was given the captaincy of not only his club and country, but of the Great Britain side that was assembled against the Rest of Europe in 1947 for a special match at Hampden Park. Hardwick's team won easily, 6-1. His England captaincy came to an end with an injury, after which Wolves' Billy Wright took over. Charming and debonair, George Hardwick is fondly remembered.

Playing in that same game against the Europeans, and scoring two of the goals, was Hardwick's contemporary and teammate, 'Golden Boy' Wilf Mannion. A dazzling inside-forward, he was speedy and entertaining, sending defenders the wrong way with the slightest movement of his shoulders. One immortal home match, against Blackpool in November 1947, is now known as the Mannion Match. Without scoring a single goal in the 4-0 victory, he mesmerised spectators (of whom the author's father was one!) and opposition alike. George Hardwick captained the Boro at this time, and he explained in his autobiography that "in a virtuoso display, Wilf performed an expert demonstration of his innate footballing talents, and engaged in some outrageous individual party pieces, such as juggling the ball on his head as he was running." In many ways, Willie Fernie's admirable ball control and accurate passing was a continuation of Wilf's inside forward tradition during his all-too-short stay at Ayresome Park.

The Boro fans loved Wilf, even making a kitty for a wedding day gift. The man himself must have wished that the management felt the same, as he famously, and unsuccessfully, battled for his freedom against the noose-like grip of his contract, an unfair chain to the club that all professional footballers faced in those times. In his battles for freedom of employment, Wilf was well before his time. It wasn't until nearly fifty years later that Jean-Marc Bosman won this very liberty for footballers in a long battle against his club, Belgium's FC Liege. After five devastating years which saw him bankrupt, his marriage shattered and rumours of a drink problem, he walked from the European Court of Justice a free man. In his own words, football authorities are "people without scruples. They have no respect for the rights of others, and are basically incompetent".

Mannion's 26 appearances for England are a Middlesbrough record and he was part of what many consider England's finest forward line – Matthews, Mortensen, Lawton, Mannion and Finney. He and Hardwick are the twin giants of the Middlesbrough story and it is fitting that they have statues in their honour at the Boro's new ground, the Riverside Stadium. They welcome spectators as they stand alongside each other, deserved legends.

Middlesbrough's growth and prosperity during the nineteenth century fell on the shoulders of migrant workers, who sought their shares of the wealth in the proliferating iron and steel industry. From the 1860s to the 1870s, the population of 20,000 doubled, and now stands at nearly 400,000. Shipbuilding on the River Tees grew during the same period and was a reflection of the likewise, but superior, industry on the River Tyne, about thirty miles further north. Later, in 1926, the Imperial Chemical Industries (ICI), was established on the fringes of Middlesbrough and was the biggest industry of its kind in the UK, making paints, fertilisers, dyestuffs and pharmaceuticals, among many other products crucial to the national economy. During Clement Attlee's post-war government, immigration from the Commonwealth and South Asia was actively encouraged to help rebuild the shattered country; again Middlesbrough saw migration, this time from abroad. The Windrush generation from the West Indies was the best-known cog in the machine of that national recuperation.

Middlesbrough's railway line runs east-west through the town, and the oldest parts of the industrial community are housed north of this line and upwards to the banks of the river Tees. To this day, the area is known as "over the border"; and it was into this area that a large population of Pakistani people moved, worked and lived after the war. Slowly, gradually, suspicion and distrust grew among the souls in these streets, and in a particular one named Cannon Street. That street name was spoken of in hushed tones all around Teesside during the 1950s – the troubled times are still remembered locally. Willie Fernie arrived to play for the Boro as this friction was approaching ignition point, returning to Celtic in the year before it exploded into fire, on 18th August, 1961. The murder of local man John Hunt, by a sailor, Hussain Said, made national headlines and prompted four nights of window-smashing and clashes with police, culminating in 55 prosecutions and the exodus of many Asian families from the Cannon Street area. The local press and the MP denied racial causes, citing hooliganism and teddy boy violence.

The next match, away to Sheffield Wednesday, was no more comfortable for Willie. He was targeted by the opposing defence, who descended on him as soon as he ever got the ball. He was tripped and man-handled in various and imaginative ways, and was clearly put off his stride in the faster tempo of life in the English Second Division. These two games must have got Willie wondering if his move to Middlesbrough was the right one, but he bounced back in the next game. The long coach journey to the south coast for a game against Brighton may have given Willie time to think.

His pitch partner on the right wing for many of Willie's Boro' games was Billy Day, who was a popular player with the fans, his exciting touchline play showing control and accuracy. More importantly though, he was fast, so fast that he was sprint champion during his National Service time in Germany with the 7th Royal Tank Regiment. He was held in such high esteem by his club that they paid for him to fly back to Middlesbrough to play, then they flew him back to Germany afterwards. This happened twenty times, with Billy taking to the air on Friday lunchtime and arriving at Ayresome Park in the early hours on Saturday in time for the match. Maybe Billy inspired Willie to speed up his playing style, but whatever the reason, the two of them formed a vigorous alliance on the right wing, causing damage in the opposing ranks, and especially so in this next game against Brighton when Boro' scored six times, Clough scoring a hat-trick in thirteen minutes. The lop-sided nature of the Boro' team during these years however, with a strong attack and a weak defence, surfaced again during this match. They were leading 5-0 with less than half-an-hour to go, and won 6-4!

Nonetheless, Willie had settled into the side, earning praise from the local press in the next game, a 3-1 home win against Barnsley on Boxing Day, 1958. Willie's football was described as "cool, unflurried, and of value to the defence as well as the attack, with attractive footwork and ball control". It was a good comeback because the Barnsley right-winger, Arthur Kaye, took away the home team's breath with a goal in the first minute of the game. Boro' travelled to Barnsley to play them again on the very next day, and lost 1-0, even though Willie had a good game approaching the other goal. Boro' played precisely the same team, so maybe it's of no surprise that they lost, playing on two consecutive days, punctuated by an 85-mile coach journey. Such demands on players would not happen in the modern era.

Fidel Castro's revolution in Cuba saw in the New Year, 1959, with General Batista giving up the struggle and setting off for the Dominican Republic. On that 1 January, the Boro' were similarly too much for Huddersfield as Willie Fernie scored the first of his

Boro' goals in a 3-1 home win even though, yet again, the other team netted in the first minute. Brian Clough scored the Boro's other two goals, and forged an eye-catching link with Willie, who completely outshone Huddersfield's young Denis Law, Scottish international and shortly to turn only 19 years of age. Born in Aberdeen and selected for Scotland schoolboys, he was spotted by Archie Beattie, the Town's scout. As 1958 turned into 1959, Denis was talked of in the football world as a future superstar, but after the Boro'-Huddersfield match, a spectator was heard to say "If Law's worth £40,000, what's Willie Fernie worth?" The latter scored his impressive goal just before half-time, to add the icing to a cake of effective football. Just over a year later, Denis Law was transferred to Manchester City for £53,000, then a record. Denis became a legend of Scottish football and is missed, not only for his footballing ability, but for his charming and witty comments.

The co-author remembers, although the year escapes him, a Law quip while commentating on an England-Scotland match at Wembley when his playing time was long over. Well before the kick-off, the stadium accommodated many thousands of cheering, be-kilted Scots. Denis Law's companion pundit wondered where all the England fans were. "Maybe they'll all come in one big coach", he said. "Maybe they'll all come in one big car!", Denis quickly returned.

Boro' were in action again on a freezing 10 January, when they tackled Birmingham City in the third round of the English FA Cup. Over 34,000 Boro' fans wrapped up tightly and watched their team hold their own against the First Division club. With the score at 1-1, the match was abandoned after 60 minutes with an icy pitch becoming a danger. Brian Clough's goal was hence chalked off the record, and one can only imagine the goal-hungry centre-forward's angst! Birmingham City, scoring the only goal of the match, won the replay exactly two weeks later.

Morale was still low throughout the team for the next game, a goal-less draw against Stoke City at Ayresome Park. The pitch was muddy and heavy, a familiar sight in those days as groundsmen struggled to keep wintry playing surfaces in good condition. Even Edwin (Eddie) Holliday suffered. Boro's Leeds-born left-winger, whose ferocious, pinpoint crosses were a big part of the team's attacking play, was left in the cold as his team-mates could not feed him with sufficient passes. Willie also left room for improvement as his passes forgivably went astray, and it wasn't until the last five minutes that the game came alive. Dejected by then, most of the spectators had set off for home! Boro's cheerless spell continued with a 3-1 home defeat at the hands of London team, Charlton Athletic, though Willie was named among the best three home players, along with Arthur Fitzsimmons and Ray Yeoman.

A regular inside-left since 1952, Arthur had lost his place as Clough's striking partner to Alan Peacock in the previous year, but was recalled for this Charlton match at the unfortunate Eddie Holliday's expense. Fitzsimmons, born in Dublin, won 26 international caps for the Republic of Ireland, equalling Wilf Mannion's total for England, though both endeavours dwarf in comparison to Boro's goalkeeper Mark Schwarzer (109 caps for Australia) some fifty years later. Maybe Brian Clough's disenchantment with Willie Fernie on the pitch stemmed from his playing time with Fitzsimmons, who would easy beat two or three defenders then sky the ball over the goal's crossbar. A famous story is often recalled in the Boro's football circles how Clough once bellowed at Arthur on the pitch "You make the bloody goals, and I'll score them!" Looking at Brian 'Ole Big 'Ead' Clough's scoring record of 251 goals in 274 games for Middlesbrough and Sunderland combined, it's a credible tale!

Incidentally, Clough's nickname for Willie – "My Ball Fernie" - was also well-known. Ramon (Ray) Yeoman, gritty and tough-tackling full-back turned half-back, was born in Perth, and first played for St. Johnstone. He made his Boro' debut in Willie Fernie's second league match. Born only 15 miles apart, Willie, at Kinglassie, and Ray no doubt entertained each other with accounts of their early days in their home area. Remarkably, that was the beginning of a run of 207 consecutive games for Yeoman, beaten only by David (Spike) Armstrong with a phenomenal 358, in 1980. He played for England on the left wing.

A 1-0 win over Grimsby Town in March, on the back of a fourth-minute Brian Clough goal saw an upward turn in the red shirts' fortunes, even though the next game saw a 3-2 reverse at the hands of Fulham. That was a game the Boro' should easily have won, with chances squandered. Clough and Fernie both missed opportunities that were easier to convert than turn down, though the latter was easily the best ball-player on view, and that included Fulham's Johnny Haynes, an England World Cup international and about to become captain of his country. The next game saw a Fernie goal, four from Clough and a penalty from wing-half Bill Harris as they swept away Swansea 6-2. Even though Willie did not have his full range of skills on display, he still had a hand in more than one of the goals, and his own was described by the press as a "gem".

The next game saw Willie and Bill Harris as the best players on show as the Boro' won 'on points' in the 0-0 draw at Roker Park, Sunderland, though two days later, the team crashed 5-1 to Huddersfield. A hiccough it was though, as Fernie's new team scored three victories consecutively, described as their finest wins of the season. They began with a 4-2 home win over Leyton Orient, with wing-half Bill Harris again on the score sheet. It must be noted that in the modern game, teams play different formations according to their battle plans; for example, 4-4-2 or 3-5-2. In Fernie's day, the usual plan was 2-3-5, with two full backs clearly the last line of defence, three half-backs (left-, centre- and right-) and five in the forward line. Ray Yeoman played the left-half position (shirt number 6) but was a defensive player, whereas Bill Harris was a right-half (shirt number 4) but carried the ball forward when he was in possession of it. The

Yeoman wing-half would be in today's back line, where the Harris wing-half would be in midfield! Willie Fernie wore the number 8 shirt, the classic inside-right position in the forward line, but today he would be in midfield as a game-maker.

Modern teams change formation from game to game, and sometimes during a game, according to the opposition, but curiously, and almost humorously, George Hardwick, arguably Boro's finest-ever player, recalled that managers rarely studied the opposition for its strengths and weaknesses; they never produced the now-infamous Don Revie dossiers. He said that, leading his side out from the Ayresome Park tunnel, he sometimes glanced to the other end of the pitch to see who they were playing! The next game was midweek, against Liverpool at Anfield, with the Boro' impressively scoring a 2-1 victory. Finally, on the day that Bobby Charlton scored the only goal in a 1-0 victory over Scotland at Wembley in the now discontinued Home Internationals, Boro' beat Derby County 3-0 at the Baseball Ground.

The next match saw the end of this pleasing run of victories with a 2-2 home draw against Derby County, two days before Winston Churchill announced he would, at the age of 85, stand again for the Westminster parliament in the election of that year, 1959. He was re-elected to his Woodford constituency with a slightly reduced majority, retiring at the 1964 election. His death in 1965 was marked by a state funeral and one wonders if he knew that his funeral had been in planning since 1953.

The final three games of the 1958-59 season came and went without a win, but at least Willie Fernie had contributed to a rise in league position since his arrival - Boro' finished thirteenth. The following season, Willie's only full period with the Boro', began in style in August and September, with spectacular wins (7-1 against Derby County at the Baseball Ground, Plymouth Argyle's loss of 6-2 on Boro's home turf, and four against Hull without reply, also at Ayresome) and only two losses. Five days after the drubbing of Hull, Boro' faced them again in the league, and drew 3-3 – the Ironsides were now second in the league. The sky was the limit and indeed, on 12 September, the Soviet Union launched Lunik II, the first man-made object to hit the moon, which it did the day after blast off. The Russians' first attempt, Lunik I, in January, was not so accurate. It missed and went into orbit around the sun, but the huge radio telescope at Jodrell Bank, Manchester, followed Lunik II's signal all the way to the moon, a quarter of a million miles away, and there was no doubt about the plucky space probe's fate when its signal suddenly stopped. Willie Fernie's aim was equally true in October's first game. He scored in the 3-1 home win over Scunthorpe.

Fernie's versatility was shown during this spell in the game against Cardiff at Ayresome Park on 2 September. Boro's right back in this game, a position that always carried the number 2 shirt, was Ray Barnard, a loyal, no-frills player and former England schoolboy international. He played in 113 league matches from 1950 to 1960, but was left with a leg injury on the hour in this 1-1 game. Unfortunately, this was six years before substitutes were allowed, and Ray was moved out of harm's way onto the right wing in a game where defences were playing a crucial part: ice-cool Bill Harris at right-half (number 4) took Ray's place at the back. Boro's right-winger, always a number 7, thus displaced, was moved to inside-right, number 8. Willie Fernie, the actual inside-right, was bumped back to Bill's place at right-half. All in, Willie was Boro's best forward until this comedy of musical positions, and was also judged to be also the team's best half-back!

Meanwhile, Willie's wife, Audrey, was finding it difficult to settle on Teesside. She missed the family atmosphere of Parkhead where she had been secretary to manager Jimmy McGrory - a position which put her on first name terms with the whole club almost. She returned north to see friends regularly, and even travelled to Glasgow, Redlands Nursing Home, to give birth to their second child, a boy, Alec, who could then look up to his older brother, Billy.

Willie generously granted though that Middlesbrough FC had looked after the family very well, giving them use of a club-owned house in Heythrop Drive, Acklam, a comfortable suburb of Middlesbrough.

It's an area that the co-author knows well. He was a ten-year-old football-mad schoolboy at the time, and the auntie of his best pal lived in ... Heythrop Drive! On one of the chums' visits to auntie, they were told of a new neighbour, a Middlesbrough footballer! Grabbing an autograph book, they whizzed down the road, breathlessly knocking on Willie's front door. To their jaw-dropping, eye-popping astonishment, he opened the door and amiably signed their book, a moment that has stuck in the author's memory like a barnacle. Maybe those two boys brought a smile to Audrey in her homesick days. Indeed, when the author looks back at boyhood football matches with his father at Middlesbrough's Ayresome Park, they seem like dark, ancient, black-and-white events, almost alien, in a world gone by. Entry to the ground was through narrow, wrought-iron, clicking turnstiles, manned by flat-capped retirees behind a wire mesh. They would smile and nod at me - "Just lift him over the barrier" – and over I would go, into the match for nothing! There was a concreted section at one corner of the ground known as the Boys' End. I would be directed there by Dad. Matches were played in conditions that would not be contemplated today; on heavy wintry days, the pitch was often like a First World War trench, and the author remembers a press report carrying a picture of Brian Clough scoring a goal in a snow storm! Your writer also remembers autograph-hunting at Ayresome Park during weekdays, and the signature of Brian Clough is one which he wishes he still had today!

Probably the most memorable match at Ayresome Park during Willie Fernie's stay was the home match against local competitors Sunderland on 10 October, 1959. Historically a ship-building and glass-making port town, the city of Sunderland is now famous for its car-making industry – Nissan began production there is 1986. Even though the favourite chant of the Boro fans during such a contest is "We Hate Sunderland", the Boro's rivalry with Sunderland is probably more imagined than real; Sunderland's fierce football enemy is actually the much bigger city of Newcastle, about ten miles further inland. Likewise, the Boro's battles with Newcastle are taken much less seriously by the Tyneside club. The authors were present as Middlesbrough suffered a 2-0 defeat at St. James' Park, Newcastle's huge, hallowed stadium, in December, 2009. As they scoured the programmes, books and souvenirs in the fans' shop near the stadium before the encounter, they mentioned to the jovial shop manager how earnestly and seriously the Boro fans viewed their rivalry with the Geordie team. He roared with laughter. "Not at all", he yelled, "the real foe is Sunderland. That's when war breaks out!", and he was right.

Two days before the teams locked horns, the political parties did likewise; in a general election. Stockton-on-Tees, a satellite town of Middlesbrough across the dirty waters of the River Tees, can claim Harold MacMillan as a former member of parliament. Supermac was prime minister by the time of this election, and his Conservatives held control with a big majority. Margaret Thatcher was a new MP, and the day before the big match, she took her seat in the Commons.

This home match against Sunderland attracted more than 47,000 spectators, and was the last time the Boro's ground held more than a 45,000 crowd. The home team were presently playing attractive football, with Brian Clough scoring four times in the 6-2 thrashing of Plymouth Argyle, and Alan Peacock netting four in the 7-1 defeat of Derby County on their own pitch. It has to be said that during these years of goals aplenty, Boro' nevertheless failed to win trophies. The defence usually leaked more goals than were scored! It was well-known that Brian Clough, particularly, bemoaned this unfortunate lack of balance in the side. (A prime example was the home defeat at the hands of Cardiff City in the League Cup not long after Willie returned to Celtic. Clough and Peacock bagged the Boro's three goals, but they lost 4-3!) Nonetheless, as the size of the crowd attested, this match against Sunderland was the talk of the town, as Clough and left-winger Eddie Holliday had just been called for England international duty. Loud and throaty cheers greeted both teams as they ran out of the tunnel. It was a warm and sunny autumn day. Willie did what he did best, organising the Boro's attacks from the middle of the park with style and authority, and the home team took the lead in the 19th minute. Eddie Holliday slipped in from the left wing to score with a pass from right-winger Billy Day that was intended for Clough but fell behind him. They all count! On a wave of vocal support from the crowd, Boro' pressed on, forcing the pace, but Sunderland counter-attacked in the 59th minute, scoring an equaliser through Amby Fogarty past the Boro' keeper, Peter Taylor, the very same who would achieve management success much later in partnership with Clough himself. The home team continued to control the game, but had to settle for a draw.

After the fireworks of the Sunderland clash, thirty league games remained of the 1959-60 season. Fernie was an ever-present, but for two games near the end, and his command of the support role in Boro's attack contributed to thirteen victories, six draws, and a fifth place in the league - pleasing improvement over the threat of relegation before he arrived. If an impartial observer needed proof of Fernie's successful stay at Middlesbrough, the statistics provide it.

Willie's wife Audrey was the driving force behind the family's welfare and future, and circumstances coalesced ominously at the start of the 1960-61 season. Willie was in his usual number 8 shirt for the first three games, against Bristol Rovers, winning 3-2, Derby County, falling 2-1, and Liverpool, ending at the 1-1 level, but he then found himself in the reserves, possibly after a minor injury, and was later quoted in the press with the sentiments – "we have been well treated by Middlesbrough, but my wife and I would like to settle back home". Ears immediately pricked, and Celtic, Rangers (!), Kilmarnock, Hibernian and St. Mirren were said to be interested though none confirmed so.

At about 5.30 in an early October evening, Boro' manager Bob Dennison drove over to Willie's house in Heythrop Drive and told him that Jimmy McGrory, his opposite number at Celtic, had called him. "Would you like to go back to Celtic?", Bob asked. Willie and Audrey didn't take long to decide. The two men promptly forged north, arriving at an Edinburgh hotel to meet Jimmy. Willie agreed terms and signed papers by midnight, arriving back with Bob at 4.30 the next morning. The transfer fee was said to be £12,000. A local press reporter later called on Willie, hopefully at a respectable time giving Willie chances for a good sleep! He found Fernie packing a case for the train journey to Glasgow from Middlesbrough railway station that very day - Celtic's intention on this new start was to play him against St. Mirren on the morrow afternoon. Here's where another one of those spine-chilling coincidences occurs – Willie's debut for Celtic during his previous incarnation ten years previously was against...St. Mirren!

CHAPTER SIX

THE RETURN (1960-1961)

The Celtic that Fernie returned to in October 1960 were in some ways a shambles. Talent was there, no-one could dispute that, and the support were enthused by all this, but there was a distinct lack of what is now called "game management skills". In short no-one seemed to know how to translate good football talent on the field to actually winning matches.

For example, the team had started with a bang in their all-Glasgow Scottish League Cup section in 1960. They had also defeated Rangers in the Glasgow Cup, and after four games of the six in the League Cup, they had lost only one point and it was difficult to see them not qualifying. Disturbingly the word "arrived" was used a lot in the context that the "Kelly Kids have arrived" and were now going to dominate Scottish football. They then managed to lose to Partick Thistle and then fatally to Rangers in the rain in the final game of the section at Celtic Park.

Failure then breeds more failure and in September they went down 1-5 to Rangers in an appalling performance in the League, and lost the Glasgow Cup final to Partick Thistle on the Holiday Monday. It was the Saturday after, that there occurred the single most bizarre episode of the whole Kelly years involving a youngster called Willie Goldie, a promising reserve goalkeeper. The reserves had no game, and Willie was going to Broomfield, Airdrie to see the first team and there he was, Celtic scarf tied round his neck standing waiting for the service bus to Airdrie.

The Celtic team bus then came along, and Mr Kelly recognised him, ordered the bus to stop and gave Willie a lift. It would save him his bus fare! So far so good, but when they got to Airdrie, to the consternation of John Fallon the goalkeeper, Willie Goldie was suddenly told he was playing! It was barely believable, but absolutely true. Not surprisingly, the move was not a success, the team lost 0-2, and the shattered and overwhelmed Goldie never played again!

That was on 1 October 1960, and that was the club that Willie Fernie returned to. He was signed on Friday 7 October after a "dramatic midnight dash" (according to *The Evening Times*) by Jimmy McGrory to sign him, after much talk about Celtic being interested in Tommy Bryceland of St Mirren, and the move was greeted with much enthusiasm by the support.

Fernie had been sending out the signals for some time that he would not be averse to a return to Scotland. Words like "homesick" were bandied about in the Press. This seems hard to believe, for his family were settled among the warm folk of North Yorkshire, and indeed he was something of a cult hero among the Boro supporters. But on the other hand, the call of Scotland was a strong one, particularly to his wife Audrey who wanted back, as indeed was the attraction of a return to the club he loved and which he had served with such distinction.

Some of the support – indeed most, if not everyone - felt that he should never have been allowed to go in the first place. Some felt that he would come back from England a better player with more experience under his belt, and the general feeling was that now almost 32, Fernie was just the man needed as an "auld heid" to calm down some of the youngsters and to bring out the best in them as a sort of father figure to the talented but callow Hughes, Carroll, Divers, Auld and Gallagher.

Celtic Park on 8 October 1960 was therefore the place to be for all Celtic supporters to see the return of the hero. The opposition were, ironically enough in view of later events, St Mirren. (By an odd coincidence, St Mirren had also been the opponents in his debut a decade earlier in 1950). Veteran supporters recalled the return of Tommy McInally in 1925, (the man who had "pined for home" and he was only a couple of miles away at Third Lanark!) and great were the expectations of Willie Fernie. They were not disappointed. 32,000 turned up and there was a strange field invasion before the game even started as thousands of youngsters charged on to the field to pat him on the back and ask for his autograph!

Fernie immediately delighted his fans by going on a mazy run, and within 5 minutes Celtic scored, through Bertie Auld, their first goal in a month. It was 3-0 at half time, and 4-2 at full time, Right half Crerand (a very impressive young man) had picked up an injury, but now that Willie Fernie was back home again, that was no problem, and Willie simply moved from inside right to right half.

It was a long time since the fans had left Celtic Park so happy, and there followed three good wins including a particularly impressive 6-0 over Hibs at Easter Road. November brought a return to the old inconsistent ways, including a defeat from this year's bogey team Partick Thistle, and Fernie had a few injury problems with his hip in particular. New Year was reached with the team nowhere in sight in the League race, but with the expectation, however, that the old Celtic Scottish Cup magic might yet return in the New Year.

In view of what was to happen in the future, the game at East End Park, Dunfermline on 19 November was not without its significance. Fernie would have been glad to meet again with his old colleague Jock Stein, now Manager of Dunfermline and clearly making a difference to the impoverished Fife side. The game, played in a heavy mist which affected other games that day, notably Rangers' game at Motherwell, was an entertaining 2-2 draw. Two players had a good game that day. One was the Pars goalkeeper Eddie Connachan, and the other was Willie Fernie. Stein would have noticed that his old friend and team mate still had his dribbling and ball-playing ability. He would have learned from that. Celtic, however, did not learn lessons about Dunfermline's young goalkeeper, who told them all afterwards that he was a Celtic supporter.

The New Year fixture at Ibrox on 2 January 1961 was a 1-2 defeat but a very unlucky one as Fernie was deprived of a good headed goal wrongly disallowed for offside by referee Wharton after Fernie had clearly run past Caldow to head home a Divers lob. Then a goalkeeping error by the likeable but ill-starred Frank Haffey gave Rangers a scarcely deserved victory. A few days later, the Celtic death wish against Glasgow teams continued with a defeat by Third Lanark and with Fernie injured again, prospects for the Scottish Cup beginning at the end of January did not look bright. But the team rallied again, went to Pittodrie and beat Aberdeen who were having one of their best seasons for a spell, and they were boosted by the news that Fernie would be back for their Scottish Cup tie at that most difficult of grounds, Brockville in Falkirk on 28 January 1961.

Falkirk, Scottish Cup winners in 1957, were now in the Second Division but that did not in any way lessen the enthusiasm for this game, and of course it would not be a Falkirk v Celtic game at Brockville if there were not some crowd misbehaviour. 21,000 were packed into the ground, and they saw a thrilling Cup tie, which Celtic won 3-1 with two goals from Bertie Peacock (one a penalty) and one from Bertie Auld, but it all started from Willie Fernie.

Fernie was not playing in the next round of the Scottish Cup when they beat an overawed Montrose 6-0 before 26,000 at Parkhead, but a far more difficult game was expected in the next round when they were drawn at the more challenging venue of Stark's Park, Kirkcaldy to play Raith Rovers. Fernie was back in the team to play his fellow Fifers before a packed crowd of 19,359, but this was a Raith Rovers team which had passed their best and were now beginning to struggle after a great few years in the 1950s.

The game was remarkable for one of Fernie's really great goals. It was in the 25th minute that "the wizard of trouble", as the local Press bizarrely described him, held off a challenge from Easson, ambled forward a couple of strides and hammered home from about 25 yards and "it was a goal all the way". The other goals in the 4-1 victory were scored by John Hughes and Steve Chalmers and then veteran Raith defender Andy Leigh got in the way of a ball from Charlie Gallagher to Steve Chalmers and conceded an own goal.

Performances like this led to an increasing belief that this might be Celtic's year in the Scottish Cup. League performances had picked up about this time as well, and the team and support were given a great boost when Rangers were removed from the Scottish Cup by Motherwell. It was generally agreed that the return of Fernie was making a huge amount of difference to the raw Celtic youngsters with Charlie Gallagher, Fernie's right wing partner in particular benefitting greatly from the promptings of the old maestro. Charlie himself in his later years was very conscious of this and very grateful to Willie for "taking him under his wing" as Charlie put it.

After Clyde and Ayr United were put to the sword in the League, a huge crowd of 56,000 appeared at Celtic Park on March 11 to see Hibs try their luck in the quarter final. There was a spring in the step of the supporters that had not been seen for a long time with loads of songs about the 7-1 victory of 1957, of which there were now only two survivors in Willie Fernie and the now ageing but still game Bertie Peacock. The very impressive young Billy McNeill at centre half was also clearly benefitting from the presence of Fernie, and already he was being touted for a place in the Scotland team against England at Wembley in April.

Hibs were an odd side. The Famous Five had long gone, and they were struggling sometimes. They had been in the final of the Scottish Cup in 1958 but had lost to Clyde, and were clearly suffering from the success of Hearts at this time (It is an odd phenomenon in football that when one team's rivals do well, the other team seems to go into a sulk as it were and does badly!) But Hibs had a brilliant forward and goal scorer in Joe Baker. They also had ex-Rangers favourite Sammy Baird who still had a little football left in him. Around the same time as Fernie had returned from Middlesbrough, Hibs had signed a goalkeeper from Newcastle United called Ronnie Simpson, and this man, clearly released prematurely by the Geordies, was having a great game for Hibs today.

Celtic, spurred on by the huge crowd, had been the better team in the first half but it had been Hibs who scored early in the second half through Kinloch, after some fine work from Baker. This was now a severe test of Celtic. Fernie tried hard but the Hibs defence held firm, and it began to look as if Celtic's hopes for the Scottish Cup were going to be shattered. But then well within the last ten minutes of the game, after a severe battering of that Railway End goal, Peacock slipped the ball to McNeill who launched a long one to find Alec Byrne. Byrne then flicked the ball on to the fast running Steve Chalmers who finished the job to a huge roar of relief and acclamation. Such were the scenes of joy and celebration that the BBC film cameras doing their recording of the game for the evening's programme, actually turned their antiquated cameras to show the happiness of the fans. The important thing was that Celtic were still in the Scottish Cup, even though they now had to go to Easter Road for the replay.

Serious overcrowding was a problem at Easter Road on Wednesday night with well over 40,000 inside the ground at kick off time and many more arriving later because of traffic jams, as more and more fans now went to games in motor cars – such was what was called in 1961 the "affluent society". Celtic had a late call off when captain Bertie Peacock went down with a knee injury, (a significant injury as it would turn out in the context of Peacock's career and indeed the destination of the 1961 Scottish Cup) and his place was given to young John Clark, a man who had played only a handful of games for the club but tonight very definitely earned his spurs. The standard of football was not necessarily all that high, but the pace was relentless, something that told on veterans like Willie Fernie and Sammy Baird.

The game was goalless after 90 minutes, but in the extra time period the youth of so many of the Celtic players became an advantage. But they still needed the "auld heid", the manipulator, the general in the shape of Willie Fernie, and eventually they wore Hibs down. The goal came late in the first half of extra time when Alec Byrne took a short corner and the ball came to Clark who scored his first goal for the club (he was not destined to score very many more!) to put Celtic into the semi-finals. Fernie was of course delighted and was even more convinced than ever before that he had made the right decision to return to Celtic. The supporters, for some time, had had no doubt on that score

Celtic were due to play Airdrie in the semi-final on April Fool's Day at Hampden while Dunfermline took on St Mirren in the other semi at Tynecastle. It was difficult not to be swept along by the tide of optimism and confidence that was emanating from Parkhead with photographs appearing regularly in newspapers, and great stress laid on how well youngsters like Gallagher, Byrne, Hughes and Chalmers were doing in the forward line now that Willie Fernie was there, and what a mighty half back line Crerand, McNeil and Clark were going to be. Clark indeed had been drafted in to replace Peacock before the Hibs replay, and now that Peacock was fit again, he was actually keeping him out, playing so well that he could not be dropped. This may well have been a mistake, as we shall discover, but the atmosphere was all euphoric in that spring of 1961. The grim years seemed to be ending, and the word "arrived" began to appear once again to describe the Celtic youngsters.

The Scottish Cup did appear to be Celtic's for the taking. Rangers had gone out to Motherwell who themselves had been beaten by Airdrie. Hibs were now out, as indeed were Hearts, Aberdeen and Dundee, the big city teams. Of the teams left in, the big danger would appear to be St Mirren, always a tricky Cup team and one who had beaten Celtic 4-0 in that shocking Scottish Cup semi-final of 1959. Their opponents Dunfermline came to Celtic the week before the semi-final and had actually scored first before Celtic hit back and won 2-1 in the second half. The Pars were still however, it was believed, a team playing above themselves, even though ex-Celt Jock Stein, given a good reception that day at Parkhead because he was still much loved for his great deeds in 1953 and 1954, had done well for them. Before the start, those who arrived early to this game saw Fernie and Stein enjoying a long conversation on the field.

But it was Airdrie who were the immediate concern. They usually gave Celtic a good game at Broomfield, that strange little ground with a pavilion in the corner that looked as if it should be at a cricket ground rather than a football ground, but Celtic usually got the better of them in Glasgow. They had a great goalkeeper in Scotland International Lawrie Leslie, and at centre forward had an interesting player in ex-Celt Jim Sharkey who might have had a great career at Parkhead, but was never really given the opportunity, in particular when he was passed over in that awful Cup final of 1956 which Fernie remembered well. Airdrie were not a bad side, but the smart money was on Celtic.

And rightly so. 72,612 were there in upbeat mood at Hampden for the semi-final to see a remarkable first half of vintage attacking Celtic football. Celtic went in at half-time 4-0 to the good with two goals from Hughes, one from Chalmers and a brilliant one from Fernie himself from almost the by-line just before half time. The crowd rose to applaud the brilliant passing of Crerand and Gallagher, the running and intelligent footwork of Alec Byrne and above all the sheer craft and guile of Willie Fernie who orchestrated it all.

Young spectators compared him to Stanley Matthews and Ferenc Puskas, while the old timers were even more lavish in their praise by likening him to Patsy Gallacher and Jimmy McMenemy. One wonders what McMenemy himself, still alive, 80 years of age, in good health and a regular attender at Celtic games, thought of Willie Fernie that day. One rather thinks that Napoleon was impressed.

Airdrie, funnily enough, had not played badly that day. Indeed, Jim Sharkey had brought out several great saves from Frank Haffey, one in particular, but they had no real answer to Celtic. The 4-0 half-time score stayed the same all the second half to the disappointment of some of the crowd, who expected a real goal feast. But Celtic remained on top, as they reached their 28th Scottish Cup final.

And now that most dangerous of emotions took over – optimism. Optimism in itself is not necessarily a bad thing, but it can lead to complacency. Fernie, now by some distance the oldest and most experienced man in the team – and the only man who had played in a Cup final – was probably able to realise that things were far from a foregone conclusion. The news that Dunfermline had beaten St Mirren in their replay (narrowly and possibly even luckily) was looked upon as another good sign, for this would be Dunfermline's first ever Scottish Cup final. But Willie was very aware that his old friend Jock Stein would have something up his sleeve for this game. Nevertheless it was difficult not to look back on Celtic's demolition of Airdrie in the semi-final and take heart from that.

The weekend after the Airdrie semi-final, they were in the city of Dundee to play at Dens Park on the Saturday, and then on the Monday at the new Tannadice Park that was being developed and the stand was not yet ready, compelling the Celtic team to arrive in their bus already stripped for action! They had stayed at Arbroath over the weekend. They did not play particularly well in either game 1-0 v Dundee and 1-1 v United, but the support were there in great numbers, cheering the half time score at Pittodrie where

Rangers were losing, and singing the old songs from the 7-1 game (including the famous adaptation of Lonnie Donegan's "Putting On The Style") and talking as if the Scottish Cup were already won.

But then an event occurred which (we never know) may have affected Celtic more than it seemed at the time. Scotland with two Celtic men on board, Billy McNeill and Frank Haffey, went down to Wembley and lost to England in the infamous 9-3 game. The Celtic men were not exclusively to blame, for the full backs were Shearer and Caldow of Rangers, but beneath all the jeers of the Rangers supporters and their moronic chants of "Haffey! Haffey" as they appeared to rejoice in the discomfiture of the Celtic goalkeeper and the defeat of Scotland, there was a certain amount of hurt among the players. McNeill was young enough and able to get over it, but there were times when one wondered about Frank Haffey who, by allowing himself to be photographed under a station platform sign which said 9, appeared to be rather enjoying the publicity.

And after the jokes about the orange ball – the Celtic players were afraid of it and the Rangers ones didn't want to hurt it – died down, these two Celtic players had now to buckle down and work for the Scottish Cup final the following week. How this affected the other young Celtic players we don't know, but Fernie certainly took it as an example of how unfortunate things can happen on a football field, and one mustn't take things for granted. But euphoria was still in the air and difficult to dispel.

In the run-up to the final, the world may well have flirted with nuclear war as the Americans invaded Cuba. "Invaded" was an exaggeration and "botched" didn't quite cover it, and within a few days the Americans were on their way home again, their tails between their legs and deservedly earning the contempt of the Soviet Union and even their western allies, not least Great Britain who perhaps now felt that their own Suez fiasco of 1956 was not quite so bad after all!

But for Celtic fans, it was all about the left half spot – the young and so far blameless John Clark or veteran captain Bertie Peacock. It was not an easy decision, for Clark had not done anything to deserve to be dropped, but Peacock already had two Scottish Cup medals and two Scottish League Cup medals and knew how to win games at Hampden. In addition, he possibly knew a little about Jock Stein's mind and one suspects that Fernie would have preferred Peacock, just for his experience. Stein from his viewpoint in the other dressing room certainly preferred Clark, one feels. Anyhow, Clark it was, and Fernie was also delighted for the earnest youngster who clearly knew a great deal about the game.

For the Pars, Tommy McDonald took ill with appendicitis and was out of the side but Celtic had not a single injury (there had been minor scares about Billy McNeill and Alec Byrne) and 113,328 were there to see a final which is described as being full of good football, but without any goals. Each side had a few chances but there were no real sitters missed, and each goalkeeper Eddie Connachan and Frank Haffey (the latter not showing any apparent signs of lack of confidence after last week's experience) coped with what came their way. Dunfermline's centre half Jackie Williamson was off injured for a spell, and some felt that Celtic might have made more of that opportunity, but near the end it was the Pars who almost snatched it when Frank Haffey saved from George Peebles.

But 0-0 it was. Conventional wisdom was that, although Dunfermline had shown that they were not overawed by the big occasion, Celtic should now do it. If anything, it had been some of the young Celtic players who had shown a little more nerves than the Pars, but it all remained to be settled on the night of Wednesday April 26 with a 6.15 pm kick-off, Hampden still not yet having floodlights. But in the meantime, fate played a hand and Celtic made a decision which was maybe not the best, and once again one would have liked to have known what Willie Fernie's feelings about this one were.

John Clark, as we have said, had been preferred to Bertie Peacock on Saturday. Clark had not let anyone down on Saturday and was rightly retained for Wednesday night. Bertie Peacock had been allowed to go to Bologna in Italy to play for Northern Ireland in a friendly. This had been agreed before the first Cup final was drawn, and Celtic, crucially, did not change their mind on Saturday evening after the 0-0 draw. Peacock was allowed to go to Italy.

The folly of this decision became apparent on the Tuesday when Jim Kennedy the left back was taken ill with appendicitis and operated on that night. It was an odd coincidence that it was the same problem with Tommy McDonald of Dunfermline on the Saturday, but the question was now posed to Celtic "Should Peacock be recalled?" This would have allowed Clark perhaps to move back to left back and Peacock to come in at left half. It was a possibility. The logistics of getting Peacock back to Hampden were difficult but not impossible if a telegram had been sent immediately. He might even have played at Bologna and got a night flight back to London and then to Glasgow. The problems could have been overcome, but Celtic decided instead to give a game to 20-year-old Willie O'Neill who would be thus making his debut! Celtic's left back and left half were therefore both rookies thrown into a Cup final!

In fairness to everyone, it was not an easy decision to make, and it must also be said that O'Neill did not let anyone down, but it is usually experience that wins trophies, and one cannot help taking the view that Stein was very happy NOT to see his old friend Bertie Peacock there, and Willie Fernie would have preferred to see him in the team. No-one could have predicted the illness of Jim Kennedy, but it might have been better in any case if Peacock had been withdrawn from the Irish squad on Saturday night, once it became apparent that a replay was necessary. It was only a friendly, and Danny Blanchflower and Jimmy McIlroy had already been withdrawn because of club commitments. As it was, Peacock played in Bologna and starred in a losing cause as Northern Ireland went down 2-3 to Italy.

Which brings us to the tragic and cruel events of 26 April 1961 which even 60 and more years later bring more than a pang of pain to the Celtic chronicler. In a funny sort of a way, the seeds of future Celtic greatness were planted there that night – it was the night that Jock Stein emerged as a first rate Manager – but at the time, there was little more than excruciating agony for our supporters. Celtic should have won, and anyone who has ever followed any team at any level will agree that the worst sort of a defeat to endure is one in which the team has 80% and more of the pressure, but simply can not score. This is exactly what happened here when a hellish cocktail of brilliant goalkeeping, inept finishing, lack of game management skills and yes, sheer bad luck denied the club and their supporters the trophy which they had craved for so long. And oh, more than 60 years down the line, how much it grieves to recall this game!

87,866 turned up on the dull, murky night – the weather mirroring the events on the field – when referee Hugh Phillips of Wishaw blew his whistle at 6.15 pm. The teams were;

Celtic: *Haffey, MacKay and O'Neill; Crerand, McNeill and Clark; Gallagher, Fernie, Hughes, Chalmers and Byrne*

Dunfermline: *Connachan, Fraser and Cunningham; Mailer, Miller and Sweeney; Peebles, Smith, Thomson, Dickson and Melrose*

Fernie saw his role as encouraging the youngsters. A special word for young O'Neill, encouragement for the half back line of Crerand, McNeill and Clark which seemed to have such a great potential and future ahead of them and then the necessity of geeing up the young forwards who were visibly shaking before the start. He himself was confident enough, but it was a confidence tempered by the thought that Dunfermline had proved themselves on Saturday, that they certainly would not "freeze" on the night (Jock Stein would see to that), and that in young Connachan between the goalposts, they had a goalkeeper who looked as if he might have an International future ahead him. This immediately brought his thoughts back to Frank Haffey. He would clearly never play for Scotland again, and needed someone to cheer him up.

And why did Fernie feel that he had to do this? He knew that in the other dressing room, Jock Stein would be going around patting everyone on the back, saying things like "This might just be your night" and "let them see what you can do" even adding things like "Is your wife here tonight?" "I think I saw your father in the stand. He's looking well after his operation!" And even when some player said "My father is a Celtic supporter", Jock looked at him with a twinkle in his eye and said "Well, of course, so am I!" and everyone had a laugh and relaxed.

Other than Fernie, Celtic had no-one who could do that. It was not McGrory's style. Much respected and much loved, as he would be for the rest of his life, McGrory was no Manager. Fernie realised that, but could not of course publicly acknowledge it. The success of the mid-1950s had all been achieved by men like himself, Bertie Peacock who should have been playing tonight and of course, Jock Stein, who was now in the other dressing room! Captain Dunky MacKay was able to do a little of the "geeing up" as well, but he was a man who was himself under a great deal of pressure to produce the goods. And Mr Kelly? He was upstairs with the official party! He was Chairman of the SFA and his wife was going to present the Cup at the end.

This did not mean that Celtic could not do it tonight. Indeed they were clear favourites, and started off playing towards the King's Park goal. Fernie quickly realised that Pat Crerand behind him, clearly a man of undeniable class, was on song, but that the men in the forward line were struggling, choosing the wrong pass option, dithering rather than shooting, and then shooting from a difficult angle. Connachan had already had a few good saves, and a great deal of routine ones before the half time interval. Dunfermline had played as they did on Saturday, competently and compactly, not giving anything away, recognisably playing for each other but not as yet seriously threatening the Celtic defence for whom young Willie O'Neill was showing up well.

Half time was spent in serious thought. The Scottish Cup was just so close, and surely one of these shots just had to go in some time. The BBC radio broadcast on the Home Service (and the World Service) which started at 7.00 pm brought thousands more Celtic fans (including one of your writers) to the game, as it were, and thus the agony was shared throughout the world.

John Hughes started off the wrong way by getting himself booked (the 1960s equivalent of the yellow card) for a silly foul on Fraser in the very first minute of the second half, and the pressure intensified. Crerand was superb throughout, and Fernie was equally productive, spraying passes to his other forwards. But there was a lack of co-ordination with the wingers far too inclined to cut inside and lose the ball rather than making space on the outside and crossing. Chalmers tended to be bundled off the ball too easily and Hughes had the infuriating habit of bustling through the defence and blasting the ball straight at Connachan when a moment's thought might have persuaded him to place the ball out of his reach.

But there was bad luck as well. Celtic might have had a penalty for hand ball in the box, but to their credit did not make a lot of it, and there were times in the many goalmouth scrambles that a Dunfermline foot got there first. Fernie was still obvious, clapping his hands and urging everyone on, but increasingly frustration was beginning to take over.

And then in the 67th (yes, the 67th!) minute things took a decisive swing away from Celtic. Celtic simply had too many men up the field when Dunfermline broke away and a cross found Dave Thomson who earned his one and only moment of glory with a low diving header.

Things are often like that, Fernie reckoned, but even he must have been just a little downhearted as time now began to slip away.

The assault redoubled, but Connachan with a mixture of skill and luck kept them out. One shot from Crerand at the edge of the box was singled out by *The Glasgow Herald* as an example of "glorious goalkeeping" but the same writer Cyril Horne also talks about "forward deficiencies". The minutes now raced away as Celtic pursued extra time, but then almost at the death, Frank Haffey misjudged an easy ball and allowed Charlie Dickson to score Dunfermline's second and decisive, killer goal.

The full time whistle brought scenes of desolation that were hard to parallel in Celtic's long history. To their credit, the Celtic players showed total sportsmanship with Fernie visibly seeking out his old friend Jock Stein in his white raincoat to congratulate him, but the supporters were a great deal less praiseworthy with showers of bottles raining down from the terracings and imperilling the lives and persons of other Celtic supporters as well as the triumphant Pars. Some did shake hands with the still incredulous (and definitely not gloating) Dunfermline supporters, but more left for home in the gathering gloom, devastated and betrayed, to face the horrors of the jeers of Rangers fans at their work the following day and worse still, the realisation that Celtic still did not have a team. "Fancy big Jock daein that tae us!" "Aye, he should have been oor Boss!"

As Mrs Kelly, the wife of SFA and Celtic Chairman Bob Kelly, put a brave face on it and presented the Scottish Cup to the Dunfermline captain, and Fernie and the others trudged disconsolately to the dressing room, with curses and angry silences, there was little that anyone could say. This 12-year-old boy who went to bed early that night and cried himself to sleep with an apparently everlasting hatred of Dunfermline, Eddie Connachan, Jock Stein (and how I hated that white coat!) and even anything to do with Dunfermline like Andrew Carnegie or Malcolm Canmore, was not the only one who despaired of Celtic that night, almost as if there was a prescience that more horrors still lay in store before the corner could be turned.

And yet, it is interesting to speculate what might have happened if that result had gone the other way. Jock Stein might have stayed the Manager of provincial Dunfermline before moving on to some team like Motherwell or Bristol City; Eddie Connachan might have played professional football for a year or two before finding a job elsewhere; Pat Crerand might have stayed with Celtic rather than depart to Manchester United in 1963; Celtic might have competed for honours in Scotland and indeed won a few; and Willie Fernie would have stayed on, eventually becoming a Coach and then maybe even Manager when Jimmy McGrory took his honourable retirement.

As it happened, Fernie did not have much longer to go as a player at Celtic Park. The season still had a few games left, and Willie even won another medal (of sorts) when he played in the final of the now moribund Glasgow Charity Cup on 9 May. Their opponents were relegated Clyde, and the low key game finished 1-1 before 12,000 spectators, and when extra time failed to provide a winner, the teams were declared joint winners.

And so ended the awful 1960/61 season. But hope springs eternal and Celtic supporters, as always, able to delude themselves that things were getting better were back at the start of the next season to see the League Cup section involving Hibs, Partick Thistle and St Johnstone. It is not often that Celtic have a complex about St Johnstone, but the Perth men beat Celtic home and away 1-0 and 2-0. Fernie did not play in the first two games – a win at Partick Thistle and the home defeat by St Johnstone where the forward line of Carroll, Jackson, Hughes, Divers and Chalmers was described by Gair Henderson of *The Evening Times* as "too bad to be true" – but he was restored for the next game, a 2-2 draw at Easter Road where there was at least some improvement in the sweltering heat. This was the day that St Mirren's Tommy Bryceland broke his leg, something that would be significant for Fernie.

Fernie was now retained in the side, but the team without Pat Crerand, suspended for several offences including one, incredibly, at a Five-A-Side tournament at Falkirk (!), struggled, and Fernie played in the notorious game at Muirton Park, Perth on Wednesday 30 August 1961. It was notorious for two reasons. One was the poor performance of the team "Fernie tried desperately to make the forward line more effective, but the openings were thrown away", but even worse was the hooliganism at the ground, on the way to the station, at the station itself and on the trains back to Glasgow. It was shocking and made much of in the Press, and although Celtic were by no means the only team with thuggish supporters, they were by far the worst, and one wonders whether Fernie may have wondered if it was all worth it.

That night was indeed bad, and one recalls the panes of glass broken at the railway station, the pathetic sight of a respectable St Johnstone supporting family of a decent man, an attractive wife and two terrified boys in tears sheltering in a shop doorway as yobs in green colours threw bottles, kicked cars and threatened to fight everyone including some of their own persuasion who were appealing to them to stop. A pleasant faced middle class, middle aged lady coming out of her Women's Guild meeting at her Church was abused, spat at and called an Orange MAN (!) It would have been funny, if it had not been so sad – and frightening!

Fernie was moved to the left wing after that game, and then Celtic beat Hibs and Third Lanark before having real hard luck in a League game at Ibrox on September 16 which ended up 2-2. Rangers scored first and last, Celtic were the better team and Fernie scored Celtic's second goal, but the real significance of this game was in two other respects. One was that at the end of the game, two fans were killed coming down the stairway – and incredibly lessons were not learned from this – and the other was that it was Willie Fernie's last game for Celtic.

Fernie was out ill for a spell after the Rangers game, and when he recovered, he found that he couldn't get back in, because the team had suddenly started to play well with a settled forward line of Chalmers, Jackson, Hughes, Divers and Carroll, and goals began to flow, not least when St Mirren came to Celtic Park on Wednesday 15 November and lost 7-1. It was possibly that night that Manager Willie Reid sounded out McGrory and made a polite enquiry about Willie Fernie, now back and fit and playing for the reserves.

There had been other enquiries as well from Falkirk and Airdrie, but a formal bid of £4,000 was made on Wednesday 22 November. Celtic agreed, and Fernie after taking some time to let it all sink in, agreed to join the Buddies on Friday 24 November. The attraction lay in the promise of first team football. There certainly seemed to be little point in hanging about the Celtic reserves at this stage of his career, when he could be playing for a first team. Fernie went straight into the St Mirren team the following day against St Johnstone at Muirton, scored and was instrumental in their 3-0 win. In the meanwhile, Celtic travelled to Pittodrie and drew 0-0. Not for the first time, Celtic had let Fernie go when he still had a lot of football left in him. And how they would suffer for that!

CHAPTER SEVEN

ST MIRREN AND THE END OF HIS CAREER (1961-1965)

The St Mirren team that Fernie joined in November 1961 had seen better days and were struggling near the bottom of the First Division table. They had won the Scottish Cup in 1959, but since then things were slowly going downhill, and the win that they achieved on Fernie's first day against St Johnstone at Muirton was much needed. Indeed, its value would prove to be vital by the end of the season. One could even argue, correctly, that the Buddies effectively saved themselves from relegation that day of 25 November.

St Mirren would have a bad December with defeats from Third Lanark, Hibs and Dunfermline, but they did manage to grab a point where it was least expected. This was when Dundee came to Love Street. Dundee were topping the table having defeated Celtic (luckily) and Rangers (comprehensively) in November, but there was still a fragility about them away from home, and the usual lack of belief in themselves that often affects provincial clubs who seem to feel that they are not entitled to be top of the League. On this day, 23 December on a pitch "dappled with frost" Dundee scored first, but Fernie earned an equaliser for the home side when, surrounded by three Dundee defenders, he swept the ball into the net, and the score stayed that way.

It was a different St Mirren team from even a month ago. Manager Willie Reid had fallen on his sword after the poor performances in early December and had been replaced by ex-Dundee man Bobby Flavell. Flavell had immediately brought in Tommy Henderson from Hearts, and this pre-Christmas result gave St Mirren a boost which was much needed, but they were still very definitely in the relegation pack. It was the Saturday where it was believed that Celtic were now in with a chance of the Scottish League because Rangers had lost to Aberdeen that day and Celtic themselves were on the crest of the wave with a 4-0 win at Raith Rovers following some other very positive results. It was thus a Merry Christmas in Celtic households and a qualified feeling of optimism in Paisley ones.

But any euphoria that St Mirren might have felt was immediately dispelled when they went to East End Park, Dunfermline on 30 December. The weather was awful, although the hard packed snow gave players a good footing, and Jock Stein's side simply went berserk as Charlie Dickson scored six goals in a 7-0 thrashing of a dreadful Saints' team. It was by no means the best way to end 1961 and Fernie must have wondered what he had let himself in for! And once again, albeit in vastly different circumstances from April, Stein had got the better of Fernie in that eventful year of 1961.

But 1962 turned out to be quite a different year for the Buddies, with some remarkable games. January was a mixed bag as far as the League was concerned with wins over Raith Rovers and Kilmarnock but defeats at the hands of Hearts and Rangers, thus preventing them from getting totally away from the relegation zone. The Hearts game was a 0-1 defeat at Love Street on a difficult pitch with Fernie totally out of sorts and even being booed by some of the sillier Saints supporters who did not appear to realise that a class football player like Fernie needs a good surface to play on. St Mirren however did raise a few eyebrows with a 2-1 win over Dundee at Dens Park in the Scottish Cup.

It will be recalled that Saints had earned a point against Dundee in December, and since then the Dens Parkers, while still winning, had shown signs of slipping and the commonly held belief was that sooner or later they would blow up and allow Rangers (or possibly even Celtic) to take over.

This in fact happened but Dundee recovered and would go on to win the League, as we shall see. The start of Dundee's temporary decline, however, could certainly be dated to their defeat in the Scottish Cup to St Mirren.

Dundee, clearly buoyed up by their recent successes, had a pipe band playing and the weather was good at Dens Park before a crowd of about 12,000 including quite a few from Paisley. Fernie was early on the ball, setting up a good chance for George McLean which he fluffed, then Fernie himself managed to scoop a ball over the bar when it looked easier to score. St Mirren eventually did score a deserved goal towards the end of the first half when McLean scored from a Henderson cross to send the Paisley men in 1-0 up at half time.

A Dundee offensive was now expected, but did not really materialise and Fernie was able to use all his experience to hold on to the ball, to run the clock down and to ensure that St Mirren made it through to the next round of the Scottish Cup to the delight of their small band of travelling supporters. The next round of the Scottish Cup put St Mirren to Stark's Park to play Raith Rovers, a team still in the First Division but like the Saints, in no way confident about where they would be playing their football next season.

The game had a remarkable beginning, and a difficult one for St Mirren. Bobby Adamson scored for Rovers, in so doing collided accidentally with goalkeeper Jimmy Brown so badly that Brown had to be carried off and looked out of the game altogether. Jim Clunie had to wear the goalkeeper's jersey for a spell before Brown, with his leg heavily bandaged, was able to return about 20 minutes later. By that time, the 10 men Saints were back on level terms, and it was a wonderful free kick taken by Fernie. Fernie often seemed to play his best on Fife grounds, and this was beautifully struck free kick from about 20 years which *The Evening Times* said was "so hard and low that it struck the back stanchion as Thorburn was still in mid-air". This account was actually confirmed by an eye witness over half a century later who told me that the sound of the ball hitting the stanchion resounded through the ground a split second before the goalkeeper hit the ground as the St Mirren supporters then went mad with joy.

St Mirren, now clearly the better team, might well have won the game there and then, but the triumph was only delayed until the Tuesday night replay at Love Street. The Saints won it at a canter 4-0 and Jimmy Dunbar of *The Evening Times* was eloquent in his praise of Fernie. "He was simply splendid. If he made a mistake, I did not see it. One minute he was making all the moves up front, the next he was back harrying and chasing in defence." Those who had been critical of him in that 0-1 defeat by Hearts in January were now eating humble pie. The reward for this win over a poor Raith side, was an interesting tie against another Fife team. Jock Stein's Dunfermline who had thrashed the Saints in the last game of 1961 would be coming to town. Willie v Jock yet again! And of course, Dunfermline had beaten St Mirren in last year's semi-final as well.

It is interesting how the paths of these two, Fernie and Stein, crossed since they had played together in that fine, if inconsistent, Celtic team of the 1950s. They had met in last year's Scottish Cup final in which Willie had definitely come off second best; this year it would be different. This quarter final game was played at Love Street on March 10 before a crowd of about 10,000 and unusually for clubs like Dunfermline and St Mirren, there were reports of crowd misbehaviour before the start with one or two less than totally mentally equipped youths being "frogmarched" out of the ground before the game even started. The Scottish educational system, often in the 1960s claimed to be the best in the world, still had its deficiencies, apparently!

The game itself was universally described as dull with Dunfermline, as always under Jock Stein, organised and methodical and clearly quite happy to take the game to East End Park for a replay. St Mirren on the other hand had Fernie and he could always be relied upon for a few mazy dribbles or telling passes, but the team in general lacked the penetration necessary to break down the Pars defence. In particular the talented George McLean exasperated the fans with his inconsistent play. He certainly could take a goal, but couldn't do it often enough, and today the Pars defence read him very easily.

Until, that is, a cross ball from Fernie found Henderson on the wing, and the winger made room, crossed and McLean was there to do the needful. That was about the 75th minute. It was now that Fernie came into his own. Now his ball winning and ball retention skills came to the fore as the frantic Dunfermline tried to get back in the game, but the full time whistle came with St Mirren the winners by 1-0.

The draw for the semi-final paired the Saints against Third Lanark or Celtic who had played out an astonishing 4-4 draw at Parkhead. The replay was held at Hampden (not Cathkin for safety reasons) and clearly St Mirren now had an opportunity to watch their semi-final opponents. The game turned out to be a 4-0 win for Celtic, but it was not as clear cut as it sounded. Fernie and the rest of the St Mirren team were at Hampden that night, but Fernie knew in any case all that anyone would need to know about the sometimes world-beating, brilliant Celtic, but sometimes the disorganised, shambolic, dysfunctional outfit that they could be. The simple word "inconsistent" did not seem to come anything close to covering Celtic in 1962.

Fernie knew them all. They were all still young, and that tended to mean unpredictability. It usually meant that if they were on top, they could stay on top, but once things started to go badly, they could continue to go badly. In particular the loss of one goal could very easily lead to the loss of another. And yet in the three Cup games they had played this year against Morton, Hearts and Third Lanark, things had gone badly for a spell... and yet they had fought back to triumph eventually. Their supporters, and of course, that included Willie himself who still followed their results obeying the old dictum "Once a Celt, always a Celt", did not know where they were with them. On a good day, they could beat anybody, but on a bad day...

And of course, their support was a major factor. Huge, cheerful, upbeat, naïve on occasions about their team's potential, and on other occasions depressed, bitter and disillusioned. They had certainly been through the mill for a long time, betrayed by incompetent leadership, nursing a huge inferiority complex about Rangers and also with a nasty element in them which could easily turn to hooliganism. But the main characteristic of Celtic supporters was the age-old one of their impatience and intolerance of young players who were, after all, just learning their trade. "Give them time" had been the cry a few years ago when the "Kelly Kids" first appeared... but they had now been given time, and needed to deliver trophies.

Willie understood all these dynamics, and he played a huge part in the quite amazing events of the last week of March 1962. The Manager of St Mirren, as we have seen, was Bobby Flavell, a good man...but the mastermind was undeniably Willie Fernie.

The facts are that on Monday 26 March at Love Street, Celtic beat St Mirren 5-0 in a League match, and that on Saturday 31 March at Ibrox, St Mirren beat Celtic 3-1 in the semi-final of the Scottish Cup. It has been naturally assumed by Celtic historians (and indeed their supporters at the time) that this is what is known as an "ambush", whereby a team deliberately loses a game in order to lull their victors into a false sense of security for a more important game in the future. (A similar thing was believed to have happened between the same two teams in February/March 2009 when Celtic beat St Mirren 7-0 on 28 February, then went down 0-1 in the Scottish Cup on 7 March).

A glance at the League table on the morning of Monday 26 March 1962 would indicate however that this fanciful theorising about an "ambush" was simply rubbish. St Mirren's position, just outside the relegation zone was just too precarious for them to play games like this. They had lost rather badly on the Saturday to fellow relegation candidates St Johnstone at home, and their fans had not been slow to indicate their displeasure. Rather like Celtic in 1962, they were infuriatingly inconsistent, capable of great things one day and appalling rubbish the next. But at that time, if St Mirren had been given the choice of winning the Scottish Cup or saving themselves from relegation, one feels that they would have chosen the latter.

Celtic on the other hand had beaten Aberdeen 2-0 on Saturday, and still had a remote, outside, mathematical chance of winning the League if Dundee and Rangers both hit bad patches. Rangers had lost to Dundee United on Saturday at Ibrox, and Celtic were buoyed up by that. They therefore travelled to Paisley on the Monday night in good spirits, and won 5-0 scoring four goals in the first half hour playing with speed, composure and confidence, while Fernie played one of his worst ever games against a nippy forward line including Divers, Carroll and Chalmers. He even suffered the indignity of not being mentioned at all in newspaper reports. He might have been jeered by some Celtic fans but he was still loved by most of them who contented themselves with statements like "Poor Willie." "I think he's finished" and "He would make a good coach, I believe". As Celtic had already beaten the Buddies 7-1 in November at Parkhead, there was little doubt who the smart money was on for the semi-final on Saturday.

As is often the case, it is what happens before the game, in the build-up, which influences matters. The other semi-final was between Rangers and Motherwell at Hampden, and Celtic and the supporters were even confident about that one as well. Rangers had lost to Dundee United and rumours were reaching the Glasgow press about some Rangers players wanting more money next season. The mischief making *Scottish Daily Express*, normally very supportive of Rangers for circulation reasons, carried a photograph of some of them walking to their training ground with their faces covered so that they wouldn't be recognised, for some obscure reason. Motherwell were a good and improving side with some fine players like Bert McCann and Willie Hunter and a surprise there was not impossible. But Gair Henderson in *The Evening Times* on the Friday night has no hesitation in plumping for an Old Firm Scottish Cup final.

But St Mirren and Fernie had not been idle. They received a major boost with the return of Tommy Bryceland from a broken leg sustained at the beginning of the season, and also George McLean who had not played on Monday was now back in the team. Flavell and Fernie discussed Celtic. There were weaknesses up front certainly and the weaknesses came more to the fore when things were going badly for the team. McNeill was certainly a majestic centre half and well worth his place in the Scotland team, but the defence generally could be suspect to a cross ball (the joke was often related that they weren't really very good Catholics because they couldn't face a cross), goalkeeper Haffey was appallingly unreliable (hardly Scotland's best kept secret after last year's Wembley experience) and also Fernie was able to say that there was a certain amount of internal division in the camp, if things did not go well, with one or two of the other players less than 100% behind the captaincy of Dunky MacKay.

Nevertheless, Fernie and St Mirren cannot really have been over-optimistic as they made the short journey to Ibrox that bright, but (crucially) rather windy day. The teams were;

Celtic: *Haffey, MacKay and Kennedy; Crerand, McNeill and Clark; Brogan, Chalmers, Hughes, Divers and Byrne*

St Mirren: *Williamson, Wilson and Campbell; McLean, Clunie and Stewart; Henderson, Bryceland, Kerrigan, Fernie and Beck*

Referee: *A McKenzie, Coatbridge*

St Mirren were immediately handed a free gift, and it was a bizarre one. Celtic captain Dunky MacKay won the toss and decided to play against the wind. Conventional wisdom was to play with the wind in the first half because, you never know, the wind might drop or even change in an hour's time, but it needn't have been a serious matter because you normally have to play against the wind at some point, and in any case, although the wind was significant, it was nothing like some of the gales one sometimes gets on a Scottish football field.

The problem for Celtic was that MacKay's decision was not popular with his team mates. Whether he had made that decision on a whim, or whether the matter had not even been discussed, we will never know, but Ibrox was now treated to the spectacle of some Celtic players shouting at their captain before the game even got started! In the meantime Fernie noticed this, said nothing but thought plenty and St Mirren kicked off playing with the wind with Celtic already in some disarray.

Within a couple of minutes, Haffey had allowed a ball to slip through his fingers and go for a corner kick and then Jim Kennedy had to clear off his line. Celtic fought back to a certain extent, but before ten minutes had elapsed the Saints were one up and it was Willie Fernie who scored, taking advantage of another Haffey error when, misjudging the wind, Frank failed to hold on to a Henderson cross and the lurking Fernie had the easiest of tap ins.

This need not have been fatal to Celtic, for the game was not yet 10 minutes old, but after some weak shooting by Hughes and Divers and some genuine hard luck from Crerand, the Saints scored again. This time Fernie found Beck who in turn released Kerrigan to score with a magnificent shot. Celtic were still rattled over that one, when St Mirren scored again this time through Beck, but again with a major Fernie involvement. 3-0 and Fernie was now rampant with *The Evening Times* calling him "Fernie the fabulous" and talking about his "waggle of the hips" which flummoxed the Celtic defenders. Half time came with the score a scarcely believable St Mirren 3 Celtic 0.

The Celtic team trooped off to a stunned, ominous silence. St Mirren for their part were jubilant with their small knots of supporters making plenty of noise, but Fernie and others were determined that they must keep their feet on the ground. They were now facing a desperate Celtic side who had the wind at their back. An early goal would make a huge difference. Fernie now knew that Celtic with the wind were bound to put up a better performance in the second half. But he also knew that it would be hysterical, ill-thought out pressure with a lack of any real quality ball into the box. All that St Mirren had to do was to play sensibly, keep the ball as much as possible and not make any mistakes Things were about to get even worse for Celtic.

Over at Hampden where Rangers were beating Motherwell 2-0 after an appalling tackle by Bobby Shearer had put Bert McCann out of the game, the half time score at Ibrox was greeted with incredulity as if someone at the BBC were having them on. George Davidson the BBC radio commentator had said at half time in the Hampden game that the half time score at Ibrox "for those of you who are interested (!) is Celtic 0 St Mirren 3". Cheers, but then bewildered silence. It couldn't be true.

But it was. Celtic huffed and puffed, one or two wild shots at goal, a distinct lack of knowledge of how to counteract St Mirren's offside trap, loads of effort but no great skill with one or two players looking as if they had lost heart. For Pat Crerand in particular, it was probably one disaster too many and he would be on his reluctant way within a year. It was the reaction of the fans, however, that was the sharpest blow to Celtic and their prestige.

A correctly given offside decision against a John Hughes goal seemed to be the catalyst for a pitch invasion which started at the Copland Road end and soon spread to the other end. What they intended to achieve, we can but guess – indeed rational thought did not really come into it - but the players were soon taken off the pitch. Celtic to their credit, immediately conceded the tie. It was really not good enough to talk about "a minority" when there were so many on the pitch, seeking a little fun out of a very dismal afternoon. No-one was hurt, and the pitch was eventually cleared after about a quarter of an hour. The play resumed, Alec Byrne scored an irrelevant goal for Celtic, but it was one of the saddest days in Celtic's history.

Fernie, still too much of a Celtic supporter, to be really happy about this day's events, nevertheless, reflected on four things. One was that he himself was in another Scottish Cup final on 21 April. It would be his fifth, and he was very much looking forward to it. Another factor was that one of the things that had upset him throughout his Celtic career had been hooliganism and bad behaviour – and here he had another example. And the third factor was that Celtic were going nowhere under the current regime, and that he had undeniably made the right decision by leaving Celtic to go to St Mirren. The fourth, and most immediate concern, was that the Buddies were not yet safe from relegation.

For Celtic fans, the desolation was total. Once again, they had been led up the garden path, this time it being all the more galling because, for the second year in a row, their downfall had been engineered by another ex-Celt. It had been Jock Stein in 1961 and now Willie Fernie in 1962, but the more astute of the supporters realised that in fact Celtic themselves had been the authors of their own destruction. Yet, a couple of weeks after the Scottish Cup exit, Scotland beat England 2-0 at Hampden – and the stars of the Scotland side were Pat Crerand and Billy McNeill! It was a crazy time for Celtic supporters.

But for Fernie, there was still an awful lot of football to be played this season. The Monday morning euphoria would have been tempered by a look at the League table which would have shown that St Mirren still had four League games to play, and that they were in no way clear of relegation. Stirling Albion looked doomed, but the Saints were still only three points clear of the second bottom team Falkirk, and the fear now was that the concentration on the Cup final might distract them from the bread and butter problem of saving themselves from relegation. Winning the Cup and being relegated in the same year may not necessarily have been unique in Scottish football at this time, but it was not something to be aspired to!

They had a game in hand over their competitors but that was used up on the Wednesday night in a 1-2 defeat against reasonable opposition in Hibs at Easter Road. St Mirren were given a generous round of applause by the Hibs crowd, ever jealous of Celtic, for their achievement on Saturday, and scored first on a heavy pitch in more or less incessant rain. But Brian Marjoribanks scored twice for Hibs down the slope in the second half and they won 2-1.

That game didn't necessarily set the alarm bells ringing but the next one did. This was on Saturday 7 April, and it was a 2-1 win for Third Lanark at Love Street. Fernie had a poor game, missed at least one reasonable chance and Third Lanark scored a late winner to plunge the 8,000 crowd into deep depression. It was not the St Mirren result in itself which caused the problem as much as the other scores which the dressing room radio told them. Raith Rovers, St Johnstone and Falkirk all won, and this meant that although Stirling Albion were now definitely relegated, Airdrie and Falkirk were on 22 points and St Johnstone, Raith Rovers and St Mirren were all on 23.

At this critical point, the League was now put on hold for 18 days as far as St Mirren were concerned, for there was the Scotland v England International at Hampden on April 14 and then the Scottish Cup final against Rangers on 21 April. League football would resume on Wednesday 25 April and St Mirren were at Dens Park against, of all people, title chasing Dundee! The season then finished with, of all teams, Dunfermline Athletic at Love Street. The paths of Jock Stein and Willie Fernie were destined yet again to cross!

Scotland duly beat England 2-0 in one of Scottish football's better days. Astonishingly 25 years had passed since Scotland had last beaten England at Hampden in 1937, but here in typical Hampden conditions of sun and wind, Davie Wilson and Eric Caldow with a penalty kick sunk the Englishmen. These two players would of course be back at Hampden next week to play for Rangers against St Mirren.

Rangers had won the Scottish Cup 15 times, still two behind Celtic, as against St Mirren's two triumphs in 1926 and 1959. The odds really had to favour Rangers, and Willie Fernie, who had clearly revelled in destroying Celtic in the semi-final would have loved to do the same against his old rivals Rangers. He was the man that the St Mirren supporters looked to, but although it was one thing to destroy the talented but disorganised and dysfunctional Celtic of 1962, Rangers with their power, ruthlessness and grim Presbyterian determination and professionalism were a different matter altogether. Newspapers in the build-up, however, did say that in Fernie, St Mirren had the best player on the field (although Baxter and McMillan were close rivals) and a flash or two of genius might make all the difference. "Despite the passing of the years, Fernie is still something of a genius in making openings for the other forwards".

The morning newspapers were sympathetic to the Saints and in particular *The Scottish Daily Express*, normally rabidly pro-Rangers, had done their best for them by stirring up yet again the story about a pay dispute at Ibrox over next season's terms and conditions, and it was even suggested that some of the Rangers players might use this game as an opportunity to make a point to their rich, sleazy Directors, thus giving Saints a chance. On the other hand, playing at their best might make the same point and far more effectively! It was a dull, grey, windless but mild day as 127,970 made their way to Hampden to see the following teams take the field;

St Mirren: ***Williamson, Campbell and Wilson; Stewart, Clunie*** *and McLean; Henderson, Bryceland, Kerrigan, Fernie and Beck*

Rangers: *Ritchie, Shearer and Caldow; Davis, McKinnon and Baxter; Henderson, McMillan, Millar, Brand and Wilson*

Referee: *Mr Wharton, Clarkson*

The game was depressingly predictable. It would not be true to say that St Mirren "froze" on the day, as often happens with provincial teams in Scottish Cup finals against Glasgow teams, for they did try hard and had a few moments when they might have scored. Fernie had a few good moments and the booing of him by the Rangers supporters showed that they rated him as a potential menace and that they had not forgotten the 7-1, but it was also true that Rangers were the better team throughout, scoring through Brand late in the first half and through Wilson on the hour mark, and finished the game as comfortable winners.

It is always a great honour to take part in a Scottish Cup final, but it was not one of the highlights of St Mirren's history or of Willie Fernie's life. He now was the possessor of four Scottish Cup final loser's medals in 1955, 1956, 1961 and 1962, each one of them painful experiences as Scottish Cup final defeats always are. Things did not improve for the Buddies when they heard the other results in the League that day. Falkirk had excelled themselves by beating Hearts at Tynecastle, and Raith Rovers had won 1-0 at a desolate and angry Parkhead over a Celtic team which had given up for the season, and could not, in any case, cope with not being in the Scottish Cup final that day. This meant that, although these two teams had not exactly saved themselves mathematically as yet, St Mirren were now in serious relegation trouble, and had to pick themselves up very quickly before Wednesday night's important game at Dens Park.

Wednesday 25 April 1962 was the night on which the League Championship turned in Dundee's direction. More importantly for Fernie and St Mirren, it was the night that put St Mirren into the second bottom place, meaning that they had to win their last game against Dunfermline, and even then not being absolutely confident of escaping relegation, a fate that one did not often associate with St Mirren.

Dens Park has seen many dramatic occasions in its time, but this was one of the best, and if you are a Dundee supporter, you will never forget it. St Mirren were not without optimism as they headed the road and the miles to Dundee, for they had beaten them in the Scottish Cup there in January. What worried Fernie and other people like Manager Bobby Flavell and captain Jim Clunie was the effect of the Scottish Cup final. It had been an emotionally exhausting, tiring and draining experience. It might have been different if they had won, but the Saints had lost comprehensively. Such occasions, even though it was always an honour even to play in a Scottish Cup final, would, Fernie feared, have an effect on the players.

So it turned out. Dundee, by any standards a good side, and buoyed up by an eager expectant support, started off playing well. For the Saints, a George McLean header hit the post but it was Dundee who took the lead through Alan Cousin, and that was the way that it was at half time. As the teams came out for the second half, Fernie was aware that the Dundee players and supporters were even more upbeat than previously, and this was because they had heard that up at Pittodrie, Aberdeen were beating Rangers 1-0.

But there was still a tense second half to play, and St Mirren, for whom a point would not necessarily have been a total disaster, pressed and pressed as Dundee's defenders began to get panicky and argue with each other, always a sign of stress and worry. Fernie was magnificent in his foraging and "fetch and carrying", and then as the pressure intensified, they earned a penalty when the great Gordon Smith, back helping his defenders, conceded a penalty for hand ball. It was a controversial moment, but referee Mr Syme,

Wedding day in the late October sunshine of 1956 for Willie and Audrey.
It was a 'match' that lasted the rest of their lives.

Willie at home with Audrey and brother-in-law Norman Douglas looking at his scrapbook.

Willie Fernie in full flight at Celtic Park.

Three wonderful Celtic stalwarts of the 1950s photographed together in February 1957.
Willie Fernie, Sean Fallon and Charlie Tully.

Willie and Bobby Collins wait to be introduced to Lord Roseberry at Wembley in April 1957.

Willie looks on as Duncan Edwards clears the ball at Wembley, with England skipper Billy Wright grounded. Bobby Collins and Lawrie Reilly are the other Scots in the photograph.

Piling on the agony, putting on the style!
Willie makes it 7-1 from the penalty spot at Hampden in the League Cup final on 19 October 1957.

Piling on the agony, putting on the style!

27 Celtic goal-scorers with the League Cup, October 1957—Fernie, McPhail, Mochan and Wilson

Irish eyes are smiling as Celtic captain Bertie Peacock and Charlie Tully receive the League Cup at Hampden in the Sun.

Celts pose with the League Cup before the match with Kilmarnock on 2 November 1957.
Back row: Peter Goldie, Bobby Evans, Sean Fallon, Dick Beattie, Billy McPhail and Willie Fernie.
Front row: Manager Jimmy McGrory, Charlie Tully, Bobby Collins, Bertie Peacock, Sammy Wilson, Neil Mochan and Trainer Willie Johnstone.

Willie and Bobby Collins threaten the Paraguay goal in the World Cup finals clash in Norrkoping, Sweden on 11 June 1958. This was Willie's last appearance for Scotland.

Celtic's annual trial match in August 1958 between first team and reserves. Observe a youthful Billy McNeill standing extreme left in the back row, behind Willie Fernie.

Willie at Middlesbrough in October 1959.

Happy Middlesbrough players training at Ayresome Park on 28 October 1959.
Left to right: Derek McLean, Ray Yeoman, Ray Barnard, Ray Bilcliff, Willie Fernie and Ron Burbeck.

The Middlesbrough team which beat Derby County 3-0 at Ayresome Park on 2 January 1960. **Back row:** Mick McNeil, Ray Yeoman, Bill Harris, Peter Taylor, Ken Thomson and Ray Bilcliff. **Front row:** Derek McLean, Willie Fernie, Brian Clough, Alan Peacock and Eddie Holliday.

Football card depicting Willie in Middlesbrough colours from 1960.

He's back! Second time around Celt Willie is the meat in the sandwich between cousins Charlie Gallagher and Pat Crerand, whilst Frank Haffey and John Clark look on.

Willie turning on the style against Partick Thistle at Celtic Park on 12 November 1960.

The happy young Celtic side which qualified for the Scottish Cup final in April 1961. **Back row:** Dunky MacKay, Jim Kennedy, Frank Haffey, Pat Crerand, Billy McNeill and John Clark. **Front row:** Charlie Gallagher, Willie Fernie, John Hughes, Stevie Chalmers and Alec Byrne.

Skip to it! A smiling Willie Fernie trains at Celtic Park in July 1961.

Celtic's forward line training in front of the old Jungle in 1961. **From left to right;** Charlie Gallagher, Willie Fernie, John Hughes, Stevie Chalmers and Alec Byrne

Celtic F.C.—1961-62

Back row, left to right: *Donnelly, Kennedy, Fallon, Kurila, McNeill, Clark.* Front row: *Carroll, Chalmers, Hughes, Fernie and Byrne*

A final photoshoot for Celtic.

Willie, Audrey and sons Alex and William leave Celtic Park.

Willie scores his last goal for Celtic, putting the Hoops 2-1 up at Ibrox on 16 September 1961. This was his final game for the club.

Willie poses with the St Mirren team of 1961/62.

Willie about to score for St Mirren against his old Celtic teammates Stevie Chalmers, Frank Haffey and Dunky MacKay in the infamous Scottish Cup semi-final played at Ibrox on 31 March 1962.

Celtic's backroom team line up in 1969. **From left:** John Higgins (Chief Scout), Willie Fernie (Coach), Sean Fallon (Assistant Manager), Neil Mochan (Trainer), John McAlindon (Stadium Maintenance), Jimmy McGrory (Public Relations Officer), Frank Meechan (Scout), Jock Stein (Manager), Jim Kennedy (Supporters Liaison Officer), Alec Boden (Coach) and John Duffy (Scout).

Coach Willie at Celtic Park c.1971.

The Godfather! Jock Stein pictured in September 1977 with some of the Celts he helped into football management. **From left:** Benny Rooney (Morton), Billy McNeill (Aberdeen), Mike Jackson (Queen of the South), Bertie Auld (Partick Thistle), Willie Wallace, Tommy Gemmell (both Dundee) and Willie Fernie (Kilmarnock).

Life after Celtic for Willie, as Kilmarnock manager (left) then taxi driver.

Two masters of their craft. Willie chats with Danny McGrain outside Celtic Park.

Three generations of Fernies at Celtic Park. Willie, son Alex and grandson Andrew.

A poignant Celtic Park farewell tribute for Willie on 13 August 2011
ahead of the match with Dundee United.

although widely believed (and not without cause) to have Rangers sympathies, was adamant, and penalty it was.

Jim Clunie ran up to take the penalty. No-one else wanted it, and he was the captain, so “noblesse oblige”. Booing and slow-handclapping were heard in that worried and angry stadium, but it was goalkeeper Pat Liney (ironically enough, himself a Paisley Buddie) who saved the day for Dundee. The penalty was well placed, high to the top right hand corner, but Liney was able to get there and claw it away. Dens Park erupted, but Fernie’s heart sank for he knew there would now be no way back. His fears were confirmed a few minutes later when Dundee ran up and scored through Andy Penman. The ground was invaded at the end by joyful young Dundee supporters, and St Mirren had to thread their way through the crowd to the dressing room. The 1-0 score line at Pittodrie had stayed the same, and now Dundee had only to earn a draw on Saturday at Muirton Park to win the League.

But where did it leave St Mirren as the last day approached? They and Airdrie had 23 points, Falkirk 24, and St Johnstone and Raith Rovers had 25. Any of the five of them could go down with Stirling Albion, but St Mirren with a worse goal average than Airdrie, would go down if everyone won, drew or lost. It was going to be a very anxious day. All five relegation teams were at home, as it turned out – St Mirren v Dunfermline, St Johnstone v Dundee, Raith Rovers v Aberdeen, Falkirk v Third Lanark and Airdrie v Partick Thistle.

St Johnstone were the unlucky ones in that they were the only team in the relegation scrapheap who were playing a team which had something to play for. One of the disadvantages of an 18 team First Division was that there were so many teams who had nothing to play for by the end of the season, and that was true of Dunfermline, Aberdeen, Third Lanark and Partick Thistle but not, emphatically not, Dundee. Dundee travelled to Perth still needing a draw to guarantee them their first ever League title, and they were very aware that on a precious occasion against Falkirk in 1949, they had blown up on the last day and had gifted Rangers the championship.

All that St Mirren could do was play their game against Dunfermline and hope for the best. They were aware that their goal average was weak (not least because they had had a couple of real hammerings 7-1 and 5-0 at the hands of Celtic) but St Johnstone's was worse and St Johnstone would go down if they lost and St Mirren won. St Mirren however still had to win against Jock Stein's Dunfermline who had had a comparatively disappointing season after last year, but were still no-one's idea of pushovers, and indeed would be looking for revenge for their Cup exit at the same venue. A win for Dunfermline would certainly relegate St Mirren, no matter what happened elsewhere. Once more, therefore, these two great Celts, Jock Stein and Willie Fernie faced each other with an awful lot at stake.

8,000 were at Love Street, and it started badly. After Fernie had put McLean through once or twice and McLean shot straight at Connachan, Fernie must have had a déjà vu of last season's Scottish Cup final in which John Hughes repeatedly did the same thing. And then Charlie Dickson scored for the Pars to put the Buddies right in the soup. An ominous silence descended on the ground that was broken only when Willie Fernie scored to equalise.

It was a controversial one as well, for Tommy Bryceland looked to be offside when he collected the ball. Indeed, he was flagged for offside by the linesman but referee Mr Massie of Dundee waved play on and Bryceland crossed for Fernie to score. The Dunfermline players protested for offside and also a half-hearted appeal for handball against Fernie, but Mr Massie was inexorable and the goal stood.

It was then that it appeared that Providence wanted St Mirren to be saved. Not only was John Fraser of Dunfermline carried off after an accidental collision with one of his own men, but then, while Dunfermline were trying to reorganise, their centre half Jim McLean had the misfortune to slice a clearance past his own goalkeeper. 2-1 now for the Saints, and then just on the half-time whistle Tommy Bryceland scored a third in a goalmouth scrimmage.

The job was not yet done, however. The half times brought discouraging news from Stark's Park, Broomfield and Brockville, but at Muirton Park, St Johnstone were 0-1 down to Dundee. That would be enough to save St Mirren, and indeed things got better in the second half when Dundee scored another twice and young Drew Provan scored another at Love Street. The Buddies were saved!

And thus ended Fernie's first ever relegation dogfight. He had played a significant part in saving the Saints, and he rated that as much a cause of pride as anything he had achieved at Celtic and Middlesbrough. Full time came and he was touched by the amount of fans who ran onto the park to congratulate him and say "well done", for it was the other Saints, the men of Perth who were relegated as their game finished 3-0 for Dundee who were of course now the Champions of Scotland. That also pleased Fernie and other Celtic-minded people, for if Dundee were the Champions, then Rangers weren't!

Years later, a story emerged that an attempt had been made by a consortium of Dundee and Perth businessmen to fix the Perth game as a draw which would of course have suited both teams in giving the Championship to Dundee and saving St Johnstone. One would have to be naïve in the extreme to believe that corruption and match fixing never happens in Scottish football, but there is a reassuring lack of evidence to back up this particular claim, and in any case, mercifully, this attempt, if it ever happened, was disregarded by the clubs concerned. But, if the Perth game had been drawn, St Mirren would have been the team which suffered.

And thus, another year of Fernie's footballing career finished. He was now nearly 34. How long could he go on for? The answer was not really very long. He stayed for a spell with St Mirren, he had a few games with Alloa, Fraserburgh and Coleraine in Ireland, but to all intents and purposes, Fernie's serious footballing career finished in 1962.

He had to find himself a job – not easy for a man who had done nothing but play football for well over ten years. The only other job he had done was farming in the mid-1940s, but there was no real call for that in the middle of Glasgow! However he turned to the motor trade, eventually becoming Parts Manager at Milngavie Motors which was owned by the Steedman Brothers. This lasted until he got his full time job at Celtic Park in 1970. From 1967 until 1970 he was able to do his part time job at Celtic Park in tandem with his job in the motor trade.

CHAPTER EIGHT

BACK TO PARKHEAD AGAIN (1967-1973)

1967 was of course Celtic's greatest year. The triumph of May 25 can never be beaten, and will probably never even be equalled, (no club in any country has yet managed to win a clean sweep of all their domestic trophies and the European Cup in the same year, nor are they likely to) and Willie Fernie would have been as happy as any ex-Celt with the triumph of Jock Stein and his men.

But Jock was aware that it was one thing to win the European Cup; it was another to keep them at the forefront of Europe. He was also aware that Celtic, although by no means a poor club, were not in the habit of buying players – at least not on the scale of some clubs in England and Europe. He had always been of the persuasion that young players needed to be developed and brought on, and of course he himself had played a huge part in this in the late 1950s, but he was also aware that someone reliable was needed to bring them on. He needed a man whose specific remit was to manage the reserve team. He thought of Willie Fernie.

The morning papers of 19 June 1967 gave us the news that Willie Fernie had been appointed on a part-time basis as manager of the second XI and he was also given the remit to look after the third XI players. There were now five members of the 1954 Scottish League and Cup winning team at Parkhead – Jock Stein as Manager, Sean Fallon as Assistant Manager, Neil Mochan as Trainer, John Higgins as Chief Scout and Willie Fernie as Reserve Team Coach. It had been a successful team in 1954, and it would continue to be a good team now.

The Celtic View of 21 June 1967 has the headline "Welcome Back, Willie!" and tells us that Willie has been given "the task of looking after and tutoring the Celts of the future, the youngsters of the second and third teams who will some day form the nucleus of the side being shaped to bring further honours and glory to Celtic Park". It goes on to say that there "were few more popular figures than Willie Fernie. His swerving runs, his astute passing and his amazing coolness, no matter the pace, made him one of the best loved Celts from the famous nursery of Fife" and it also goes on to say that he was "one of the mildest mannered players ever to wear the colours." The idea in the first instance would be that Willie will attend the Tuesday and Thursday evening sessions at Celtic Park where 100 schoolboys will get the benefit of "up to date Celtic coaching methods"

Stein felt that Fernie would be good in this role. Several of the players knew him and had played with him in 1961 and they all testified to his qualities. Charlie Gallagher in particular talked about how Fernie had "taken him under his wing" and nursed him along, and told how disappointed he had been when Fernie left for St Mirren in late 1961.

And yet in some ways Fernie was a most unusual person to be a coach. He had been a very naturally talented player himself and did not rely on any complicated coaching methods. He would not have been a "blackboard" coach. His emphasis was on attacking, natural football and he was certainly in the right place at Celtic Park for that, because the place was teeming with young talent desperate to emulate the achievements of the men who had brought home the European Cup from Lisbon. His methods would have been to talk to the young players individually, tell them how good they were and bring out the best in them that way. He was a natural "father figure" (even though in 1967 he was not yet 40), and an impeccable role model. Like Stein he was a strict teetotaller.

Ward White, one of the lesser known of Fernie's proteges has this to say about him. "Willie Fernie was a big influence because he was football mad. He just loved football. He didn't like training or anything. He just liked playing football." Billy Murdoch, brother of Bobby, says that he just loved working under Fernie, for his honest approach and infectious enthusiasm for the game, and that he could do anything with a football. Sometimes at training, the players had to try to get the ball off him and it was never easy. In this way, Fernie had a marked similarity to Jimmy Johnstone. Even the other Lisbon Lions found it too difficult to separate Jimmy from a football!

The sheer amount of talent that Willie had to work with was phenomenal. Dalglish, McGrain, Hay, Connelly, Davidson, Macari and many, many others. What they did in the game is eloquent and evident proof of Fernie's contribution. Sadly, so many of them did not do it all for Celtic, and the career of Kenny Dalglish, for example, although there are very many happy memories for us, must always be tinged with sadness at the thought that so much of his spectacular success was achieved elsewhere. He is the most egregious example of this, but it was and remains a common phenomenon.

But then again there was a key difference in age. The Lisbon Lions had mostly been born in war time (some of them before the war) and their early years were the grim, albeit slowly improving years of the late 1940s. The Quality Street Kids or the Quality Street Gang, on the other hand, were all BORN into the National Health

Service and the Welfare State. They thus grew up into a different world, a better world certainly, but also a world in which there was an emphasis on self-improvement, and possibly less need to be dependent on any one institution, even though the institution happened to be Celtic Football Club which still meant so much to so many people. It was a development to be welcomed in many ways, but it did have its effect. Celtic, in this sense, had a great deal less control over young men.

For example, were there any of us who were not just a little bit upset at the departure of Macari in 1973, Hay in 1974 or, particularly, Dalglish in 1977? Non-Celtic supporters would be totally unsympathetic and employ specious clichés like "Everyone has the right to choose" and "Wouldn't you go to England for more money?" "Don't you want to better yourself?" Such things are difficult to argue against, but they ignore the basic love that we all have for the Celtic and our desire to have and to maintain a good team.

The fault of course lies with the Celtic Board who were always keen to bring in more money from transfers, even when there was no obvious lack of money. And they also failed to spot that in Celtic in the early 1970s, winners of the European Cup only a few years previously, they had a great product which could attract new talent. More relevantly, they had a great product to retain the talent that they had developed. This, of course, meant paying their players enough (and yes, we were all shocked even in the 1970s at some of the wages that players could earn!) to keep them where they were. It remains my firm belief that another European Cup could have been won in the 1970s, if Celtic had worked with and kept the players that they had, and whom Willie Fernie had developed. As it was, they reached the final in 1970, the semi-final in 1972 and 1974, so they weren't necessarily all that far away. But things had changed, and the Board began its slow slide to its 1994 nemesis as early as the 1970s when they were happy to rear players and then sell them on – for money. Ironically, there might have been more money in the kitty if they had developed and retained what they had.

But all this happened several years after they had left the hands of Willie Fernie. Kenny Dalglish arrived in 1967, more or less at the same time as Willie Fernie himself. As Fernie himself had been farmed out to Kinglassie Colliery, Dalglish was farmed out to Cumbernauld United for whom he scored 37 goals in season 1967/68. Clearly there was some talent here, and although Stein himself was keen for Dalglish to stay at Cumbernauld for another year, Dalglish preferred to move to Celtic Park. He therefore played for Fernie's reserves in seasons 1968/69, 1969/70 and 1970/71 before breaking into the Celtic first team on a regular basis in 1971/72. He thus had three years of working with Fernie.

It was in the aftermath of the other European Cup final, the considerably less successful one in 1970, that The Celtic View gave the news that Willie had been appointed to the same job but on a full-time basis. It was in some ways a strange Celtic Park to work in in 1970. Celtic historians Tom Campbell and Pat Woods are happy to quote Charles Dickens A Tale of Two Cities "It was the best of times; it was the worst of times". The team had swept all before them in Scotland to win the Scottish League for the fifth year in a row (although they had lost the Scottish Cup final in contentious circumstances to Aberdeen) and were the unofficial champions of Great Britain having beaten the dreadfully unpopular Leeds United (to the delight of most of England) in the European Cup semi-final.

That was the good side of it. The bad side was the curiously lacklustre and totally un-Celtic like performance in the European Cup final in Milan where they broke the hearts of their bewildered supporters by losing to Feyenoord. It was simply not good enough to say that the Dutch were better. Feyenoord were indeed a great deal better on the night, but it was the reasons of why they were so much better that puzzled the fans. The wrong team had been chosen perhaps, Feyenoord had been under-estimated, the defeat of Leeds made them all think that they simply had to turn up in order to win – all these things were true, but it was also obvious to everyone that the relationship between Manager and players was not what it ought to have been.

A disastrous tour of America had followed with poor results, Manager Jock Stein departing suddenly and flying home on his own over the Atlantic leaving Sean Fallon in charge, then two players being sent home for bad behaviour. Rumours of Stein going to Manchester United persisted and would not go away, some players were clearly going to have to be sorted out and newer ones had to be brought in, the supporters were angry and upset but mainly puzzled and bewildered – and yet their team were the best in Britain and second best in Europe with a style of play that made them the envy of the world!

Such was the strange, contradictory, unprecedented atmosphere at Celtic Park when Fernie went full time in July 1970. But The Celtic View tells us that "Now the management have decided that this key task demands a more concentrated approach than can reasonably be expected from a man with a job outside football. Their (the Directors') decision to offer the position to Fernie is a tremendous boost for the ex-Celt. It is a resounding vote of confidence in the skill, drive and all-round enthusiasm he has brought to his part in the coaching scene at Parkhead in the past three years. Now, with no business or professional commitments outside Celtic Park, Willie will be exerting an even stronger influence on the development of the club's potential stars. Manager Jock Stein says 'Willie will concentrate on the younger players on the staff. His task will be to speed up the process of getting youngsters up to first team standards. The younger players will continue to train with their senior colleagues because they benefit from the experience. From now on, however they will be constantly under Willie's eye."

For his part Willie said that he was flattered to be asked to do this important job and was delighted that his old friends and colleagues had such faith in his coaching abilities. Inevitably it would be a case of "many are called but few are chosen". Fernie said not all would make the grade, but those who were not good enough for Celtic might still be good enough to make the grade elsewhere.

It was also quite a wrench for Fernie to leave his job in the motor trade. He was clearly a success there, and it was definitely a far more reliable job than anything vaguely to do with football management. He was now nearly 42 and had a young family of four boys, and there was an element of risk here. On the other hand, he was working with men like Stein and Fallon whom he respected and liked, and he was doing something that he had always wanted to do. He was not really interested in anything other than football, and he now had a chance to combine what he loved doing with the way he earned his living. Audrey, supportive as ever of both her husband and Celtic FC, was delighted.

It was clear that Celtic now saw the development of youngsters as a major part of the future of the club. It was certainly true that although all the Lisbon Lions were still with the club, they would not last much longer. Simpson would retire soon, Clark and Chalmers would soon go elsewhere, Gemmell, Wallace, Hughes and Auld had never really regained the confidence of Stein following the events of summer 1970, and already Hay, Brogan and Connelly were regulars with the breakthrough of Macari and Dalglish not far away. It is often said that Stein managed one club at Celtic between 1965 and 1978, but about three different teams – 1965-1970, 1970 – 1975 and 1975 – 1978. For the development of the 1970 – 1975 team, Stein would rely heavily on his old colleague Willie Fernie.

There is a curious and flattering parallel here between Willie Fernie and the great Jimmy "Napoleon" McMenemy. Napoleon's playing career had been legendary. He had been the same sort of player as Fernie – a tricky dribbler with an astonishing ability to pass a ball – and in the 1930s he came back to work as Trainer with the excellent team which won the Empire Exhibition Trophy in 1938. Maley was still the Manager, but now old, remote, curmudgeonly, hypochondriac and sheer awkward but in practice, it was McMenemy who ran the team with his ability to relate to youngsters and to bring out the best of them with the odd "quiet word" and permanent encouragement. Fernie was often like that in the early 1970s, one feels, at Celtic Park, acting often as a conduit between young players and the formidable Stein who still retained the ability to inspire awe and even fear in some of his players.

CHAPTER NINE

MANAGER OF KILMARNOCK (1973-1977)

Kilmarnock is a team that is very much woven into the fabric of Scottish football. Founded in 1869 when Gladstone was Prime Minister, they are the second oldest club still alive following Queen's Park, and they are a team who, although traditionally badly supported by their locals, always feel that they should be near the top of Scottish football. They had two marvellous successes in the Scottish Cup in 1920 (the first full official season after the Great War) and then again in 1929 when they beat Celtic in the semi-final and Rangers in the final. These were the great days of "Matta" Smith, the grandfather of Gordon Smith who also played for Kilmarnock before moving to Rangers and Brighton. But their only League success was in 1965.

It was an epic occasion for Willie Waddell and his men, sadly for them overshadowed by the fact that it was on the same day that Billy McNeill propelled Celtic to glory in the 3-2 win over Dunfermline in the Scottish Cup final. Kilmarnock had had to go to Tynecastle and beat Hearts 2-0, and they did just that, making it a great triumph for their supporters. This had followed several years of always being the bridesmaid and never the blushing bride with a particular tendency to "blow up" in crucial games in February and March and to thus allow Rangers to win the League again. In the calendar year of 1960, they had played Rangers in the Scottish Cup final in April and the League Cup final in October, and lost on both occasions, and in October 1962 just at the height of the Cuban Missile Crisis, only a controversial refereeing decision from referee Tom Wharton had denied them extra time in the Scottish League Cup final against Hearts.

They had had a few reasonable experiences in Europe as well, notably in 1967 when they nearly became the third Scottish team to reach a European final that year – the Inter Cities Fairs Cup – where they had many impressive performances before losing to Leeds United. It is a shame that people tend to forget about Kilmarnock in 1967, overshadowed as they were by the mightier deeds of Celtic. But then, as is the way with provincial clubs, a steady decline, not helped by a lack of ambition at Board level, had set in, and in 1973, Killie found themselves in the Second Division where they had not been since 1954.

The sergeant-major methods of Walter McCrae did not always go down well with everyone and he and the club parted company in autumn 1973 with Davie Sneddon and Hugh Allan in temporary charge until such time as a new Manager could be found. On Wednesday 10 October Willie Fernie was an "interested spectator" at the League Cup game against St Johnstone, a thrilling game well won by Killie. The following day, Thursday 11 October, he was announced as Manager.

It would have been a difficult decision to leave Celtic Park, but the attraction of having a team of his own to run must have been a very potent one. He had done a great job with the Quality Street kids at Celtic Park, and he left with all the best wishes of everyone at Celtic. He became at least the third Celtic man to become

Manager of Kilmarnock, others being Jimmy McGrory and Malky MacDonald, but he would have been under no illusions about the difficulties of the job. For one thing, the team was now part-time. Fernie himself was appointed full time, of course, but there were problems involved in managing a part-time team which he perhaps had not been totally aware of before he arrived at Rugby Park.

No doubt he consulted Jock Stein before making the decision. He was doing an excellent job at Celtic Park but the time had perhaps arrived for him to branch out on his own. He had now seen at first hand how a good professional team was run. He was aware however that there were several worlds of difference between a high-flying successful team which still had European pretentions and a Second Division club with not very much money and which had (temporarily) fallen on bad times.

The world was in turmoil in many ways in October 1973. The President of the United States, Richard Nixon, was under increasing pressure for his part in the cover up of the Watergate burglary, war was going on in the Middle East in what was known as the Yom Kippur war, a miners' overtime ban and eventually strike was about to take off, and inflation showed every sign of getting totally out of control – but, more importantly than all that, Scotland had qualified for the World Cup! And a week after Fernie was appointed at Kilmarnock, England didn't. Willie might have chuckled at the discomfiture of his old colleague Brian Clough who on television described the Polish goalkeeper as a "circus clown with gloves" but then that same man defied England and effectively knocked them out of the World Cup!

Saturday 13 October saw Willie's first game in charge. He was given a great reception from the 4,000 fans (a considerable increase from previous home game when attendances had dipped to below 2,000 on occasion) and the Killie fans saw a fine 4-0 win over Airdrie. The team was Stewart, White and Robertson; McSherry, Redman and

Maxwell; Cook, Fleming, Morrison, Sheed and Smith. Obviously players, who have been lethargic or even deliberately playing badly in order to get their Manager sacked, will suddenly raise their game to impress the new Manager, but even so, this was a good start. It was Airdrie's first League defeat of the season, and from now on Kilmarnock never looked back and never lost again in the Scottish League Second Division until 2 March 1974.

The left winger was called Gordon Smith. He must of course be differentiated from the other Gordon Smith of more than a decade previously who was part of the Hibs "Famous Five" forward line and who has the honour of having won League medals with three separate clubs – Hibs, Hearts and Dundee. This Gordon Smith of Kilmarnock was the man who would eventually go on to play for Rangers and (infamously) Brighton and Hove Albion missing the "Smith must score" chance which would have won the English FA Cup in 1983, but at the moment he was a very talented left winger, well anchored in Kilmarnock. His grandfather had been the already mentioned Matt or Matta Smith of the 1920s, a real Kilmarnock legend.

Kilmarnock were still involved in autumn 1973 in the League Cup. The quarter finals saw Killie drawn against Albion Rovers for the two-legged contest. Thus brought Fernie up against ex-Rangers Ralph Brand who was now the Manager of the wee Rovers. One could say that these teams had both seen better days – one in particular when they both contested the Scottish Cup final of 1920! - but the Rovers' ability to keep going in very adverse circumstances was truly astounding. It was an interesting League Cup competition this year with an experimental offside rule, whereby a player could only be offside in a box which saw the penalty box extended to the touchline. Whether this was anything to do with it or not, no-one will ever know, but Albion Rovers won the first leg 2-0.

In between the two games, Fernie gave an interview to The Weekly News saying how much he was relishing the new challenge. He stressed that there was no real difference in atmosphere between Celtic Park and Rugby Park because at Celtic Park he was in charge of the reserves whose games were not well attended. He also said that he was not really new to management because he had been a manager in the motor trade and "The connection isn't obvious but it's certainly there. You see, management is all about getting the right people to do a job for you, whether it's in football, a garage or a factory".

This was good stuff. Good managers can't do it themselves, but they must be able to motivate others to do it for them. It was indeed a totally different story in the second leg. Power restrictions caused by the miners' overtime ban meant that this game was allowed to be played on a Saturday, (astonishingly and inexplicably, the two teams had played a League game on the previous Wednesday!) but it was a very windy Saturday and Killie who had won the League game as well in midweek, won the League Cup quarter final second leg 5-2 to put themselves into the semi-final to play Dundee. Goals were scored by Robertson, Morrison, Cook, Fleming and Maxwell with a penalty.

The semi-final ought to have been played on Wednesday 28 November but it was snowed off. Sensible administrators might have decided to postpone the whole Scottish League Cup until the spring, given the uncertainty of the weather and the power situation, but the game went ahead on Monday 3 December at Hampden and attracted an attendance of 4,682. Words like "lonely" were used to describe the spectators at Hampden and the atmosphere was likened to a public library (only a lot wetter and colder than normal) while *The Glasgow Herald* cruelly describes the game as the "ghost semi final" and Dundee won 1-0. The goal was scored by Tommy Gemmell, (whom Fernie knew well from his Parkhead days, of course) but Kilmarnock, the Second Division side, were as good as Dundee in the opinion of most of the Press.

The defeat, although disappointing, meant however that the team now had a lot more confidence in themselves that they were capable of getting to the First Division, and this was what they set about doing. And Fernie very soon earned the respect and confidence of writers like John Mackenzie and Jim Reynolds for the way that he set about his business, and in an interview with Ian Peebles, he stated categorically that "My first duty is to put an attractive and entertaining team on the field because I believe this is what brings people to a football ground. We had a team recently at Rugby Park and it was clear their only aim was to earn a point at all costs. They had no interest in making a game of it. I think they let the public down and after the match I felt like saying so to their manager. Then I remembered I had only been in the job a few weeks and realised I might be tempted to do the same thing before the season was out. But I hope not". The team in question seems to have been Raith Rovers, but Fernie gave a remarkably forthright and honest interview.

It was also fine, traditional Celtic stuff. Celtic, even in their bad days, were never a defensive team. That would have been against their ethos, their tradition and even their DNA, and clearly Fernie had inherited and taken this philosophy with him. Bertie Auld would often tell the story about how "Mr McGrory" (as Bertie would call him reverentially) would stand at the door of the dressing room door and say "Entertain!", while Jock Stein would frequently remind his players about the boring jobs that so many of the supporters had, and how they looked forward to Saturday for some entertainment.

The Scottish Cup came round in late January and put Killie to Easter Road to play the strong going Hibs. It was exactly the challenge that Fernie wanted for his ambitious squad, for he felt that, even though they lost to Turnbull's Tornadoes, they would certainly learn something about football, not to mention crowds and atmosphere.

They certainly did. The game was played on Saturday 26 January when the country was now definitely on a three-day week as Prime Minister Edward Heath pursued his somewhat unwise fight with the miners on whom he was trying to blame everything including his own Government's now rather obvious shortcomings. The three day week was a fairly blatant attempt to demonise the miners in the eyes of the rest of the working class, but whatever the reason, the three day week meant that large sections of the working population were working all day on a Saturday, and therefore for the first time ever, Sunday football was allowed. Celtic immediately embraced this idea, but Rangers, Hibs and Hearts didn't and thus we had the rather foolish situation of Hearts and Hibs both playing at home on the Saturday when one or other of them, with a little common sense, might well have moved their game to the Sunday.

But 14,241, the largest crowd that quite a few of the Kilmarnock team would have played in front of, turned up at Easter Road, and those from the many buses that had come from Kilmarnock had great cause for joy when their team, playing down the slope took command and Eddie Morrison put them two up with two headers within the first twenty minutes. It was too good to last however, and a minute later Alex Edwards had pulled one back, and by half time it was 3-2 for Hibs. The final score was 5-2 for the Edinburgh men, but it was no disgrace to lose to this strong Hibs team who would finish second in the League this year behind Celtic, (about whom they tended to have a death wish), although many commentators felt that, man for man, Kilmarnock were just as good as Hibs that day and possibly better. It was a point conceded by Hibs' Eddie Turnbull who said that Killie were just as good as many teams in the top tier.

But Kilmarnock were still involved in a four way race for the Second Division Championship with Airdrie, Hamilton Accies and Berwick Rangers. A spectacular 8-2 hammering of Alloa Athletic was followed by a tight and tough goalless draw against Airdrie at Broomfield. It is not often that a goalless draw can be said to thrill spectators, but this one did with Kilmarnock indebted to a wonderful display of goalkeeping from Jim Stewart, and Fernie fulsome in his praise of his defence. It meant however that Kilmarnock were still third in the League, and there was very little room for error.

Indeed, the only bad result came at Stark's Park, Kirkcaldy when in spite of a Jim Cook goal, they went down 1-3 to a strong but inconsistent Raith side. It was a game played on 2 March 1974 in a strange atmosphere, where people were wondering just what was going to happen in the governance of Great Britain. The General Election had taken place on the Thursday, but it produced a hung Parliament with Harold Wilson's Labour Party having the most seats. A feature of this election was the appearance of seven Scottish Nationalist MPs. On this day Edward Heath was desperately trying to get a deal or a coalition with the previously despised Liberals, while Labour waited in the wings to form a minority Government. The Liberals refused to play ball and the upshot was that Harold Wilson was invited to form a Government on the Monday. This was a relief to everyone but of more immediate concern to the Fernie family, Kilmarnock now were three points behind Hamilton Accies with a game in hand and 11 games to go.

Fortunately for Killie, their games tended to be against poorer opposition like East Stirlingshire, Forfar Athletic, Brechin City and Albion Rovers, but they rose to the challenge. They had a difficult game at Station Park, Forfar when the 3-3 half-time score line raised a few eyebrows but they won through 5-3, but apart from that, the defence was solid enough and goals came from Morrison and Fleming at the right times.

April was a busy month with eight games, but Kilmarnock rose to the challenge. Often there is a lot of journalistic nonsense about players being "tired" and "jaded", but for other players it is an exciting, stimulating and motivating experience to play so many games close together particularly if there is something like promotion to play for, and Fernie and his men rose to the challenge. They were very fortunate in managing to avoid injuries, and promotion was eventually achieved on 27 April. 27 April was a rather remarkable day, for Celtic drew with Falkirk to win the Scottish League for the ninth season in a row and in England, Manchester United were relegated, their relegation confirmed by a goal from Denis Law, now playing for Manchester City! But that was of little intimate relevance to those 6,000 or so who attended Rugby Park and saw Kilmarnock clinch promotion by beating Stirling Albion 2-1.

Ian Archer in *The Glasgow Herald* says that this was the "Nicest success story of the season" as the champagne flowed in the dressing room. Fernie, of course, a strict teetotaller, abstained, but was still happy enough to talk to journalists and admit that "We've played better" with reference to the Stirling Albion game in which they had gone behind until Fleming and Morrison scored to give the crowd a 2-1 win.

It mattered not, for Killie were now back where all their supporters felt that they should have been all along. When Fernie had joined the club in October, they had been ninth or tenth, but he had clearly given them a boost. He had not made a great amount of changes in personnel (Kilmarnock had a small squad and no great amount of money to buy more players) but the main difference had been in tactics (if it could be described like that, for Fernie was no blackboard tactician) but more in attitude and encouragement of players to do what they themselves wanted to do on the field. The players and supporters had maximum faith in him, and summer 1974 saw football much enjoyed in the town in the shape of the World Cup but with the added ingredient in the prospect of the return of First Division football to the town next year.

One wonders how Willie reacted to the 1974 World Cup. Scotland did well, almost beat Brazil and returned unbeaten and unlucky. It was a very respectable business, and was in total contrast to the shambles of 20 years before when Willie had been involved in the awful events of Switzerland 1954 which reflected credit on no-one. Clearly now under the leadership of Fernie's old friend and rival Willie Ormond, things had improved for Scotland.

But he had little time to dwell on such matters, for the fixtures were out for the new season. Willie Fernie would not have been Willie Fernie if his first thought hadn't been "When do we play Celtic?" And the answer was first in each half of the season – Celtic Park on 31 August and Rugby Park in the midwinter fixture between Christmas and New Year on 28 December. But the League Cup sectional fixtures came first in August with Kilmarnock drawn with Montrose, Queen's Park and Stranraer.

It was going to be a strange League season. For some time dissatisfaction had been expressed about the two League structure of 18 and 19 teams, and the decision had been taken to move to 10, 14 and 14 from 1975/76. The meant that in 1974/75 there would be no promotion or relegation as such, but the placings of teams in the Divisions would depend on where where they finished up. In practical terms it means that for Kilmarnock to reach the Premier League, they would have to reach 10th position in this season's First Division. For a club that had just come up out of the Second Division, this was a tall order, especially as the club was still part-time.

Fernie may, at this stage, have approached the Board of Directors at Kilmarnock with a desire to go full-time, as far as some players at least were concerned. Disappointingly, the Board said no, possibly however dangling the carrot that if they did reach the Premier League at the end of the season, it might be a different matter. The lack of ambition was something that would eventually disillusion Fernie with the club, but in the meantime he had a job to do.

Just as the football season was starting, we had the unprecedented sight of an American President resigning office. "Resigning" was a euphemism. Richard Nixon was a millimetre away from being removed from office for repeated lies about the burglary at the Watergate in 1972, and there were clear signs that he was becoming unhinged. (Last November, he had put his troops on a "low key nuclear alert" in response to the war in the Middle East!) His departure was little lamented, for there was blood on his hands for what he had done in Vietnam, Chile and the Middle East. The loss of America's prestige and respect was permanent.

Meanwhile back in Ayrshire, the form in the League Cup, against Second Division opposition, was impressive. The only blip was a draw against Montrose after the section had been settled. The trouble was that this did not really prepare the brave part-timers for their first League game – against Celtic at Parkhead. It was the day that Celtic unfurled their ninth League flag in a row, and wearing canary yellow, Celtic beat Kilmarnock 5-0 with goals from Vic Davidson, Kenny Dalglish, Paul Wilson, Jimmy Johnstone and a penalty from Stevie Murray.

It was not one of Fernie's happier visits to Celtic Park, although it was nice to see Jock Stein, Neil Mochan and Sean Fallon again and to get a rousing cheer when he came out to take his seat on the Kilmarnock bench. But looking at the array of Celtic talent in comparison with his own honest, hard-working part-timers, he realised that the result was no great surprise and that the success or otherwise of Kilmarnock's season would be determined by opposition other than Celtic.

It was even worse when Rangers came to Rugby Park to deliver a 6-0 hammering. Against that, however, there was a narrow 1-0 win over Aberdeen (not perhaps as good as it sounded for Aberdeen had fallen a little since their great days of the early 1970s) and the all-important (for an Ayrshire club) 3-0 victory over Ayr United. The Aberdeen game would have been watched out for with particular interest in Kinglassie, Fife, for the Managers, Willie Fernie and Jimmy Bonthrone, were childhood friends from the same street in that small Fife village! Bonthrone was a great player and then Manager for East Fife, but found Aberdeen a step too far. He was often described cruelly as the man "who led Aberdeen back into the wilderness" but this comment must not be allowed to detract from his heroic achievements as a player and Manager with East Fife.

The 3-0 game against Ayr United on 7 September was the one that meant most to the Kilmarnock supporters. Ronnie Sheed scored twice and Ian Fleming once. The match brought together two managers of totally different temperaments – Willie Fernie, the quiet man as distinct from the exuberant Ally MacLeod of Ayr United. At the end of the game it was as if the roles had been reversed, for Willie was "sparkly and euphoric" whereas Ally was morose saying "We didn't play well, we didn't play at all". Not until his spectacular downfall in Argentina in 1978 would we see such a subdued Ally.

Fernie on the other hand deserved all the praise that came his way. Ian Archer of *The Glasgow Herald* having claimed that Rugby Park is the cleanest and tidiest ground in Scotland, goes on to say "Kilmarnock play football to match, neat and spruce, not smudged or stained. Willie Fernie's influence has been remarkable, his motto surely one of the game's oldest injunctions: make it simple, make it quick... Fernie's management is a little marvel, proving the essential simplicity of the game. He plays 4-2-4 with wingers rather deep, insists on the ball being worked from the goalkeeper outwards and prefers that the pass is given in that split second when the brain tells the feet what to do – and not a moment later". It was clear that Fernie had acquired a valuable ally in the perspicacious and much respected journalist, Ian Archer.

In the midst of all this impressive start to the League campaign, there was a spectacular League Cup quarter final first leg game against Hibs at Rugby Park which ended up 3-3. Kilmarnock were winning 3-1 at one point, and then Fernie made a substitution which divided the support. He took off Jim McSherry and put on Ian Fallis, a forward instead of a defender, when some supporters thought that he might have been better off shoring up the defence. Fernie's thinking was that it might be better to go for a larger lead to take to Easter Road, but his thinking failed and Hibs managed to bring it back to 3-3.

Advantage Hibs then, but Kilmarnock were still in the game when they went to Easter Road a fortnight later. Hibs scored first, then Kilmarnock equalised through Morrison. Jim Stewart was outstanding in the Killie goal, but eventually in the last quarter of an hour, full time training told, and Hibs ran out 4-1 winners. But everyone agreed that Kilmarnock had played well, and that they had some fine players who were capable of bringing their team to the magical position of 10th in the First Division to ensure qualification for the Premier League. The good times were returning to Rugby Park, although there was still no obvious improvement in the attendances at home games – the constant problem with Kilmarnock, and something that went a little way towards explaining the Board's reluctance to go full time. The problem was basically the fundamental one that although Kilmarnock had a strong and loyal core support, there were simply not enough of them who turned up and paid their money on Saturdays.

When Celtic came to Rugby Park on 28 December 1974, they won by a solitary Kenny Dalglish goal, but *The Glasgow Herald* was full of praise for Kilmarnock and their "likeable Manager Willie Fernie" who refused to blame everything on "luck" and said that Killie had themselves to blame for "not putting away their chances" of which they had probably more than Celtic did. This meant that Killie went into the New Year in 12th spot. They were well in the mix for 10th position and attracting praise for the brand of football that they were playing.

The Scottish Cup, however, was another one-game flop for Kilmarnock who went down 0-2 to Hearts at Tynecastle on a Wednesday night after a postponement on the Saturday. An astonishing crowd of 21,054 appeared to see these two old rivals but this time it was Drew Busby who scored for the Jambos. And yet Kilmarnock had tough luck when Ian Fleming may have been impeded by a defender as his lob went over the bar, and then veteran Hearts goalkeeper Jim Cruickshank had a brilliant save from Gordon Smith. It was generally agreed that Killie were worth a draw, but Fernie was philosophical about the whole business.

One had always to be very suspicious of statements like "we can now concentrate on the League" as if they were wanting to be knocked out of the Scottish Cup in any case, but in early 1975 with League reconstruction very much on the agenda, every single League match for every club was vital. Normally mid-table clashes can be boring with little at stake even as early as February, but not so this year.

Early 1975 was the time that probably thwarted Killie from making the cut to the Scottish Premier League for it was 22 February before they recorded their first win since December. It was not that they always played badly, for there was a creditable draw against Hearts and a very exciting 3-3 game against Rangers at Ibrox, but against that there was a painful defeat at Somerset Park, Ayr in the New Year's Day local derby and two heavy defeats across on the east coast against Aberdeen and Dundee.

It was probably true to say that life in early 1975 was showing signs of a slow return to normality. Labour had won the October 1974 General Election with a small majority, and the confrontational approach to solving industrial disputes had now gone. The disputes involving miners, dustmen and teachers were all reasonably quickly solved, but no solution was found to that of inflation which was now showing serious signs of getting out of hand, running at a rate of about 25% per annum. There were winners and losers in all this. The winners were those who borrowed money for mortgages and cars, for £5,000 borrowed in 1970 was fairly easily paid back in 1975. By the same token those who had saved all their lives suddenly found that their next egg had dwindled in value. In addition there was a general lack of confidence in the value of money, and everything was all very unsettling. But it has to be said that, much as people complained about their lives, things were improving under the benign Harold Wilson, who was much vilified and ridiculed, but turned out to be one of the best Prime Ministers of them all.

The weather was not too bad by Scottish standards, but there was an awful lot of rain with the concomitant wet and heavy pitches, and as a rainy, windy Scottish winter turned into a rainy, windy Scottish spring, things began to look good for Kilmarnock with a particularly good win over Hibs at Easter Road on 1 March, and two other good wins over Morton and Clyde at home.

The game at Easter Road was a very fine performance, and all the better because it was unexpected. Hibs were still in the race for the Championship but this game effectively killed them off and came close to giving the League to Rangers, Celtic having blown up some time ago. The first goal came on the stroke of half-time and was made on the wing by Gordon Smith who zoomed past John Brownlie and crossed for Eddie Morrison to have the simplest of tap-ins. Ian Fallis was the man who scored the second goal after some fine team work involving Davie Provan and Eddie Morrison.

5 April saw Kilmarnock at Gayfield, home of bottom club Arbroath. The game was a dreadful 0-0 draw on a typically cold Arbroath day with a snell wind blowing in from the North Sea some ten yards or so from the far touchline, and Kilmarnock might have expected to do better on this occasion, but the point gained meant that Kilmarnock were now in ninth spot with only three games left against Dumbarton and Dundee United at home, and a trip to Airdrie.

In the meantime, tragically, Celtic's run of nine League titles had come to an end. All good things must come to an end, of course, but it was particularly sad to see it happen with even the normally energetic Jock Stein showing signs of weariness. They were still going strong in the Scottish Cup however and indeed would eventually win it, beating Airdrie in the final.

Another thing that was coming to a conclusion, to mark the end of an era, and this one was a great deal more tragic for it had cost thousands of lives over the past ten years was the War in Vietnam. South Vietnam would eventually surrender to the North at the end of April, but it had been coming for a long time, and although the USA had long ago realised that they were on a loser and had been trying to disengage with some sort of self-respect, the humiliation was total.

All these things were happening when Kilmarnock made their unavailing bid to join the Premier League. On 12 April, wearing red shirts, they took on Dumbarton at Rugby Park. The game was given the honour of being chosen for the STV programme Scotsport the following afternoon. Sadly Kilmarnock lost 1-2, being 0-2 down at half time to goals scored by the brothers Tom and Colin McAdam, who would go on and play for the Old Firm, Tom very successfully for Celtic and Colin, less happily, for Rangers. Veteran defender John Cushley who had been McNeill's deputy about ten years ago, was still playing for Dumbarton, and the Dumbarton defence were good enough to hold out for a victory even after substitute Ian Fleming pulled one back for Killie.

This did not go down at all well with the 6,000 crowd, and chants of "What A Lot Of Rubbish" were heard, according to the writer of *The Evening Times*. One would have to be very naïve to ignore or minimise the undercurrents of feeling in the ground and in the town about whether the Board were really as upset as they ought to have been about this. Many of the Kilmarnock support recalled the great days of 10 years ago when they were the Champions of Scotland and were convinced that the team should be in the Premier League – which of course meant being full time. The Board on the other hand were very aware of the pressures of being full-time and often seemed to lack ambition and to be glad to be where they were. Fernie was of course in the middle of all this. He did not pretend otherwise than that he wanted to run a full time team, but generally his position as Manager compelled him to keep a low profile on this issue.

The second last game was at Airdrie. On a gloomy day of wind and rain, (again!) this game, featured on BBC Sportsreel this time as well as top billing on the back pages of most newspapers, saw a thrilling 2-2 draw which meant that everything depended on the last day. For a long time, Kilmarnock looked really good with Gordon Smith in particular impressing. Having lost the first goal, they fought back with goals coming from an own goal and Ian Fallis, before Airdrie grabbed an equaliser.

And so the last day of the old League structure saw a three way struggle between Motherwell, St Johnstone and Kilmarnock. The weather was good, and all three teams were at home, Motherwell entertaining Dumbarton, St Johnstone having their biggest game of the season against Celtic, and Kilmarnock facing the strong and steadily improving Dundee United. The Tannadice men who had reached the final of last year's Scottish Cup were now managed by Jim McLean, the brother of Motherwell's Willie McLean and also of Tommy McLean who had once played for Kilmarnock but was now with Rangers. Of the three teams, only two could qualify. Basically, Kilmarnock needed to win and to hope that one of the other two would drop points.

It did not turn out well for Kilmarnock. They were at one point 0-3 down well before half time as Andy Gray, Paul Sturrock and Iain McDonald scored for Dundee United. The crowd were beginning to show every sign of turning on Kilmarnock, but the team rallied and pulled two back before half-time through Ian Fallis and Ian Fleming. Sadly half time brought bad news from the other grounds and Paul Sturrock scored again for United, which meant that Kilmarnock were the team that missed out. The victories for Motherwell and St Johnstone merely confirmed the position, Celtic's performance at Muirton against St Johnstone being a very poor one indeed and one which even had many people wondering whether their status as favourites for next week's Scottish Cup final against Airdrie was justified.

But even in the disappointment of defeat, the Press were sympathetic to Kilmarnock with Alan Davidson of The Sunday Mail saying that Killie went down in style, their faults lying in defence rather than in their basic approach to the game, and Alec "Candid" Cameron of The Daily Record similarly sympathetic, and predicting a great season ahead for Kilmarnock in the new First Division.

But round about this time, Willie gave a very frank and disarming interview to Chick Young in The Scottish Daily Mail. Born in 1951, Young was not old enough to have seen Fernie as a player although he had heard him described as "the master of the body swerve" and a "football purist" and had seen enough of the Kilmarnock team in 1974 to be impressed by his footballing knowledge. But Fernie gave him a valuable insight into the realities of management of a provincial club. "As it is, we are running no more than a football factory at Rugby Park. We take boys on and coach them to the best of our ability and wait till someone comes along for them... Sometimes I feel like a Soccer salesman. Make no mistake about it. Every player at Rugby Park is for sale if the price is right."

In this he was only speaking the truth. Kilmarnock had rates to pay and needed their floodlights updated. Money was necessary for the club whose supporters were very loyal and committed, but did not always turn out in as large numbers as one would have liked. Like many provincial clubs, Dunfermline and Dundee springing to mind in recent years, Kilmarnock had had their moments in the sunshine, but it was a very brief interlude. But Willie remained determined to do the best with what there was of the limited resources, and was sure that a team from the new First Division could do well in the Scottish Cup or the Scottish League Cup.

1975/76 was another strange year in Scottish football in a curiously unsettled time which mirrored all that was going on in the outside world with inflation reaching silly levels while all the time fashion seemed to be going out of fashion, as it were. A picture of any football team in the mid 1970s will show long hair, beards, moustaches and loads of players looking more like Mexican bandits than Scottish professional football players. How often does one look at photographs from that decade, shake one's head and say "They don't even look like a football team!"

The top ten having been creamed off to the Scottish Premier League, Kilmarnock found themselves in the new First Division of 14 teams. The Scottish League had decided that they would play each other twice – which was sensible – but the snag was that this only made for 26 fixtures and was all over by the end of February. To supplement the season, the authorities introduced a Spring Cup. In theory it sounded like a very good idea, but for some reason it never took off and was quietly abandoned after one season. The reason was that it was more or less a carbon copy of the Scottish League Cup, but without the big teams, and frankly, by this stage of the season and at this stage in history, there was little appetite for any new development in the game. The competition was played however, and although it was a disappointment for Kilmarnock who might have been expected to do well, Airdrie have the distinction of having been the one and only winners of the Scottish Spring Cup.

The replacement idea was hardly any more satisfactory, for it involved the teams playing each other three times per season with two home and one away. That would begin in season 1976/77 but fortunately, as far as Kilmarnock were concerned, it was not their immediate concern. Kilmarnock were by then in the Premier League, thanks to the events of 1975-76 in which they earned promotion, meaning that Fernie had achieved that honour twice in three years

But before the League started, there was the Scottish League Cup. Killie found themselves in a very difficult section involving St Johnstone and Dundee United (who were both now members of the Premier League) and Partick Thistle. Kilmarnock's form would have to be described as mediocre at best, for they earned only 4 points out of a possible 12.

The season opened in nice sunny weather on 9 August with Kilmarnock hosting the team who would in many ways prove their nemesis this year – Partick Thistle. It is often said that the 1970s were a decade of industrial militancy, but there was a bizarre twist to this motif when East Stirlingshire arrived that day at Shielfield Park, Berwick to play Berwick Rangers and refused to strip until such time as a payment dispute was settled. One scratches one's head about this, because one was hardly likely to extort much money out of the Shire, and the phrase "Ye cannae tak the breeks aff a Hieland man" comes to mind. The dispute was settled and East Stirlingshire won 2-1! It is sad to note in passing that although both of these teams are still in existence, their days in the Scottish League have now gone.

There were no such tantrums at Rugby Park in the strong sunshine, but there was a major disappointment for Killie fans as the team went down 1-3, two of the Thistle goals coming from Joe Craig, a man who would, next season, make his mark in the green and white. Bob Paisley the Manager of Liverpool was seen in the stand that day, reputedly interested in left winger Gordon Smith, a man who had made an impression last season.

Things did not prosper for Killie after that, and two unsuccessful trips to Tayside followed – 1-2 at Muirton Park, Perth and 0-2 at Tannadice Park, Dundee, the game at Muirton being distinguished by little other than that there were four men called Smith playing (three for St Johnstone and one for Kilmarnock) and the one at Tannadice seeing the talented young man called Andy Gray scoring twice.

Kilmarnock were thus out of the Scottish League Cup at the halfway stage of the sectional campaign, and disillusion reigned with a few questions beginning to be asked about Willie's management skills. But he then steadied the ship a little, beating Dundee United and St Johnstone at Rugby Park in front of small and unhappy crowds. A young man called David Provan was now beginning to turn in impressive performances for the club.

The League season began on 30 August, and form was generally good with Fallis, Morrison, Smith and Provan all impressing, and by the New Year, there had only been four defeats. One was the crucial one to the team who would win the League this season – Partick Thistle, two others were to the Angus teams of Montrose and Arbroath who were relishing the First Division, but the other was a team who were clearly not doing so well in the League structure. This was Dunfermline Athletic. Ten years ago, Kilmarnock and Dunfermline regularly attracted praise for their sustained challenges to the Old Firm on a limited budget. But ten years is a long time in football and Dunfermline were relegated to the Second Division at the end of the season. It was sad to see such a fine Scottish side in such straitened circumstances.

The last game of 1975 saw a good 3-2 win over Morton, and then New Year's Day 1976 brought an equally good performance against Airdrie. 3 January brought 11,500 to Firhill to see the undeniable game of the day with the attendance a great deal better than several Premier League crowds that day. Thistle's Manager at the time was the irrepressible Bertie Auld and one wonders whether he was the person responsible for the loudspeaker announcement that offered Kilmarnock congratulations for joining Thistle in next year's Premier League. Such a statement was premature to put it mildly, but it was borne out by events for Thistle won the League by six points ahead of Kilmarnock who, in turn were five points ahead of Montrose. Today, it was Bertie who got the better of Willie by beating Killie 2-0.

Eventually on 21 February in the second last game, Kilmarnock, watched by politician Jim Sillars, a Kilmarnock supporter who had founded a short lived new political party called the Scottish Labour Party, beat Falkirk at Rugby Park in an astonishingly lacklustre game, the only goal being scored by Ian Fallis to clinch promotion in the second spot. It was an anti-climactic way of doing it, but it was deserved nevertheless, and the celebrations from the small crowd were justified, even though they were tempered to a certain extent by the worry of whether they had a team at the moment that was good enough to stay in the Premier League. There was a worry that they might just come straight back down again.

Jessica Barret in *The Scottish Daily Express* runs an article on the wives of the managers Liz Auld, wife of Bertie of Partick Thistle and Audrey Fernie. The teams of both their husbands had been promoted, and although both wives agreed that Saturday night's happiness depended on how well (or otherwise) the team had done, Liz Auld tended to take a back seat about football. Audrey Fernie on the other hand was a self-confessed football fanatic and says "Actually I'm the one who gets most upset if Kilmarnock lose or play badly. Willie will go over the bad moves and the mistakes quite rationally. But me, I get terribly annoyed. You should hear me sometimes" She also said that, although she had had experience of a huge club like Celtic when she was the Secretary to Jimmy McGrory as Celtic, she liked the "homely" atmosphere of a provincial club like Kilmarnock and would hate to leave. But "you never know with football".

Kilmarnock had a reasonable Scottish Cup run in 1976. Saturday 24 January was a remarkable day. Celtic were 2-0 up at Motherwell, then blew up spectacularly to lose 3-2, there was unusual, possibly even unprecedented hooliganism at Alloa (of all places) involving Aberdeen supporters and the locals, while not all that far away from Alloa, at Ochilview the home of Stenhousemuir, Kilmarnock were held to a 1-1 and according to some accounts, they were lucky to get off with the draw. They weren't a great deal better at Rugby Park in the replay, either, but Gordon Smith scored the only goal of the game to put Killie through to play Falkirk in the next round on St Valentine's Day.

There was also crowd trouble at this game, for Falkirk, who had beaten Dundee in the previous round, brought a large support with them, two of whom did not see the game out, being marched away by the Ayrshire Police for throwing some bottles after Killie had scored their first goal. The game was tough and hard fought, but ended up with a clear 3-1 win for the home side with two goals from McDicken and an own goal. The week after that, Falkirk returned for the game that clinched Kilmarnock's promotion.

The draw for the quarter finals of the Scottish Cup on March 6 1976 saw Kilmarnock avoid the obvious dangers of Rangers, Hearts and Hibs but it paired them against Dumbarton at Boghead. In theory this was a fairly easy game, but it proved to be anything but. It was a real hard luck story for the Kilmarnock fans in the 7796 crowd, for the first goal was a severe deflection which couldn't be stopped by Jim Stewart in the goal, then Ian Fallis scored an equaliser from a Davie Provan cross. But then a late goal saw Dumbarton scrape through, and Kilmarnock did not have enough time to get what would have been a deserved equaliser.

The season now fizzled out with no success in the miserable Spring Cup, but there was still a great deal for fans to look forward to in summer 1976. The major topic of conversation however centred on the decision of the Board not to go full time. It did seem to be unnecessarily timid, given the fact that there would now be four games against Celtic and four against Rangers, not to mention the two Edinburgh teams, and possibly most important of all, four games against Ayr United. It would also be a very tight League with no room for any loss of form. This year, St Johnstone had been out of it from an early stage, and the other team to go down was Dundee, a team now paying the price for having a Board which was at once timid and supine, and also greedy and acquisitive who saw short term gain in the selling on of star players when they really didn't need to. And yet, like Killie, they had won the League in the 1960s! There was a lesson there about lack of ambition.

Another item that entered the heads of supporters was the position at Celtic Park. Jock Stein had had a bad road accident in summer 1975 from which he took a whole season to recover. The job had been done by Sean Fallon, who, frankly, was not a great success. The question was often put that if Jock had not recovered sufficiently or if he had decided to give up (as a lesser man might well have done), whether Fernie might not have been the worst idea in the world as his successor. He knew the Celtic Park set up, he retained his love for the club - "once a Celt, always a Celt" and he was doing a creditable job in not the easiest of circumstances in Ayrshire. It might have happened, but it didn't, for Stein came roaring back and season 1976/77 was possibly one of Jock's best in terms of decision making and creating a good team by some incredibly shrewd transfers.

Season 1976/77 was a lot less kind to Kilmarnock and Willie Fernie. No-one said that it was going to be easy for Kilmarnock to stay in the Premier League, especially as two teams out of the ten were to be relegated. The fairly obvious weak links, apart from Kilmarnock, were Ayr United, Partick Thistle and possibly the inconsistent Motherwell. In the event the team that were relegated along with Kilmarnock were one that no-one could have predicted, namely the illustrious Heart of Midlothian for whom even their enemies were said to be sorry, when it happened. Indeed, it was sad for those of us with long memories to recall that 12 years previously, Hearts and Kilmarnock had met at Tynecastle on the last day of the season to decide the League title! Now, Hearts, like Kilmarnock paid the penalty for having unwise Directors in charge of the club.

The odds had been stacked against Killie almost from the start. The decision of the Board not to go full-time was one that irked Fernie, and it meant that there were all sorts of problems involved with players getting off their work for training sessions etc. and also those who wanted a full-time footballing career feeling frustrated and all the more willing to listen to the seductive voices of full time and English teams. It was hardly the best kept secret in the world, for example, that Rangers, as well as a veritable host of English clubs, were interested in Gordon Smith.

But there was another factor which militated against Kilmarnock in their fight to avoid relegation. Fernie, imbued with the Celtic tradition of attacking, entertaining football found it difficult to adapt to the more defensive game that is appropriate and sometimes necessary to survive in the Premier Division. For example, a goalless draw against someone like Motherwell or Partick Thistle in front of about 3,000 disappointed and frustrated fans at Fir Park or Firhill might be looked upon as a good result by some people – but it was anathema to the style of Willie Fernie and indeed most of the Kilmarnock players and supporters.

The League Cup section might have been better. Drawn in a tough group of Aberdeen, St Mirren and local rivals Ayr United, Kilmarnock could only achieve two victories out of six games, but they were good ones – one was against Ayr United on the first Wednesday night, a 2-0 triumph with goals from Provan and Murdoch which delighted the supporters, and the other was on the last Wednesday night over an Aberdeen team which had already won the section. It was a strong Aberdeen team (as was proved when Killie lost 0-2 on the opening day at Pittodrie) now under the ebullient Ally MacLeod who in fact went on to lift the trophy that year.

The League season opened on 4 September in reasonable weather at Rugby Park. It was a tough encounter against Motherwell and ended up a 1-1 draw. It was a tolerably good performance although Kilmarnock felt that they were worth a little more especially after Paul Clarke (brother of Steve who is now Manager of Scotland) opened the scoring. And then Kilmarnock excelled themselves the following week by going to Ibrox and earning a 0-0 draw. It was the day of Rangers' somewhat vainglorious celebrations of what they had achieved last season. They included a visit from Miss United Kingdom (something that feminists were already beginning to ask questions about) and an embarrassing piece of sycophantic crawling before a Saudi Arabian oil sheik, (fortunately neither the beautiful lady nor the rich gentleman from the Middle East were Roman Catholics!) but when the business began, Fernie's Kilmarnock proved themselves the equals of Rangers whose supporters were already, even at this early stage of the season beginning to wonder about how good their team really was.

But that was about as good as it got for Kilmarnock in September because a couple of heavy defeats against Aberdeen and Celtic followed, the Celtic game at Rugby Park, a 0-4 defeat, being punctuated by one of these outbreaks of hooliganism, incomprehensible to the rational mind, but nevertheless common in the 1970s and proving, yet again, the failures of the Scottish educational system! October was better with draws against both Edinburgh teams and then a result which possibly deceived the naïve into thinking that everything was going to be all right. It was a 6-1 thumping of Ayr United at Rugby Park on 30 October with the highlight being an Ian Fallis hat-trick.

The following week 6 November was a bad day for the Fernie family. Not only did Celtic lose the Scottish League Cup final in a travesty of a game where Celtic applied all the pressure but simply could not score and Aberdeen nipped in to score at vital stages, but Kilmarnock played an astonishing game against Motherwell at Fir Park and lost 4-5! Fallis had scored twice in the first half to give Killie a 2-0 lead, but then both defences collapsed, Kilmarnock's in particular as they managed to lose 5 goals in 45 minutes. The Motherwell fans and the neutrals were euphoric and talked about "great entertainment" and "Scottish football at its best" and so on, but Kilmarnock fans were less charitable.

It was now as if someone had pulled the plug and let the bathwater out, for Kilmarnock won only one game (against Dundee United the week before Christmas) until the middle of February. Some were creditable defeats - 1-2 against Aberdeen and Celtic, for example, but there were a few severe hammerings as well, but the defeat on New Year's Day to

Ayr United at Somerset Park was the one which really hurt.

And yet, at this stage, there was a cluster of teams at the bottom and survival was still a possibility. On 3 January, for example, they fought back from being two goals down to Motherwell to earn a draw, but once again form collapsed, although it has to be said once again that part-timers against Celtic, Rangers and Aberdeen was hardly a level playing field.

A Scottish Cup run might have made a difference to morale and finances, but Killie went out at the first time of asking to Motherwell on 29 January, and February brought only one victory against fellow strugglers Hearts. The team were now doomed, but there was one sting in the tail which showed what they might have done this season.

This was on 26 March, when Kilmarnock beat Rangers 1-0 at Rugby Park. Killie were definitely on the way down (but not yet mathematically) and Rangers, reeling from being outmanoeuvred on the field and on the diplomatic front by the resurgent Jock Stein, brought one of their poorest supports of all time to Rugby Park. Skipper Alan Robertson scored one of his rare goals when he lobbed in a Gordon Smith cross. Sadly, although this goal raised the rafters at Celtic Park when news came through on the transistor radios, it made no difference to Kilmarnock. Celtic beat Dundee United 2-0 that day, and one of the highlights was debutant goalkeeper Roy Baines saving a penalty taken by the other goalkeeper, Hamish McAlpine! It would have been difficult to make that one up!

By the time that Kilmarnock came to Celtic Park on 9 April, relegation was confirmed but Ian Paul of *The Glasgow Herald* makes the perceptive and encouraging point that "If the Premier League will be poorer financially with the exit of Hearts, it will be just as poor aesthetically for the disappearance of Kilmarnock. Their uninhibited style against a team which does not itself hang about made for an open, always interesting match"

Everyone seemed to be sorry to see the loss of Kilmarnock from the Premier League, and of course Fernie was distraught. He might have expected to be dismissed, the frequent fate of relegated Managers, but for some reason that did not happen. He remained convinced however that had the team gone full time and had he been given some money with which to strengthen his squad, things would have been different.

In fact, he was given some money at the start of the 1977/78 but it was hardly the way in which he would have wanted to be given it. It came from the sale of Gordon Smith to Rangers for some £65,000. Smith, now a Scotland Under 23 International, had been wanting away for some time, for he had been one of the few unqualified successes of the previous season. It was still a blow for Kilmarnock and their fans, coming as it did a few days after an awful 0-3 defeat to Morton on the opening day of the season. It is not often that one hears mutterings among the discontented fans at this early stage, but the unhappiness would simply not go away.

The beleaguered Fernie was in good company, for his old team mate Jock Stein was in the same boat. Stein had been compelled by his grasping Directors to sell Kenny Dalglish for £400,000. As in the case of Gordon Smith, there is not really all that much that one can do if the player wants to go, but the money must be immediately re-invested, particularly when, in the case of Celtic, Stanton and Conn were injured on the opening day, and McGrain a few weeks later. Celtic's supporters were thus condemned to a whole season of torment as Rangers had been effectively gifted the treble virtually before the season even started.

Kilmarnock's fans were similarly to be given a season of disappointment, but for Fernie at least, the torture did not last long for he was sacked on 21 October 1977. Following the opening day disaster, things went from bad to worse with three more defeats in the League and an early exit from the League Cup. There was an air of desolation hanging over the ground with crowds struggling to reach 2,000. Even by Killie standards (it is generally agreed that they do not have a huge support at the best of times) this was poor.

The first win came on 17 September over lowly Arbroath at Rugby Park, and then there was another win a month later on 15 October at Recreation Park against Alloa, but the prevailing mood was gloom. The gloom was not confined to events on the football field either for on Monday 3 October, Ian Fallis was killed in a three vehicle crash near Drumpellier Loch, Coatbridge. It was a dreadful blow for the club, and although Fallis was now struggling to retain his place after a few very successful seasons, he was much missed in every sense. Fernie was devastated, as indeed was the whole club, as the gloom intensified.

It was a gloom that was in total contrast to the general mood of the country, for Scotland were in the throes of qualifying for the World Cup. Wins against Czechoslovakia and Wales had lifted the whole nation to something approaching hysteria, and Manager Ally MacLeod did little to dampen down the feeling that Scotland were going to go to Argentina and come back with the World Cup. It was a great time to be a Scotland football fan...except in places like Kilmarnock. It was a curious "book end" to Fernie's career as manager of Kilmarnock. He had arrived when Scotland had just qualified for the 1974 World Cup, and he left just as they were in the throes of qualifying for another.

It was the night of 19 October which brought matters to a head. It was a miserable draw against St Johnstone (by another coincidence, the same team that Killie had played the night before Fernie took over the job in 1973). Before marginally fewer than 2,000 frustrated fans at Rugby Park. Killie had the bulk of the pressure but could not score, even though Billy Murdoch hit the bar. Boos, catcalls, and "What a load or rubbish" was heard all over the ground with this time, a certain amount of venom aimed at Willie Fernie himself rather than the three Directors. This clearly could not go on.

The following night the Directors met and Fernie was informed that his services were no longer required. He came to the ground on the Friday morning to clear his desk and to say his goodbyes particularly to his loyal lieutenants Davie Sneddon and Hugh Allan. He was naturally disappointed and told *The Evening Times* that "I feel that I have a lot to offer football and I want to stay in the game – preferably in a managerial capacity." He then added cryptically "Perhaps I have been too honest in my approach to the game. Maybe it's not the best policy. However, I hope that other managers can learn from what has happened to me."

One often wonders what Willie meant in his parting words. He may have been hinting at something going on in the Kilmarnock Board of Directors, but in any case, the Board must take a share of the blame for the calamitous situation that they were in. Over-ambition can lead to disaster, but so too can a lack of ambition. The good people of Kilmarnock, albeit guilty then as now of not turning out in sufficient numbers to support their team, had reason to expect that their team, Champions in 1965, should, at least, still be in the top 10 some 12 years later. This required the team going full time, one feels, and Fernie was right to be bitter and unhappy about the situation.

But he had brought a gleam of light to the club. He had encouraged them to play attractive football, and he had played a great part in the development of flair players like Davie Provan and Gordon Smith. The general view in Scottish football was that everyone was sorry to see the departure of Willie Fernie, and the hope was expressed that he might get a job somewhere else. That season 1977/78 saw an improvement in Kilmarnock who reached the quarter final of the Scottish Cup, beating Celtic one snowy night in early March at Rugby Park in a game which saw the young Roy Aitken sent off. One wonders what Fernie's reaction was when he heard that result.

CHAPTER TEN

SCOTLAND (1954-1958)

Willie Fernie played 12 times for Scotland. It was his misfortune to play at a time when, although there were many good players, the organisation was particularly shambolic and the team and the nation suffered dreadfully as a result. He played in two World Cups in Switzerland in 1954 and in Sweden in 1958, and on neither occasion could it have been said that Scotland had a Manager! There was one called Andy Beattie in 1954 but he resigned halfway through because of interference from SFA members (incredible but true!) and in 1958, there might have been one in Matt Busby but he was still recovering from the Munich Air Disaster - and no-one really got round to appointing a replacement – or even thought it might be necessary!

The way that a Scotland International team was selected beggars description. It was a cabal of usually about seven Selectors, usually Chairmen of clubs like Queen of the South or Ayr United. Such men, with all due respect, were not necessarily experts on football tactics, but they nevertheless were tasked with the job. Often the choosing was done on a vote of the Selectors for each individual position, possibly by a majority vote of 4-3! It was hardly surprising that team selection occasionally bordered on the crazy! Or that results were frequently disappointing.

It is not uncommon for Celtic supporters to say that there is some sort of discrimination against Celtic as far as selection for Scotland in concerned. As a general rule, this does not hold water – McNair, Quinn, McMenemy, Evans, Dalglish and others had no problem earning Scottish caps, for example – but it must be owned that some things are not so easy to explain, such as why Jimmy McGrory who scored for Scotland against England at Hampden in 1931 and 1933, was never chosen to go to Wembley for Scotland in 1928, 1930, 1932, 1934 or 1936! It is hard to rationalise this but is perhaps due to sheer incompetence rather than conscious discrimination. Willie Fernie too might have felt entitled to shake his head, now and again, at the folly of Scottish selectors.

He had been the travelling reserve at Wembley in 1953, but had been passed over for all the Home International games in 1953/54, an International season which had finished with a dreadful 2-4 defeat at Hampden at the hands of England on 3 April. Fernie had already played in a low-key Scotland "B" game against England "B" at Roker Park, Sunderland in early March 1954 and then he was picked for the Scottish League game at Stamford Bridge on 28 April 1954. Sadly that game turned out to be a 0-4 thumping which did not seem to do the chances of Fernie and other participants in that game any good at all.

However, the World Cup was to be held in Switzerland in summer 1954. The SFA, their somewhat sinister Secretary George Graham in particular, showed every sign of wishing to disregard this phenomenon and were only compelled to enter because of pressure from the public, the players and the Press. There were three warm up games. Fernie was in the party but not chosen for the 1-0 win over Norway on 5 May at Hampden, but then he was chosen for the two game tour of Scandinavia – Norway in Oslo and Finland in Helsinki.

Fernie was once again in the stand when Scotland drew 1-1 in Oslo – a game which included a bizarre attempt by the Norwegians to sneak on an illegal substitute when a man was injured! – but Scotland played terribly, changes were made and Fernie was given his first International cap against Finland in Helsinki on what would, in later years, become a famous Celtic day of 25 May. The game would be played in the Olympic Stadium, Helsinki the one that had resounded two years previously to the frenzied chants of "Zat – o – Pek" "Zat – o- Pek" in honour of the famous long-distant Czech athlete called Emil Zatopek.

This was a far better game than previous Scotland performances that year and was won 2-1, the goals scored by the Hibs duo of Bobby Johnstone and Willie Ormond. The verdict of The Courier on Fernie is that "he played some delightful football but rather spoiled things by overdoing it" a comment that was frequently used about Fernie. He did however play well enough to enjoy a Scotland win on his first appearance and he was also considered to be good enough to join the party for the World Cup in Switzerland.

The teams on Fernie's International debut were

Finland: ***Rintanen, Lindman and Lentinen; Henriksson, Sundback and Sommarberg; Vanhanen, Hiltunen, Forss, Lahtinen and Nygard***

Scotland: ***Anderson (Leicester City), Wilson (Portsmouth) and Cunningham (Preston North End); Evans (Celtic), Cowie (Dundee) and Mathers (Partick Thistle); McKenzie (Partick Thistle), Johnstone (Hibs), Brown (Blackpool), Fernie (Celtic) and Ormond (Hibs)***

A couple of days later when the players had returned to Scotland, the squad for the World Cup was announced. Several aspects of this process, from a viewpoint of nearly 70 years later, are, frankly, quite staggering. The party contained 13 men, when they were allowed to take 22! Apart from the 13, another 5 were told to "stand by" and yet another 4 were registered for "emergency use". The 13 were ***Martin (Aberdeen), Cunningham (Preston North End),***

Aird (Burnley), Evans (Celtic), Docherty (Preston North End), Davidson (Partick Thistle), Cowie (Dundee), McKenzie (Partick Thistle), Johnstone (Hibs), Brown (Blackpool), Mochan (Celtic), Fernie (Celtic) and Ormond (Hibs).

No Rangers players were involved. Rangers were indulging in one of their periodic quarrels with the SFA and had taken their players off to America. The squad had been chosen by three Selectors (not seven, as there often were), and Manager Andy Beattie does not seem to have been consulted. But the main objection was that the whole thing was done on the cheap. 13 players were not enough, even though there were only two games in the first instance, and there was only one goalkeeper in Fred Martin. What were they to do if he injured himself? There was no recognised centre forward, and although the excellent Neil Mochan would probably fill that role, once again there could be a potential problem in the event of an injury. As it happened, Bobby Johnstone of Hibs called off through injury and George Hamilton of Aberdeen was drafted in. Just as well, we agree. They might have been down to 12.

There were other problems as well. The party flew out on 12 June to their headquarters at Lucerne, and the first game was 16 June! There was a total party of 23 – 13 players, one Manager, one trainer and eight "hangers on" who included the much disliked, dictatorial Harry Swan of Hibs and the equally odious George Graham the Secretary of the SFA, a man for whom very few people had a good word to say. He was the man who took on Bob Kelly about the Irish flag – and lost, but, in spite of his Freemason connections, he had also upset Rangers as well on several issues. *The Evening Times* however does try to cheer up its readers by telling them that all the thirteen players were looking fit and athletic.

The strips provided were the thick cotton ones with heavy collars, long pants and thick stockings – ideal for a grim Scottish day at Arbroath in February, or Motherwell in November, but the heat in central Europe in midsummer was stifling! Not only that, but there was no training gear provided, so the players had to bring along their own! It was appallingly amateurish and clearly done "on the cheap" by the SFA whose game against England a few weeks earlier had brought in huge receipts from a crowd of 134,000. The SFA attitude was in total contrast to the mood of the country who were actually looking forward to following the games, with even a few lucky and rich supporters able to follow the football on the new infant medium called television. The mood generally was upbeat, and in spite of the appalling result against England in April, optimistic.

The tournament itself was half-baked. There were sections of four, but each team played only two games. Two teams were "seeded" by some arcane and mysterious process and the two seeded teams in Scotland's section were Austria and Uruguay. Czechoslovakia were the other team in the section whom Scotland would never meet. Possibly just as well.

The first game was against Austria on Wednesday 16 June 1954. It was not on television, the viewers being treated to Yugoslavia v France instead. Scotland decided to leave out Bobby Evans and George Hamilton and thus the teams were

Scotland: *Martin, Cunningham and Aird; Docherty, Davidson and Cowie; McKenzie, Fernie, Mochan, Brown and Ormond*

Austria: *Schmied, Hannapi and Barchandt; Ocwirk, Happel and Koller; R Korner, Schleger, Dienst, Probst and A Korner*

Referee: *L Franklen, Belgium*

Peculiarities included both Austrian wingers being called (appropriately) Korner! It was an honourable defeat in some ways – many folk thought that Scotland should have had a penalty including referees Charlie Faultless and Jack Mowat, (writing for various newspapers), and the England team who were watching the game on TV, but the telling comment is that in The Courier where it says that "the Scots did not time the 90 minutes too well". Basically, they had exhausted themselves in the first half and could not cope with the intense heat that they had never experienced before. Mochan might have scored near the end to get a draw, but Fernie after a good first half faded in the second half.

Nevertheless, although it was a defeat which rendered chances of qualification almost infinitesimal, it was not a disaster. The disasters were yet to come. The game was not broadcast on the radio, although there was a sports programme which gave the score and a brief account, and it was not really until the morning newspapers on Thursday that people back home learned about the game in detail.

The first disaster was the resignation of Andy Beattie the Manager. An International Manager resigning in the middle of a tournament would be hard to parallel in world football, and it was likened to General Custer resigning his commission as the Red Indians appeared on the horizon or, more pertinently to Scotland, Robert the Bruce abdicating when the spider failed to attach his web at the first attempt. Beattie did say however that he would stay until the end of the Uruguay game!

He did not say exactly what the problem was but a reasonable guess might be the chaotic arrangements and the constant interference by Swan and Graham in what he wanted to do. So, all was not well in the Scotland party which had not yet been together for a week! Many historians have talked at length and tried to analyse the traditional Scottish "self destruction" complex. This was one of the best examples of them all, and could reasonably be described as a "collector's item" of Scottish incompetence, possibly even to be compared to the Darien scheme of the 1690s.

What Fernie and the rest of the players made of all this, one cannot imagine. This was meant to be the apex of their career, something to remember all their lives and here it was unravelling in front of their very eyes, as Scotland rapidly became the laughing stock of world football, and the puzzlement and frustration of their supporters back home. The Press certainly did not miss anyone and hit the wall instead. And there was more to come.

For the game on Saturday at the Sankt Jacob Stadium, Basle against the unknown South Americans called Uruguay (they were however the current World Cup holders!) Scotland announced an unchanged team which meant that Evans and Hamilton were once again spectators. Presumably the Selectors chose the team (there were one or two of them there among the hangers on) and Andy Beattie gave the team talks, but the whole thing was a shambles as Scotland paid the penalty for allowing amateurs to take over.

So the teams were:

Scotland: ***Martin, Cunningham and Aird; Docherty, Davidson and Cowie; McKenzie, Fernie, Mochan, Brown and Ormond***

Uruguay: ***Maspoli, Santamaria and Martinez; Andrade, Varela and Cruz; Abbadie, Ambrois, Miguez, Schiaffino and Borges***

Referee: ***V Orlandini, Italy***

The game was shown on television back home and it is fair to say that it is little wonder that so many youngsters like one of your authors were traumatised by what they saw. The result was Scotland 0 Uruguay 7 and it was one of those games where you could honestly say that Scotland were "lucky to get nil". It was a hammering of the most monumental proportions and Scotland's ball players never got going, hampered by their heavy shirts, their huge boots and the general lack of organisation. Uruguay were a good side, but Scotland did not need to be quite so bad as all that.

Better organisation and even taking the tournament more seriously might have earned a respectable defeat at least or even a draw. As it was, Fernie returned home a few days later, having learned how not to run a football team.

And yet there was the funny side as well. One Scottish player told the story of how the heat was so intense that you could not run for more than ten yards at a time, and even walking was difficult. The Uruguayans, more used to such heat and in any case wearing lighter and more appropriate gear, were zooming past Scotland as if they didn't exist in the same way as a racehorse will overtake a carthorse. Scotland couldn't get near the South Americans, they were suffering from heat exhaustion, sunstroke and dehydration – and a voice was heard from the touchline shouting "Come on Scotland, get stuck in!"

Fernie was chosen for the first Scotland International of the 1954/55 season. It was against Wales at Cardiff on Saturday 16 October. He would have been understood, one feels, if he had turned reluctant and awkward about committing himself to such a shambles as he had been part of in the summer, but he still looked upon it as a great honour to be chosen for his country, and his form for Celtic at this time was such that it would have been difficult to omit him. There were a few changes since Switzerland, not least in the appearance of two Rangers players and the welcome addition of two Aberdeen players in Yorston and Buckley, reflecting the excellent start that the Dons had made to the season.

The teams were:

Wales: *Kelsey (Arsenal), Barnes (Arsenal) and Sherwood (Cardiff City); Paul (Manchester City), Charles (Leeds United) and Bowen (Arsenal); Reed (Ipswich Town), Tapscott (Arsenal), Ford (Cardiff City), Allchurch (Swansea Town) and Clarke (Manchester City)*

Scotland: *Fraser (Sunderland), Young (Rangers) and Cunningham (Preston North End); Docherty (Preston North End), Davidson (Partick Thistle) and Cowie (Dundee); Waddell (Rangers), Yorston (Aberdeen), Buckley (Aberdeen), Fernie (Celtic) and Ring (Clyde)*

Referee: *W Ling, England*

The crowd was 60,000 of which at least some 6,000 had come from Scotland. As is often the case with Internationals, the standard of football was not high, as good players in each side cancelled each other out, and in any case, players playing for their clubs with their own team mates are often less proficient at dealing with unfamiliar colleagues. There was also the undeniable fact that Scotland still did not have anyone who might reasonably be described as a Manager! But Scotland won 1-0 when Fernie fed Tommy Ring of Clyde who sent over a lovely cross for Paddy Buckley to head the only goal of the game. *The Evening Times* adds caustically that this was “indeed, the only big thrill in the game”. But Fernie played well enough to retain his place for the next game.

The International between Scotland and Northern Ireland was played on Wednesday 3 November 1954 at Hampden Park. It was a landmark game of sorts in the history of televised sport for the second half was televised live from 3.35 pm until 4.25 pm on BBC (the only channel that there was at that time). It was the first time that a football match had been televised in Scotland itself, but it was not exactly the game to make everyone rush out and buy a TV in the hope of seeing more football. It was a 2-2 draw, but is described candidly by *The Glasgow Herald* as a “Poverty Stricken International” with little or no football in it. The presence of TV cameras there did however oblige the referee to wear a crimson jersey and to use a white ball!

The teams were;

Scotland: *Fraser (Sunderland), Young (Rangers) and McNaught (Raith Rovers); Evans (Celtic), Davidson (Partick Thistle) and Cowie (Dundee); Waddell (Rangers), Johnstone (Hibs), Buckley (Aberdeen), Fernie (Celtic) and Ring (Clyde)*

Northern Ireland: *Uprichard (Portsmouth), Graham (Doncaster Rovers) and Cunningham (St Mirren); D Blanchflower (Tottenham Hotspur), McCavana (Coleraine) and Peacock (Celtic); Bingham (Sunderland), J Blanchflower (Manchester United), McAdams (Manchester City), McIlroy (Burnley) and McParland (Aston Villa)*

Referee; *A Bond, England.*

The 46,200 crowd failed to become animated by this game which Scotland really deserved to have lost. Even the greatest admirer of Willie Fernie (and he had plenty in the Scottish Press) could not have said that he had a good game, his greatest contribution seeming to come when he got in the way of a poor Johnstone shot and deflected the ball into the net to give Scotland their equaliser, Ireland scored at the final whistle but it was mercifully ruled out for offside. Earlier Davidson had scored for Scotland and Bingham and McAdams for Northern Ireland. One of the better players on the field was Fernie's Celtic team mate Bertie Peacock, playing for Northern Ireland.

Fernie was now out of the Scottish team for nearly two years, missing the game v England at Wembley in April 1955 (just as well, perhaps, for it was an appalling 2-7 defeat) and the whole of the 1955/56 season. Many felt that this was unfair, but at the start of the 1956/57 season, he was playing so well that he could not be ignored, and great was the joy when the team for the first International was announced and Fernie was recalled.

And yet, there was something strange about it as well, for he was picked to play on the left wing! He had not played in that position very often before, to put it mildly, but both inside men Jackie Mudie and Bobby Collins were playing so well that they could not be ignored. There was no outstanding left winger available, and Fernie was often known as "Mr Versatile". So he was invited to wear the number 11 shirt for Scotland, and it was not a mistake. The game was at Cardiff against Wales on Saturday 22 October and it ended in a creditable 2-2 draw.

Not all Internationals are great games, as we have said, because the good players on either side tend to cancel each other out, but this game was an honourable exception and characterised by a brilliant goal by the best player on the field, Willie Fernie. If anything, Wales were the better side as one would expect with mighty men like John Charles and Ivor Allchurch. All the goals were scored in the first half and Fernie's goal equalised to make it 1-1. He picked up a ball from Collins on the left, made space, cut back, beat two men and then hammered a great goal past Arsenal's Jack Kelsey in the Welsh goal. Lawrie Reilly scored the other Scottish goal, and Ford and Medwin for Wales.

The teams were:

Wales: *Kelsey (Arsenal), Sherwood (Newport) and Hopkins (Tottenham Hotspur); Harrington (Cardiff City), Daniel (Sunderland) and Sullivan (Cardiff City); Medwin (Tottenham Hotspur), Charles (Leeds United), Ford (Cardiff City), Allchurch (Swansea Town) and Jones (Swansea Town)*

Scotland: *Younger (Liverpool), Parker (Falkirk) and Hewie (Charlton Athletic); McColl (Rangers), Young (Rangers) and Cowie (Dundee); Leggat (Aberdeen), Mudie (Blackpool), Reilly (Hibs), Collins (Celtic) and Fernie (Celtic)*

Referee: *Mr RH Mann, Worcester*

Fernie's next International was 17 days later at Hampden against Northern Ireland. In those 17 days, quite a lot had happened. Fernie himself was now a married man, had won a medal when Celtic lifted the Scottish League Cup the previous Wednesday, and Britain's Suez adventure had ended ignominiously as world opinion had compelled them to withdraw, while all the time the Soviet Union was carrying out a vicious attack on Hungary. The fate of the great Hungarian football players like Ferenc Puskas who had so lit up the 1954 World Cup was now in a great deal of doubt.

62,345 turned up on the dull but not particularly cold day of 7 November 1956 to see a competent Scottish performance and a 1-0 win made all the more creditable by the fact that they were reduced to ten men when Dundee's Doug Cowie was injured. But Alec Scott of Rangers scored in the first half after some good work from Reilly, and although Ireland came more into the game in the second half, Scotland held out for a good win. Fernie was described as working hard and "running from one end of the field to the other" – possibly not as wholesome a paean of praise as one would have liked!

The teams were:

Scotland: *Younger (Liverpool), Parker (Falkirk) and Hewie (Charlton Athletic); McColl (Rangers), Young (Rangers) and Cowie (Dundee); Scott (Rangers), Mudie (Blackpool), Reilly (Hibs), Wardhaugh (Hearts) and Fernie (Celtic)*

Northern Ireland: *Greig (Doncaster Rovers), Cunningham (Leicester City) and McMichael (Newcastle United); D Blanchflower (Tottenham Hotspur), J Blanchflower (Manchester United) and Casey (Newcastle United); Bingham (Sunderland), McIlroy (Burnley), Shields (Southampton), Dickson (Linfield) and McParland (Aston Villa)*

A fortnight later, Fernie was back at Hampden playing for Scotland again, this time against Yugoslavia. It was a good victory – the first time that a British country had beaten the Yugoslavs – but it was a far from pleasant occasion with the foreigners guilty of body checking and obstruction and some of the Scots – Tommy Docherty and Jackie Mudie in particular – not above a little retaliation. But Scotland, in the main, got on with the job in hand, and scored twice without reply, Jackie Mudie in the first half and Sammy Baird in the second. Fernie is neither singled out for praise nor blamed for doing anything wrong in this game played on a placid, calm, late autumn day before 55,550 who all left happy with a good Scottish performance and win.

The teams were:

Scotland: *Younger (Liverpool), Parker (Falkirk) and Hewie (Charlton Athletic); McColl (Rangers), Young (Rangers) and Docherty (Preston North End); Scott (Rangers), Mudie (Blackpool), Reilly (Hibs), Baird (Rangers) and Fernie (Celtic)*

Yugoslavia: *Beara, Belin and Stankovic; Tasic, Horvat and Boskov; Perakovic, Milutinovic, Ognianov, Vukas and Zebec*

Referee: *PP Roomer, Holland*

Fernie's next game for Scotland was what was always referred to as the "big" International or simply "the International", the game between Scotland and England, the oldest International in the world and a game which in 1957 meant a huge amount to both nations. This year the game was at Wembley, a venue where Scotland had done quite well since World War II with two wins in 1949 and 1951, two honourable draws in 1947 and 1953 and only one defeat, admittedly a bad one and also the most recent occasion – the 7-2 thumping of 1955.

The excitement about this game dwarfed all domestic considerations in Scotland with arguments starting round about the New Year and going on for weeks and months in advance about what the team would or should be, a scramble for tickets, ferocious arguments about the way that tickets were made available, arrangements in advance about travel and saving up money for the trip for the lucky ones. In recent years, the economic affluence of the 1950s meant that a trip to London wasn't necessarily all that financially ruinous and more and more people were able to go.

On one point however, the SFA were adamant, and that was that there would be no live television of the game, on the grounds that it might deter people from going to other games that might be played on that day. The cynics argued that if the money had been upped a little, such pious concern for the protection of the lower reaches of the game might well have disappeared, but there was also a very Scottish Presbyterian facet to all this, namely that free football on TV was not unlike sexual relations. If you enjoyed something, it was bound to be bad for you!

Be that as it may, it meant that most fans had little option other than to tune in to the BBC Home Service on the radio at 3.45 on 6 April 1957 to hear the second half and find out how the following players were doing;

Scotland: *Younger (Liverpool), Caldow (Rangers) and Hewie (Charlton Athletic); McColl (Rangers), Young (Rangers) and Docherty (Preston North End); Collins (Celtic), Fernie (Celtic), Reilly (Hibs), Mudie (Blackpool) and Ring (Clyde)*

England: *Hodgkinson (Sheffield United), Hall (Birmingham City) and Byrne (Manchester United); Clayton (Blackburn Rovers), Wright (Wolverhampton Wanderers) and Edwards (Manchester United); Matthews (Blackpool), Thompson (Preston North End), Finney (Preston North End), Kevan (West Bromwich Albion) and Grainger (Sunderland)*

Referee: *PP Roomer, Holland*

It was a hard fought game and Scotland were unlucky to lose 1-2. The standard of play was not necessarily all that high – but then the tension of the occasion was not always conducive to silky football. However the game kept the 100,000 spectators and the vast radio audience on tenterhooks. Tommy Ring scored a great goal in the early stages, and Fernie had a goal disallowed before hitting the bar with a header from a Ring cross, but Kevan and Edwards scored for England, and they won 2-1. It was a great experience for Fernie, however, probably the biggest single match that he played in during his whole career, and he would remember the experience all his life, not least because it gave him the opportunity to play on the same field as Stanley Matthews. Unfortunately, he did not play well enough, in the opinion of those who mattered, to retain his place for Scotland's summer fixtures. There was however some compensation in that he was able to tour the USA with Celtic instead.

And so Willie might well have assumed that his Scotland career was finished. Not only did he not go on the Scotland summer tour, but he was not chosen for the game in October against Northern Ireland. That was a disappointing draw, however, and a couple of weeks after that, Fernie hit the headlines with his wonderful display in the 7-1 League Cup final against Rangers, and he could hardly be omitted from the Scotland squad after that. He was first chosen in the 22 for the two games in November, and, importantly, was chosen for the World Cup qualifier against Switzerland at Hampden.

It was tight for qualification for Sweden. Scotland were in a group of three countries who all, as it happened began with S - Spain, Switzerland and Scotland themselves. Scotland had beaten Spain at home and lost in Madrid. They had beaten Switzerland in Basle, and, as Switzerland had drawn one of their games with Spain, a win for Scotland over Switzerland on 6 November 1957 would guarantee qualification.

The Glasgow Herald, a long term admirer of Willie Fernie is delighted as it surveys the team "The most interesting choice is that of Fernie at right half. This immaculate ball manipulator who has played inside right, inside left and outside left for Scotland as well as for his club became Celtic's regular right half only this season, and if many of his club's supporters had had their way, he would not have been deployed in that position. Now however if will be a great disappointment if he does not present Switzerland with an insoluble problem."

The Evening Times in its report of the game shares the opinion of *The Glasgow Herald* for its headline is "Swiss Bang Fernie" and in its summing up says "No day of all round glory for Scotland, but a wonderful afternoon for Willie Fernie. He was not only Scotland's greatest half back, but greatest forward too. He literally laid on the Scottish goal for Mudie and with any luck at all would have scored one or two himself. He looked the complete footballer, which is more than could be said for some of the other players".

It was a fine mellow, fairly windless day at Hampden on Wednesday 6 November 1957 with quite a few Swiss supporters providing a colourful sight on the terracings in the 56,811 crowd and their team appearing in all orange. The teams were:

Scotland: *Younger (Liverpool), Parker (Falkirk) and Caldow (Rangers); Fernie (Celtic), Evans (Celtic) and Docherty (Preston North End); Scott (Rangers), Collins (Collins), Mudie (Blackpool), Robertson (Clyde) and Ring (Clyde)*

Switzerland: *Parlier, Kernan and Morf; Grobety, Koch and Schnelter; Chiesa, Ballaman, Meler, Vonlanden and Riva*

Referee: *R Leafe, Nottingham*

The score at half time was 1-1, Archie Robertson having scored first and then Riva equalised for Switzerland. It was then, early in the second half that Willie Fernie made his magical goal for Jackie Mudie to tap in. He beat three men as he crossed the field diagonally and then he crossed for Mudie to finish off. It was marvellous stuff, and when Bobby Collins then fed Alec Scott, with the Swiss defence waiting in vain for an offside flag, Scotland went 3-1 up and looked home and dry. Scotland never do things the easy way, however, and Vonlanden scored for Switzerland to set up a tense finish for the crowd and those listening on the radio, but Scotland, with Fernie still superb, held out for a 3-2 victory and qualification for Sweden. The following day's newspapers were unanimously of the opinion that Fernie was the best man afield.

Exactly a week later, it was back to Hampden on Wednesday 13 November to take on Wales. This was a less happy occasion. The weather was cold and bitter, the crowd was down to 42,918 and possibly as a result, the standard of football was poor. For some bizarre and unfathomable reason, the highly successful half back line of last week – Fernie, Evans and Docherty – was changed to Docherty, Evans and Fernie, and it was less successful with Fernie finding this position (his fifth!) for Scotland, just a little too difficult. Neither Scotland nor Wales lived up to their true potential, and boos and jeers rent the air as the teams left the field. Collins scored for Scotland and Medwin for Wales in a rather insipid 1-1 draw.

The teams were;

Scotland: *Younger (Liverpool), Parker (Falkirk) and Caldow (Rangers); Docherty (Preston North End), Evans (Celtic) and Fernie (Celtic); Scott (Rangers), Collins (Celtic), Gardiner (Motherwell), Mudie (Blackpool) and Ewing (Partick Thistle)*

Wales: *Kelsey (Arsenal), Williams (West Bromwich Albion) and Hopkins (Tottenham Hotspur); Harrington (Cardiff City),*

Charles (Swansea Town) and Bowen (Arsenal); Allchurch (Swansea Town), Harris (Middlesbrough), Medwin (Tottenham Hotspur), Vernon (Blackburn Rovers) and Jones (Swansea Town)

Referee: *Mr J Clough, Bolton*

Fernie may now have begun to assume, yet again, that his International career was over. He had played poorly against Wales (like everyone else) and an injury at the turn of the year allied to the gradual decline in Celtic's performances may have encouraged him in that belief. He did well to miss out the game against England in April – a dreadful 0-4 thrashing at Hampden, and he was not originally chosen for the squad of 22 for the World Cup in Sweden.

But then he received "a fiddler's bidding" when Tommy Ewing of Partick Thistle became unavailable. Tommy was doing his National Service – the two years conscription to the army – and the Army insisted on keeping Tommy and not releasing him for Sweden. Poor Tommy, but a welcome piece of luck for Willie Fernie.

Once again, as in 1954, we find that the supporters' enthusiasm for the World Cup was not paralleled by the SFA who approached the whole business with pathetic amateurism. Scotland still did not have a team manager! It would have been Matt Busby, but he was of course still recovering from his injuries sustained at Munich in February, and the SFA did not think of approaching anyone else. They might have asked Tommy Walker of Hearts or Scot Symon of Rangers or Jimmy McGrory of Celtic, but they didn't, and the closest there was to a Manager was a man called Dawson Walker, the trainer of Clyde – but of course he had no say in things like team selection!

But at home, excitement was intense. More and more people in 1958 had television, and everyone looked forward to the tournament. All four British nations had qualified and they were put in separate groups with a team from western Europe, eastern Europe and South America, in Scotland's case France, Yugoslavia and Paraguay. Brazil were the favourites to win, and that was the way that it turned out, but for Scotland, the 1958 World Cup obeyed that law of nature that Scotland must let down their fans. At least they didn't make International fools of themselves as they did in 1954, 1978 and 1990, but they still crawled back home with their tails wedged firmly between their legs.

Fernie did not play in the first game, a respectable 1-1 draw with Yugoslavia on 8 June. It was a good start, although Cyril Horne of *The Glasgow Herald* goes a little overboard when he says that "I cannot see the Scots not qualifying for the last eight, such is the calibre of this now confident blend of skill and enthusiasm". Now on Wednesday 11 June came Paraguay, a little known country and team that no-one had bothered checking up on, even though they were rumoured to be "good ball players".

Scotland had picked up a few injuries against Yugoslavia not least Stewart Imlach of Nottingham Forest, the left winger. In came Fernie to play yet again on the left wing. It did not work, Fernie being hardly mentioned in the reports of this game in Norrkoping. Scotland went down 2-3, not in truth a total disaster, but Paraguay were a poor side with a few hefty tackles and a tendency to waste time. In addition, the question must be asked as to why Fernie was not played at right half where Eddie Turnbull (no-one's idea of a right half) was deployed. He might have been a good left winger that night – but then again, of course, Scotland did not have a Manager! Imlach came back for the last game against France (another defeat) and Fernie never played again for Scotland.

The teams against Paraguay were:

Scotland: ***Younger (Liverpool), Parker (Falkirk) and Caldow (Rangers); Turnbull (Hibs), Evans (Celtic) and Cowie (Dundee); Leggat (Aberdeen), Collins (Celtic), Mudie (Blackpool), Robertson (Clyde) and Fernie (Celtic).***

Paraguay: *Aguilar, Arevalo and Echague; Achucaro, Lezcano and Villalba; Aguero, Parodi, Romero, Re, Amarilla*

Referee: *Signor Orlandini, Italy*

Fernie still, it was felt, had a certain amount to offer at International level, but he was not far off his 30th birthday now, and he possibly did well to avoid the annoyance and embarrassment that playing for Scotland tended to bring in the 1950s! It was however always considered to be a great honour to play for Scotland, and Willie remained proud of his 12 Scottish caps.

Playing for Scotland is of course a mixed blessing. It allows a player to travel, to play in front of huge crowds and let the world see what a great player he is, but it is also stressful in that a bad game or a big mistake means that you are instantly infamous. That never happened with Willie Fernie. Sometimes it is claimed that playing for the International side in midweek has an adverse effect on how one plays in the League game on the Saturday, but that never happened with Willie. Playing for Scotland was indeed a great honour – but so too was playing for Celtic.

CHAPTER ELEVEN

THE REST OF HIS LIFE (1976 – 2011)

Following his departure from Kilmarnock in October 1977, Willie never again took another job connected with football. He and his family continued to live at 292 Clarkston Road, and earned his living by driving his taxi. He was self-employed and never employed anyone else. It was a sort of freedom which allowed him to work whenever he felt like it, but he did work long hours.

It was not unknown for a fan to arrive at Celtic Park for a game in a state of excitement claiming that he had been driven to the ground by Willie Fernie. Glasgow taxi drivers are of course a breed apart. They need, obviously, to know their ways about the streets of the City, they have to be able to handle themselves with difficult passengers particularly on Saturday nights and they have to be able to show compassion to people, for example, whom they are taking to and from hospital for appointments, sometimes to be told really bad news. Above all else, he must have the patter, the ability to answer questions about Glasgow posed by passengers and to be able to seem to be a friend.

His taxi driving earned him enough to feed and clothe his family adequately. It would not be said that he earned an awful lot from his football career. Footballers in the 1950s earned more than the average, certainly, but nothing like as much as their equivalents earn today. But he was never a jealous nor an envious man. He knew that he had had a good career in football, and he had enjoyed it, making some fine friends and with the satisfaction of knowing that he had pleased quite a lot of people by his playing of the game that he loved.

He was a man who was broadly interested in most things in life, so that he could talk to his passengers about holidays, TV, entertainment and other things but had very few real interests other than football. He attended Celtic Park usually along with his sons, was sometimes recognised by fans and sometimes not, probably less so as the years began to slip away. He watched football on television all the time, had a passing interest in other sports, but generally speaking, he lived a quiet life driving his taxi and watching his football.

Willie died on 1 July 2011 aged 82. He had been suffering from Dementia, the illness that affects so many ex-football players. His wife Audrey had pre-deceased him in 2010.

THE
WILLIE
FERNIE
ALBUM